how
sweet
the
bitter
soup

how sweet the bitter soup

a memoir

LORI QIAN

She Writes Press, a BookSparks imprint
A Division of SparkPointStudio, LLC.

Published 2019

Printed in the United States of America

ISBN: 978-1-63152-614-5
ISBN: 978-1-63152-615-2
Library of Congress Control Number: 2019934765

For information, address:
She Writes Press
1569 Solano Ave #546
Berkeley, CA 94707

She Writes Press is a division of SparkPoint Studio, LLC.

To Abraham, Annabelle, and Alex:
Remember to hold to the sweet things in life,
and use the bitter, which inevitably comes,
to learn and grow.
Thank you for believing in me.
I love you more than you can imagine.
Love, Mom

And, of course, to William:
Without you, there isn't a story.
Thank you for the bitter soup,
and for adding so much joy to my life.

Part One

chapter 1

Getting married in China is nothing like what we're used to in America. For a foreign woman to marry a Chinese man is highly complicated at best—in fact, it is nearly impossible. On February 16, 2002, William and I became the ninth American/Chinese couple to get married in Hubei province. Not the ninth that month, that year, or in the last decade. The ninth. Period. As I sat there with William, the steam from the soup warming my face while I held tight to that marriage certificate, my mind drifted back to how this all began.

汤

The car seemed to have a mind of its own, perhaps wanting me to think things through before making any rash decisions, but I was done thinking. I knew what I wanted. Sort of. I wanted to go to China. But I needed to talk to Dad first. I wanted to sit down with him and explain this rare and special opportunity that had been presented to me. I wanted him to understand how important it would be for me to go, to accept this job, to do something for myself, to see what my future could be. I wanted him to be happy for me, to wish me well in this adventure. But I knew that wouldn't happen. It simply wasn't possible.

Last time I had visited—Sunday dinner just six days earlier—

he had thought I was the neighbor's daughter. Not his and Mom's current neighbor, mind you, but Sue Frocks, our neighbor from fifteen years earlier, when we lived in a small white house on the outskirts of Wisconsin Rapids.

This idea to go to China seemed perfectly normal when I could pretend my parents were not old, or poor, or sick. The reality, though, was that they didn't have enough money to support themselves, and it was up to me to close the gap between their rent and their social security allowance. The even more painful reality was that my dad was no longer playing his guitar, solving logic puzzles, or reading eight-hundred-page books; he simply wasn't able. Instead, he was a fragile man whose Alzheimer's had taken over all of our lives.

When I pulled up to their apartment, I hoped I wouldn't find him wandering outside, as I had two weeks earlier. On that day, he'd been walking around looking for their apartment. Worse than that, he had forgotten to put his pants on before embarking on this little stroll.

"I was trying to find Sparks. It was always here on this corner." He slowly lifted his finger and his gaze, pointing at nothing.

"I know, Dad," I said as I took him by the arm. "Let's go inside."

Sparks was a grocery store in Starbucks, Washington, his childhood home. My childhood was filled with stories relating back to this town. I thought then, as I walked my father into the house, that I wished I'd taken the time to visit his childhood home so that he could have shown me the places he loved and remembered.

Thinking of this moment, I was reminded that I needed to arrange full-time care for him, or Mom would need to quit her job. She'd been working as a nanny for the same family for ten years, and she was struggling to make ends meet. I told myself, though, that accepting this job in China, where I'd be earning a good salary, would enable to me to help her do just that. If we could just make it through until then. I opened the door to the apartment and was relieved to find Dad sitting at the kitchen table, eating toast. He was wearing clean blue sweat pants and a black cable-knit sweater that was a hand-me-down from me. He'd lost enough weight that he could now fit into all those once-fashionable, oversized men's sweaters I'd bought years earlier. He looked like a child sitting on a big kitchen chair, carefully using two hands to bring the buttered toast to his mouth.

"Hi, Daddy," I said, closing the door behind me.

"Hiiii," he said, dragging out the word. He'd done this ever since his first stroke. I'd become used to it. All the changes in his speech had been hard to deal with at first, but I didn't mind it so much lately. His new mode of speech made every word sound more sincere, like it was trying to stay in the air a little longer.

"How are you, Dad?" I asked, kissing the top of his bald head, my arm around his shoulder.

He looked up with a slow smile that began in his glossy eyes.

I realized I'd caught him on a good day. I moved around the kitchen, putting things away, listening to him, testing to see how coherent he was. I'd already told him I wanted to go to China when I'd called from Vancouver. I'd attended an International Teaching Conference there several days before. He'd said that was nice and then passed the phone to Mom. I knew it had not hit him, and I was sure he had no memory now of that conversation. I hoped that maybe, just maybe, if I sat down and told him in person, it might sink in. I prepared myself for two possibilities: either a blank stare or extreme sadness.

As I played out these possibilities in my mind, he shuffled toward his bedroom, sliding his hand along the wall for support. I guessed he was going to lie down, which was okay. He needed more rest. I could help with the laundry and dishes while he slept, and maybe I could come up with a fantastic way to tell him without hurting him in the process.

Just then I heard his voice behind me: "Lori, come and show me where you're going."

I spun around, almost dropping the plate in my hand. I caught it just in time and was shocked to see him holding his globe. This was what he had gone to the bedroom for. Tears came to my eyes. I could not remember the last time I'd heard such a clear sentence come out of his mouth. And to ask me this question meant he remembered my calling from the conference. That was days ago. How could he possibly remember?

I knelt down beside him and spun the globe. Wiping a tear away, I pointed to Guangzhou. "It's right here, Dad. That's the place I want to go."

He looked intently at the globe without speaking. He touched Guangzhou and slid his finger all the way up to the top of the globe, and then down the other side. He stopped right on Chicago.

"The other side of the world," he said. His grin was thoughtful.

I stared at my father. He knew exactly who I was and exactly what I needed from him. He was doing just what he'd always done as a father.

"I think you should go to China," he said.

"You do, Dad?" I asked, catching my breath. "You really do?" I was hoping I'd heard him correctly.

He raised his eyes from the globe to my face. "I really do."

I could feel the tears streaming down my face, then falling from my chin—tears of gratitude for my dad's brief moment of clarity when I needed it most. I had no idea what my future held, but now that I had my dad's blessing, there was one thing I knew for sure: I was going to China.

chapter 2

My body felt like a water tank, all swishy and huge. I'd never been on a flight that lasted over three hours; fifteen hours was a shock. Every single body part seemed to be swollen to five times its normal size, my feet being the most obvious example.

It felt good to stand up, let the numbness dissipate from my extremities, and realize that I had arrived. Now that I'd landed in the People's Republic of China, I had no idea what to expect. I felt perfectly content, though—not an ounce of anxiety.

People seemed to be in an incredible hurry to get off the plane, so I jumped right in and pushed along with them toward the exit. I could see the bus that had come to meet all the passengers. This was different. I was used to exiting a plane directly into the airport. The crowd seemed to move as one body, each of the appendages trying desperately to stay connected to the core. Stepping onto the bus, I looked around, curious as to whether there were any other foreigners. Not a one. For some reason, this fact made me smile. I felt brave and adventurous, like the person I'd always wanted to be.

汤

Walking from the bus to the terminal, I finally felt the thick air and noticed the heavy clouds. It was not yet six o'clock in the morning, but already the day was hot and muggy. My clothes stuck to me. Between the plane and the bus, the heat was oppressive enough to make my clothes wet and seemingly glued right to my skin. I didn't mind.

The airport looked nothing like my previous notion of an airport. The walls were cement and unpainted. The interior was sparse. I felt as if I were looking at an abandoned building that had once been an airport; it was hard to believe that this was an actual airport in a very large Asian city. The customs counter resembled a big metal box and was not permanently affixed to the floor. Just beyond the customs counter was the luggage carousel, and that was the extent of the international arrivals terminal.

I must have looked a bit lost, because a security guard caught my eye and pointed me in the right direction. The first thing I noticed about this man was his waist. It was so small that his belt was wrapped around almost twice. He did not look to be a day over twelve, yet something about him suggested he was actually quite a bit older than that. His dark brown eyes stared out from under his uniformed cap and he extended an arm toward the counter. He didn't really need to, of course, since there was really no place else to go except the customs line, but he seemed to want to help. He tried to look stern, but as I smiled and said my best "*xie xie*," he cracked a smile and nodded. He was still smiling, I think, as I took my place at the end of the long line.

Again I was aware that I felt completely at ease. I thought it might be the jet lag, but whatever the source, I could not believe how relaxed I was. I felt sure that later the homesickness or culture shock would set in, but in that moment, I was simply myself. I had been in this country less than thirty minutes and already felt an excitement about being there that was hard to contain. I handed my passport to the customs official and waited for my chance to pass through to the luggage carousel.

Somehow, all that mattered at that moment was that I was here. I was in China.

汤

I gathered my luggage, which was only two large suitcases and a backpack. After managing to get it on a cart, I made my way to the exit, where I saw Kassie right away.

Kassie had hired me the previous spring at the conference I'd attended in Vancouver. We'd spoken on the phone a couple of times since then, and I had felt very comfortable speaking with her. I was genuinely happy to see her outside the airport gates, waiting to take me to my new home. I gave her a hug.

I thought I knew what Chinese people looked like. I realized now how wrong I had been, because nobody looked like anybody else. Yes, the people around me all had black hair and dark eyes, but even just leaving the airport, I saw such different features and body types. Nobody was overweight, of course, but some people were much taller than others, while some were relatively short and stocky.

As we pushed my cart through the door, we almost ran over an older man who was squatting down eating an orange.

"Sorry," I said—in English, as if that were appropriate—and he fell right over. His wiry frame and weathered skin stood out to me, as did his big straw hat, rolled up pants, open shirt, and sandals.

As he caught his balance, he let out a laugh and revealed a big, almost completely toothless grin. I couldn't help grinning back. "*Ni kan!*" he shouted to his buddy. "*Ni kan! Wai guo ren!*" (Look at the foreigners!)

His friend, along with many other people, did indeed look as the two of us kept walking. I couldn't understand what they were saying, of course, but Kassie could, and she filled me in.

"You'll have to get used to that," she said.

"People staring, you mean?"

"Yes, it can take some getting used to. Some of these people have never seen a foreigner, and it really shocks them when they do."

Other people, it seemed, were oblivious to us, and I asked Kassie why that was.

"Well, businesspeople and those who have traveled abroad are used to seeing foreigners. But a lot of the people you'll see— the workers, like that man by the door, he's probably from the countryside."

Kassie and I crossed the busy parking lot, and I had to keep reminding myself that it was not even seven o'clock in the morning. There were people everywhere, and I was borderline giddy with excitement. I tried to play it cool in front of Kassie, but inside I was like a child, mesmerized by what others did not even seem to notice.

As we maneuvered my cart of luggage across the street, Kassie looked at me and smiled. "I'm glad you're here."

"It's great to be here," I said, and I meant it.

As we approached a van, Kassie pointed out the driver, Liu, and introduced us. It was clear he was a man of few words. He gave a quick "*ni hao*," swiftly put my luggage into the back of the van, and pointed toward the seats.

It was a basic utility van, with metal floors but comfortable seats. I would soon learn that this was very nice transportation compared to some of the other modes common to the area.

When we got in the van, Kassie introduced me to Cindy, the assistant principal of the school, and two other new teachers, along with their daughter, who had come in on the same flight. Since it was a huge flight, and I'd never met them before, of course, and we hadn't even noticed each other until now.

Kassie spoke to Liu in what I assumed was Chinese, and

I was genuinely impressed. She told me that she had learned Mandarin when she'd served a mission for our church in Taiwan. I was familiar with this, of course, being born and raised in the Church of Jesus Christ of Latter-Day Saints. Missionary work for young people is significant in our belief system. I hadn't served a mission—a choice I regretted a bit, since I knew it was a life-changing experience for those who did.

Kassie and Cindy wanted to give us a quick tour of Guangzhou before heading home. This gave me a chance to learn a bit about each of my new colleagues. There was Kassie, of course, who was starting her third year at the school. She was from Idaho but had lived and taught in China for years. Cindy was a retired school teacher from Nevada. The other new teachers, Sherry and Terry, were a couple and had just taught for a year in Hangzhou, where they'd adopted a little girl, Mei Li.

As we drove toward the city, Cindy told us that Guangzhou was one of the most prosperous cities in China. My senses were so overloaded with information from the sounds and voices around me that I was unable to form an immediate impression of the area. I saw a McDonald's or KFC every few minutes, along with countless little boutiques selling Western products; there were even bakeries selling cupcakes and French bread. I could smell foods that I didn't yet have a name for, and I was taking in noises I couldn't yet describe.

汤

Our first stop was an extravagant, ultra-modern, elegant hotel.

"This is the Garden Hotel," Kassie said. "When you take the bus from the Estates to Guangzhou, there are several different stops, but the Garden Hotel stop is a popular one. You'd get off right here." She pointed to the intersection. "Whenever I come to Guangzhou, this is my first stop. We love to come here to buy bread and goodies when we're craving something from home."

Kassie just kept smiling at me. She had a very calm manner about her.

Cindy, on the other hand, was nice enough, but rather loud. "Now, Lori," she interjected, "the other reason you will want to come here is to use the Western-style toilet. Anywhere else you go, you'll have to squat." She laughed loudly. "Do you know what a squatter is?"

"I've never seen one," I said, "but the name goes a long way."

At this, Sherry and Terry both let out a laugh. Terry would tell me several months later that his first impression of me was that I was so calm, that I had this easy-going look about me, as if I were thinking, *Yeah, I'm in China now, just taking it all in.*

As we walked into the hotel, a doorman greeted us with a "good afternoon" in perfect English. I had to stand still for a few moments as I took in an extraordinary mural before me. It took up the entire wall, and I could not take my eyes off it. It seemed to depict a story: there were figures in each scene doing different kinds of work—harvesting, sewing, carrying large baskets, the scenery changing according to the task. As I looked closer, I could see that the intricate design was done in solid gold. I moved on to admire the elaborate water fountain and stare at the boutiques selling things like *TIME* magazine and Liz Claiborne perfume. The five-star hotel was nicer than any building I'd ever seen in my life.

We wandered around the lobby, which seemed to go on endlessly. There were lounges, a big open courtyard area, exotic plants on display, beautiful wooden staircases, and countless elevators. I noted the businesspeople having what looked to be hurried and intense breakfast meetings, and the tourists gearing up for a day of sightseeing. I was fascinated by the variety of people in this hotel lobby. As I looked closer, I noticed quiet workers here and there, polishing this, dusting that.

We eventually found our way to the bathroom, which, like

the rest of the hotel, was elegant and beautiful. As I approached the sink, I was greeted by a woman who turned on the faucet for me and handed me a paper towel when I was finished. When I let out a laugh at this, she laughed too, revealing a mouthful of rotted teeth. She quickly covered her mouth, but her expressive eyes could not be hidden. She was even shorter than me, standing an even five feet. She was extremely skinny but looked strong at the same time under the dark brown pants and light brown jacket that comprised her work uniform. The color of her skin was somewhere in between the two shades of her clothes, and the lines in her face were deep.

I finally took the towel, though I felt strange doing so. Was this really her job, to turn on the sink for me? I watched as other women came in and out and she did the same for them. It seemed to be just part of the routine for them, nothing special. An attractive Chinese woman in a tailored suit walked up to the sink and waited for a split second, obviously anticipating that the worker would turn on the sink, which she promptly did. The woman then extended her hand for the towel, not taking her eyes off her reflection in the mirror.

Everything was so far away from my previous expectations that I couldn't speak. I saw people drinking Diet Coke. Everywhere I looked I saw signs in English. I didn't know whether to be relieved or disappointed.

汤

We climbed back into the van and kept driving. I was glad the other teachers were talking to each other, because I had no words and, at that moment, no desire to make conversation.

I had always heard that there were bicycles everywhere in China. As we drove along, I felt that I might never look at a bicycle the same way again. Apparently, bicycles in China are not just for riding; they are also for carrying. Looking out my window,

I saw an old man with bulging calf muscles. He could not have weighed more than eighty-five pounds, yet he was carrying two huge, probably queen-size, mattresses on the back of his bicycle. Sweat was dripping from his face as he pedaled along, but he was weaving in and out of traffic with those gigantic mattresses as calmly as I'd seen mail carriers back in Chicago lug around their cargo. Just doing his job.

Of course, he had modified his bicycle a bit by adding a small shelf behind his seat and plenty of cables and ropes to hold the mattresses in place. I would later notice that the majority of bicycles these workers used looked like something from a museum of ancient artifacts—but in China, people make use of things that many Westerners would discard as useless junk. Over time, I saw more than mattresses on bicycles, and the sight eventually ceased to shock me. It was nothing to see pigs, chickens, sheets of glass, groups of four or five people—it didn't matter what it was; it could all fit on a bike.

As we drove along, I saw modern buildings that would have fit in the heart of Chicago. Other places reminded me that I was in a third-world country. I had done some reading on China in the months leading up to coming, and after learning of the events of the last fifty years, I'd known I was headed for a place of contrast. I'd read about the Japanese invasions, the Guomindang armies, and the Cultural Revolution. It all seemed surreal, and I knew the China I was going to would be very different from the China that existed in the history books. I had read a couple of travel memoirs by other foreigners who had spent time in China, and that had given me a little more realistic picture of what it was like. Still, I knew I was going to a unique place. None of what I had read or heard about China matched the pages of the school brochure Kassie had sent me last spring.

Kassie had told me that the school I'd be teaching in did not represent the rest of China and that I would see a stark contrast between our gated community and some of the surrounding areas. I was anxious to see what she meant; so far I had seen only a thriving metropolis, much like my hometown of Chicago. Within minutes, however, we entered a section of town that looked quite different. It seemed older and almost forgotten—strikingly different from the downtown area we had just driven through. The buildings were gray. It seemed everything was grey. There were no trees, no grass. I saw nothing of color anywhere, and everything was run-down.

People seemed to live right on top of one another in this area. That was true in the other parts of the city I'd seen as well, but here it was different. The homes themselves hardly looked like homes. I couldn't tell for sure, but it seemed that they had no real foundation—they were just misshapen pieces of rusted sheet metal arranged to look like a house. Some didn't even seem to have doors, although most had a sheet or blanket hanging in front. People were sitting outside making food over open fires. There was garbage everywhere, and children were playing in it. When I saw the kids urinating in the street as well, I was sure my assumption about no indoor plumbing was a correct one.

"Do people actually live there?" I asked, turning to Cindy. I wondered how they lived, if they worked, and where.

She told me she didn't know—that she had never noticed those particular dwellings before. I thought that was a little strange, since she'd told me she had lived here for a couple of years. But then again, who was I to judge? Who really wants to notice poverty? Looking at these houses and the people living there made my stomach hurt. After all, we had just been to the Garden Hotel not fifteen minutes before. To see people living like this right down the street was a lot to take in.

"I know where Pizza Hut is," Cindy said, seemingly oblivious to my discomfort. "And where you can buy Maybelline."

She went on to talk about all the Western products that could be bought in town.

I smiled and thanked her and then silently looked out the window. I still couldn't make sense of all I'd seen since landing, and I was exhausted. Suddenly, all I wanted was to sleep.

chapter 3

*P*anyu was the name of the city where our school and housing development (Clifford Estates, named after the owner) were located. It was about thirty minutes from downtown Guangzhou. On our way to the Estates, which is what the teachers called our gated community, the contrasts I'd noticed downtown continued. I saw more of the metal houses, but I also saw rice farms and beautiful gardens. These people's existence looked simple but also prosperous in some sense. Their houses were also quite small, having only one room, but they were made of brick and didn't seem depressing at all. The landscape had changed and it wasn't so grey. In fact, everything was green.

As I looked to my left, I suddenly felt I had once again entered a different world. I stared at the neon billboards alongside majestic, white buildings labeled CLUBHOUSE and FITNESS CENTER. We passed a sign in both Chinese and English indicating that we had entered the Estates. Uniformed guards directed traffic, which included sparkling little buses that carried people from the supermarket to the food court. There was a food court here?

All around me, things were elegant. That's the only way I can describe it. Colorful billboards advertised the lake in the center of the Estates, as well as all the activities, such as boating and fishing, that could be done there. I saw people talking on their mobile phones. There were cars of every kind, including Mercedes and BMWs; homes that could easily be described as mansions; and everything else that would belong to the lifestyles of very wealthy people.

I'd been told that I would be living and teaching in a planned, gated community, and that this housing development catered to China's richest families, but until this moment, I'd had no clue what that really meant. Kassie told me that this kind of affluence was a rarity in China. Many of these families were from Hong Kong, but they came from all over mainland China as well.

From what I'd read about Hong Kong, I understood it to be part of China in a technical sense but with a different governmental system. Hong Kong people were free to go back and forth between Hong Kong and the mainland, but the reverse was not always true. I learned that Hong Kong was only a ninety-minute ferry ride from the Estates, so many of the people here actually worked in Hong Kong. They bought homes in this subdivision, where there were plenty of stores, restaurants, recreation, schools, security guards, and a bus system, all this luxury contained within their gates—and were still able to earn their Hong Kong incomes, which went much further here on the mainland. At the Estates, they could enjoy an upscale lifestyle at a fraction of what they would pay for it in Hong Kong.

I'd had no idea just how posh my living conditions were going to be. I had just seen kids urinating in the street and living below sheet metal, and now I was stepping into this exclusive community. I had to wonder if every foreign teacher who came here would feel as impressed with the surroundings, though. While these new surroundings were, objectively, rather luxurious, my economic situation growing up had been relatively poor. I hadn't come to China from a middle-class home in the suburbs. I wasn't used to a life where parents could pay all the expenses for their kids. I'd grown up in an apartment, and was used to a financial situation where my mom, dad, sisters, and I pooled our money and made do the best we could. Looking around, I realized that my surroundings were absolutely beautiful and highly developed by anyone's standards, but for China—this was one of a kind. From the main entrance, it was less than a five-minute drive to the teachers' apartments. The clubhouse, food court, supermarket, and bus terminal were within the Estates but open to the public; you didn't have to pass through security to enter those places. However, as we entered into the inner part of the Estates, we came upon a huge security gate the width of the entire street. Liu gave the guard what looked to be his identification card, and then we passed through. I immediately saw another elegant building labeled CLUBHOUSE, in front of which was a gigantic fountain. We turned left, up the tree-lined street, and I saw countless rows of identical white townhouses and apartment buildings. I saw larger houses in the distance, and commented at their size.

"Oh, that's nothing!" said Cindy. "You should see the villas near the lake."

"Villas? You're kidding!" I laughed. "This is unbelievable."

"It really is," Kassie said. "Just wait until you get the chance to look around."

I couldn't wait.

汤

The teacher apartments were six-story buildings located right at the edge of the Estates, up a small hill and off to the left. I was on the fifth floor of my building; Sherry and Terry would be in the building behind me, which housed the bigger, three-bedroom apartments.

I could already tell I would love the view from my place. It would be fun to be up so high, especially since the building already sat on a hill.

Liu helped me carry my luggage up the stairs and Kassie came along to see if I had any questions. The stairwell itself was plain but clean. Kassie handed me the key to my apartment, and the first thing I noticed was the strange shape: it wasn't flat, like I was used to; instead, it looked like a small Phillips screwdriver, with an end that came to a point.

In some ways, I wanted Liu and Kassie to leave right then, because this was kind of a major moment to me and I wanted to really take it in. I hadn't anticipated the moment before, of opening the door to my new home, my new home in China—but suddenly it seemed almost sacred. What would I find on the other side of this door? Would I really be able to make this my home for the next year? I had brought two suitcases filled with clothes, a few books, and a new journal from my sister Barb. She knew I loved my journals—always had. I was twenty-eight and Barb was forty-one, but it didn't feel like we were that far apart in age. We'd grown closer in recent months—right as I was leaving, ironically.

My sisters, both Chrissy and Barb, had been supportive of my decision to come to China, but I knew it was hard on Chrissy. She was four years younger than me, and she was now there with our aging parents, trying to get through school and make a little money at the same time. We'd always been there for each other, and it would be strange for her now. I felt a twinge of guilt thinking about it, and a longing to be with my family, but I held on to knowing that I was where I needed to be. With the help of my new salary, Mom would be able to afford some in-home care for Dad, and maybe even quit her job.

My new apartment had tile floors and white walls, and was fairly spacious. After entering, I immediately walked toward the glass sliding door. I didn't go out just yet; I decided to wait until I was alone. It was something I was looking forward to enjoying for myself.

"You've got a little kitchen here—that's what we all have—but it does the job," Kassie said.

The kitchen *was* small, but that didn't bother me. I wasn't much of a cook anyway, and at least there was a fridge and microwave. The hallway led to two bedrooms and a bathroom. Kassie turned on the bathroom light for me. "This also is small, but you've got a washer and dryer behind the door, which is nice."

There was a twin bed in the small room and a double bed in the larger room.

"You'll want to get a mosquito net," Kassie said, "because even with the doors shut they manage to get through and they'll drive you nuts at night."

There were ample furnishings throughout and even an air-conditioner in the bedroom and living room. There was a nice TV and VCR. The walls were too plain, of course, and as I looked around I was already thinking of ways to make it more my home.

When the tour was over, I realized Liu had already left, before I could thank him for his help. I turned to Kassie; she looked exhausted.

"I guess this has been a long day for you, making all the arrangements to pick up new teachers," I said. "You must be really tired."

"I am," she said, "but how about you? How are you feeling?"

"Right now I feel great, but I'm looking forward to throwing some sheets on that bed and going to sleep." I smiled. "What's the plan for tomorrow? I know there is some kind of orientation in the afternoon."

Kassie confirmed the time and place of the orientation and explained to me how to get to the school. We said goodnight and she headed downstairs to her first-floor apartment.

After she left, I turned around and looked at my place. I sat on the floor. There was a couch as well as four kitchen chairs but for some reason, I chose to sit on the floor. I sat in the middle of the room and smiled. *I'm in China*, I thought to myself. *In my apartment, in China.* I walked out on the balcony and took in the view. In front of me were trees and perfectly square, beautifully green patches of lawn. Beyond that, and as far as I could see, there were rows upon rows of white houses with red roofs. To my right, though, I saw something much different. My building was right at the edge of the Estates, and the contrast between the Estates and the outer community was clear. There was a line of trees and lawn and then a fence; then a field; and beyond that, I saw run-down factories and housing that looked similar to those I had seen in Guangzhou. They were structures of the makeshift variety. They looked temporary.

Wow, I thought, *all the things I've read about China being a land of contrasts is now evident from my balcony window.*

I looked around at the other balconies and wondered if the other new teachers had arrived. Who would my new neighbors be?

That thought on my mind, I came back inside and explored my house a little more. Before leaving, I had prepared myself for my first night in China. I had imagined I would be emotional and homesick; I had expected to cry tears of sadness and longing for my family. I told myself that was okay, that this was to be expected—we were, after all, incredibly close, Mom, Dad, Chrissy, and I, living together in a two-bedroom apartment, pooling our money to make the bills, getting through life.

And that's what it'd felt like for a long time—just getting through. Even with Barb helping too, taking Dad to doctor's appointments and having him hang out at her house some days, things were hard.

It wasn't until this spark of my going to China came into our lives that I saw Mom begin to light up again. Her worries about Dad and the bills and the future didn't go away, but my plans gave her a much-needed distraction. She was genuinely thrilled for me. She started reading up on China, telling me to see if I could find some of those rooftop gardens she'd read about, and find out what the deal was with the one-child policy, and a host of other questions. She'd taken to telling people at church that I was the "China girl." She was proud.

So yes, tears and homesickness would have been normal enough in this moment, but I felt nothing of the sort. I felt fine. Maybe it just hadn't hit me yet. I had told Mom I would call the following day and not to worry if she didn't hear from me. Maybe once I talked to her it would be harder. Maybe the jet lag had had a stronger effect on me than I thought and I was simply too tired to feel my real emotions. *Eventually*, I thought, *the reality of what I've done will set in and it will hurt.*

But that night, as I lay in my new bed, I felt better than I had felt in a long time. It hit me as I drifted off that I was still in my clothes and I hadn't unpacked a thing. I had mini-dreams of getting up, taking a shower, and unpacking, but none of it materialized, and soon I drifted into a deep sleep.

chapter 4

The next morning I awoke early. I looked at my watch; it was only five o'clock, but I was wide awake and could not get back to sleep.

Walking slowly to my balcony, I noticed again that I hadn't even changed out of my traveling clothes yet. Suddenly, I was screaming for a shower. I managed to find the towel I had packed, as well as the bar of soap Mom had added to my suitcase. I'd laughed so hard when she'd done that. "Mom, I think they'll have soap in China," I said, snickering.

"Well, Lori," she said with a certain air of authority, "you might not be able to get to a store right away. You don't know what kind of conditions you might find when you get there."

I made a mental note to thank her, and then spent the next few minutes trying to get the water heater to work. Kassie had briefly gone over it the previous night but that all seemed like a long time ago, and I now realized I must not have been listening very carefully to her. She had said something about turning a certain button if I wanted hot water, but it didn't seem to be working. The water was either boiling hot or freezing cold.

I made another mental note to ask Kassie to re-explain the inner workings of the water heater when I saw her. My first shower wasn't quite as relaxing as I'd hoped it would be, but at least I felt clean.

Kassie had left me some crackers and Pepsi the night before, and I made that my breakfast. As I crunched my last cracker, I decided to unpack my suitcases and begin to put some things away. I knew I needed to go shopping for household things, not to mention food, but Cindy had said something about all the new teachers going shopping as a group. I would need to find out when, because I was anxious to get my new home in order.

I had a calling card I had bought in Chicago. I put my unpacking on hold and decided to use it now to try to call home. I was surprised when the call went through without a problem. I couldn't believe how easy it was to just pick up this little red phone in my Chinese apartment and call Chicago.

"Hello?"

"Mom?"

"Hi!! Oh, thank goodness, you're there. You're there?"

"Yeah, I actually got in last night but I didn't think to call then. What time is it there?"

"Um, let's see, about seven."

"Oh, seven at night, huh? It's six in the morning here. We'll have to remember that we're about thirteen hours apart."

"So, how is it there? How was the flight?"

We went on to talk for several more minutes about my flight and what I had observed of my surroundings so far. She said that Dad was resting but was doing okay. I promised to email her and everyone else as soon as I got settled. We said our love yous and good-byes and hung up.

I felt a little twinge in my heart after saying good-bye. *I love my mom*, I thought, *and I hope she knows that*. She had always been phenomenally supportive of whatever I wanted to do. I knew how lucky I was.

As I began to slowly unpack a bit, my mind drifted back to my mom again. She had been on my mind more as I'd prepared to go to China, and for some reason I kept thinking back to our little house in Wisconsin where we'd lived before Chicago became our home base. It was way out in the countryside; we called it "the house on 80th." I was in fifth grade when we moved there and had just gotten my Gloria Vanderbilt jeans—a life-changing experience for me as a ten-year-old.

I remember a particular day, wearing those jeans. Even though it was Saturday, and I wasn't leaving the house, I was wearing them, feeling like the coolest little chick on the planet. I walked by my mom's room and noticed her sitting on the bed holding a pair of her underpants.

What was she doing? She was clearly doing something with her hands, but what exactly? And why was she holding her underwear? Her hands moved quickly and with purpose, as if she'd done whatever it was she was doing a thousand times before. As I crept closer, for some reason not wanting her to see me, I noticed that she was tying small knots to close some of the holes in her underpants.

I took the last shirt out of my suitcase and set it on the shelf. I hadn't realized how selfish I had been back then. Then again, shouldn't she have just said no to me? No, Lori, you cannot have fifty-dollar jeans when I can't even afford underwear without holes in them! But she hadn't said no. She'd never said no to me. She had always believed I could do anything. Somehow, she must have believed that setting boundaries or saying no would have limited me in some way. Hindsight is twenty-twenty, though, and it's obvious now that a clear sense of limits would have helped me tremendously.

I looked at my now-empty suitcase and realized it was time to get ready to go. I wanted to go to the school early and look around, sort of get my bearings before the orientation began.

I had read over the school's mission statement several times since accepting this job, and now I was finally going to see the school for myself. The school claimed to be unlike any other school in China, and its bold mission was to prepare its students to become elite international leaders. From what Kassie had told me through emails over the summer, few other Chinese schools employed foreign English teachers, and that fact alone did indeed make our school unique. It also made the school's tuition very high—about sixty thousand yuan per year. For the average Chinese citizen, this school was clearly out of reach; most people earned only a fraction of that amount. The families who sent their children here were wealthy, and for most of them, the tuition was not a big sacrifice. There were some families, though, that had sacrificed a great deal to be able to send at least one of their children, usually a son, to this school. They did so in hopes that their children would learn to speak English with ease, and would in turn have bright, international futures.

Kassie further explained that the students felt a great deal of pressure to do well in school, and this pressure was shared by their teachers. In fact, Chinese teachers at the school were often compensated or punished financially based upon the success or failure of their students. From what Kassie had told me, the same was not true for the foreign teachers, but I should still expect to feel the pressure of helping the kids to do well.

I hoped I was up to the challenge.

汤

As I walked to the school that morning, I noticed that the neighborhood looked different in the morning light—still beautiful, but not as surreal as it had when we'd driven through the gates the previous day. There was a bus I could take to the school, but I'd decided I would prefer to walk. It felt good to move, even though I knew it would take me twenty minutes.

Still, despite enjoying the exercise, after twenty minutes of walking, I was sweating profusely and suddenly wishing I had worn cooler clothes. Kassie had warned me about the severe humidity, but this was much hotter and stickier than I'd imagined. I looked forward to getting used to it.

chapter 5

I could see the school from several blocks away, and I suddenly realized it was more like a campus than a building. The kindergarten was behind the elementary school and was its own little campus, and there were student dormitories beyond that. Seeing those, I remembered Kassie telling me that many students lived here during the week while their parents worked in Hong Kong or other places.

The yard surrounding the school was gorgeously landscaped with flowers and even palm trees. There were several glass-enclosed displays advertising the school and the caliber of the students, all colorfully decorated with writing in both Chinese and English. The Chinese characters fascinated me; I hoped to learn more about them someday.

As I walked around, I began seeing adults (I assumed they were the Chinese teachers) carrying papers and supplies through the halls. I imagined they were setting up their classrooms and preparing for orientation. All of them wore neatly pressed uniforms—a requirement for the Chinese staff, I was told, but not for the foreign teachers. Some of the teachers nodded as they walked past me, some just stared, and a few of the women smiled.

The orientation meeting was held in a large conference room on the first floor of the secondary school building. I saw Kassie as soon as I walked in. Those teachers who already knew one another chatted in small groups as their colleagues entered the room. The room was full, and there were about thirty of us new English teachers sitting around the table and on the surrounding couches. I recognized Mr. Zhong, the school director who had interviewed me at the conference. I shook his hand and then went to find a seat.

As I walked over to the table, I said hello to a young guy who looked like he was happy to be there, but not sure what to do with himself. Just like me.

"Hi, I'm Lori," I said. "I think I saw you leaving the same apartment building today. Are you in Building Three?"

"I am!" He extended his hand, which I shook. "I'm Ryan." He smiled.

He was young—only twenty-four—and had just graduated from college in Arizona. He'd heard of the job opportunity through Cindy. Through our conversation, we figured out that he was my upstairs neighbor. I felt like we could be friends. He was funny and relaxed, as far as first impressions went.

The woman on my right was Marie, an American woman who'd been teaching in Thailand. She seemed nervous, even though she wasn't new, so I deduced that this was just her personality. She was nice enough. I was interested to hear more about Thailand.

Everything that was happening was thrilling to me for some reason. I shifted in my seat, full of anticipation, as Mr. Zhong stood up and the room became quiet.

Mr. Zhong began by welcoming us and telling us how pleased he was to see us. He gave us a bit of background about himself, explaining that he had been born in China but had gotten his graduate education in the US and had lived in Canada for many years prior to coming to the school. He kept referring to us as "Western" teachers, and it seemed to fit. I had never thought of myself as a Westerner before, but it made sense.

As I looked around at the faces of the other teachers, I wondered what had brought them to China. Were some of them as surprised by their decision to come here as I had been?

Mr. Zhong invited us to introduce ourselves, and I learned from the different teachers that some had been in China for several years while others, like me, were here for the first time. They each talked about their families and hobbies as well, so we could get a nice sense of who people really were. The younger ones actually shared their age. I wondered if I should. I thought it was kind of weird that people were sharing that, and guessed that it one of those things where since one person had done it, they were all doing it. Anyway, I figured I would share as much as everyone else had.

Most of my new colleagues had some experience as teachers, but few had advanced degrees in the field of foreign language teaching. That helped increase my confidence just in time for me to stand and introduce myself.

Here goes. I stood up, smiled, and said, "Hi, everyone. I'm Lori Frank, here on my own. I'm twenty-eight and I'm from Chicago. My parents and two sisters are still there. I earned my master's degree in applied linguistics and my BA in anthropology. I'm really excited to be here, although I'm not sure it's hit me yet that I'm actually in China!"

Everyone laughed at this as I took my seat again. I scarcely heard the next few people introduce themselves, I was so deeply absorbed in my thoughts. What had happened to me just now? I suddenly felt a great sense of freedom, even fun. Freedom because I was now whomever I wanted to be. I wasn't defined by being from a poor family. I wasn't defined by living in a run-down apartment. I wasn't defined by the responsibility of taking care of my family's finances or handling my dad's health needs. I was no longer thinking about medications, trips to the Veterans Hospital, or my own lack of a life. In this moment, the most fun thing in the world was simply to sit among these people and say that I was Lori from Chicago.

chapter 6

After lunch we were directed to meet with our individual departments. The group of teachers I would be working with was the smallest: there were seven of us, plus three teaching assistants. It looked like an interesting mix of people. As I listened to Kassie and the other teachers describe their experiences, I knew I was going to like working with them. They seemed positive and friendly, and I liked the fact that we were a small group. It felt like there would be a chance of us becoming friends.

I was pretty sure I would also like teaching second grade. It seemed like that perfect age where kids still love school yet are old enough to do more than the basics. I thought it would be fun. I'd spent the previous few years teaching college students and adults, and I was looking forward to teaching the little ones.

It was a long day—the orientation, a tour of the school, meetings within our departments, and then a visit to the accounting office downstairs, where we were each given our little envelope of cash. It was a very strange feeling to be handed a small brown bag of Chinese currency. In China, the largest bill is the hundred yuan note, and a month's pay for me was over two thousand dollars. That meant that when I picked up this money, there would be sixteen thousand yuan, all in hundreds—a huge stack of cash. I learned that this would be how we were paid every month. I was kind of concerned about keeping all that money around my apartment, but all the returning teachers said they'd never had a problem and that getting paid in this way wouldn't seem so strange after a while. When I asked where they kept it, a couple women told me they just stuck it in their underwear drawer.

Okay, I thought to myself. *Whatever.* I would have to figure out how to arrange having some of my pay taken out and wired to my bank back in Chicago; part of the reason for taking the job, after all, was to help my family financially. The more than two thousand dollars a month I was now earning was a nice chunk of change considering what we were used to. I felt proud and deeply thankful that I would be changing their lives for the better, if even a little bit.

One of the strange things that had come up at orientation was the idea of having a maid. Apparently, all the foreign teachers employed household help, or *ayis*. I had gotten an email from the school secretary over the summer asking me if I was interested and I had responded "no thank you." It seemed absurd. Who was I to have a maid? My own mother had earned her living as a member of "the help" in the past, and I could not imagine myself in a position to hire a maid.

When I mentioned this to Sally, a returning teacher, she had a different take on it.

"Well, it's actually a really good deal for them," she said. "Fifty dollars a month to us is a living to them, and they really do a good job."

Another teacher chimed in with, "Yeah, and they do everything for you—the shopping, cleaning, running errands, even cooking. After long days at school, you're going to wish you had an *ayi*."

The more I listened to their more experienced opinions, the more sense it made. Maybe I would consider it after all.

汤

That night after returning home, I sat in the middle of my living room floor once again and thought about the events of the day. I thought of my family. I thought of the past. My life had taken so many turns and had followed a route so different from most people—at least, that was how I felt. It was still hard to believe that I was in a new country and had been given such a special opportunity. I wasn't sure what this chance was for or what I would do with it, but I knew deep inside that there was a reason I was here.

chapter 7

As I prepared my classroom, I felt like a kid playing school. I knew I was spending far too much time making a sign that said "Miss Frank" for my door, but I couldn't help myself. Every few minutes I would look around my classroom with pride. Things were coming together. I had hung colorful paper on the walls and created thematic bulletin boards on each one. There was also room to hang the students' photos and drawings, as well as a place to display their work. I had distinguished the "reading corner" with a large piece of carpet so the children would be more comfortable during story time. I was having so much fun, and my lack of confidence about being able to decorate a classroom had disappeared.

After hanging my name on my classroom door, sharpening pencils and making name tags for each desk were my next tasks. I found little baskets and put crayons in one, erasers in another, and put them on the bottom shelf. I made a folder for each student and put them in piles on another shelf—one section for the morning group, another for the afternoon. Perusing my books, paper, and flashcards, I then zeroed in on the stickers Mom had bought for me in Chicago. She'd thought it might be fun to give those to the students when they had done particularly good work—such a sweet idea. I was really grateful she had thought of it. I thought it was ironic, though, that my mom spent her hard-earned money on things that these kids could easily afford to buy themselves. At least it was something unique; some of the holiday stickers she'd purchased couldn't be found in China.

It seemed that everything was in order. Now all I needed were my students.

汤

I arrived at school an hour early on Monday morning and noticed that Kassie was already in her office. She reminded me that the welcome assembly would be held at eight and the students would come up to the classroom immediately afterwards. I paced the floors of my classroom, arranging and rearranging what had already been done. Before I knew it, it was eight thirty, and I heard children's voices and lots of noise coming from the stairwell.

Kassie had encouraged us to be at our classroom doors to greet the children. The TAs were pointing them in the right direction, helping them find their classrooms.

Three kids, a tall girl and two boys, ran past me into the classroom—each one saying, "Good morning, teacher," as they did so. Clearly, they were super pumped to begin English class. They skipped around the room talking in what I could only guess was Cantonese.

"Good morning," I said. "Can you find your name tag and sit down?"

They looked at me, then each other, and then laughed.

Okay, they don't understand anything I just said. Let's try this again. "What is your name?" I asked the girl.

Again, she just laughed and looked at the other kids as if to say, "What is this lady saying?"

By this time five more students had come in and that was everyone. I had to take control from the beginning, I knew that, but suddenly it was harder than I thought. These eight-year-olds were running around the room now, shouting and laughing, and I was just standing there, helpless. I kept remembering everything those classroom management books had said about the first day being the most important, about it laying the foundation for the whole school year. *Okay, Lori, you can do this*, I told myself.

"Okay, everyone sit down," I said. I gestured to their chairs and even sat down myself to reinforce the message.

Everyone sat where they were, oblivious to my beautifully prepared name tags.

"Now, where is . . . Jia . . . Jin?"

They all laughed at the way I pronounced the name. *They ought to know a bit of English*, I thought, *they're probably just out of practice and a little nervous*. Supposedly, most of them had been taught a little English in kindergarten and spent two hours a day on it last year, in first grade.

"Are you Jia Jin?" I asked the tall girl.

"Yes. I . . . Jia Jin," she said.

"Good, okay. Now where is Liu Ping?"

A little boy raised his hand and said, "Here."

Great, I thought, *their English is coming back to them and they are settling down*.

After going through the roll, I pointed out the name tags to them and had each student sit in their proper seat. I definitely had their attention now. I noticed them sneaking peeks around the room, too, and I could tell they were fascinated by all I had put on the walls.

I had not been assigned my own teaching assistant since my class was so small. I was grateful when Lei Hong came in and asked if she could help. I knew that theoretically it was best to teach English using English; that was what all the methods I had learned in graduate school had espoused. However, on that first day, I wanted the students to be absolutely clear about a few things, so I had Lei Hong translate some classroom rules and then explain a bit about the reading corner and the program I'd designed to go along with it.

After distributing journals and pencils to the kids, I had them copy what was on the board. I thanked Cai Hong and told her before she left to tell the students not to worry if they didn't understand my words—that they should just try their best, and soon they would. She did, and they seemed happy.

汤

We took a five-minute break after the first hour, during which time I let my students go to the common room and work on a puzzle or simply talk to their friends. When they returned, they did their daily journals, which for the first several weeks would consist mostly of copying what I had written on the board.

We did some calendar activities where they practiced the days of the week and months of the year. After a second break, I read them a story, and then we played a matching game with flashcards. I had managed to keep their attention so far. I was still a bit anxious about the lesson plan—until I looked at the clock and realized I had actually over-prepared.

Phew.

At the end of class I had the kids "sit nicely" in their desks (after modeling what that meant), and dismissed them one by one. They tried too hard to sit straight, and I could tell this was a competition for them, each wanting to be the first to be dismissed. Before I knew it, they were gone and I sat alone in my classroom. I'd just survived my first class.

chapter 8

I needed internet in my apartment, so I asked the school secretary, Irene, how to do this. She gave me a form to fill out but told me I needed to pay the fee somewhere else—it was impossible to pay for the connection there. This seemed inconvenient and confusing; I'd thought I would be able to take care of both at one place. But no such luck. The post office handled internet setup, Irene informed me.

Going to the post office for internet services was a new concept to me, but I was up for it. I had to take two different buses in order to find my way to the post office; when I got there I managed, with my phrase book in hand, to find the right line reasonably quickly.

As I was waiting my turn, people kept cutting in front of me in line. I am usually an assertive person, but this shocked me because the people doing it didn't seem to think anything of it. *Is this a cultural habit?* I wondered. I tried to be patient when it happened again and again, but after the first handful of times, it started getting beyond frustrating. Being respectful of cultural differences was one thing; standing in a line all day and letting people cut in front of me was quite another. After the fourth person tried to cut in front of me I put my foot in front of him as if to say, "No way, buddy."

A shouting match in Cantonese ensued between the guy

who'd just tried to cut in front of me and another guy who was in the line next to us. I wasn't sure if the other one was defending me, or what the nature of their argument is, but as they were fighting about it, I worked my way up to the counter.

The girl took my money and said, "You come tomorrow, get information."

"Okay," I said. "What information?"

She again repeated her rote phrase without looking up at me: "You come tomorrow, get information."

Just to see if I'd get another response, I dared to ask, "What time?"

"You come tomorrow, get information," she said—this time with a slight touch of annoyance in her voice.

This was not the end of the world, I decided. Besides, now that I was out and about, I was excited to explore my surroundings and try to feel a part of things. I stopped asking questions and stepped away from the window.

汤

Three days had passed since I first went to the post office. I'd returned the previous two days to get the aforementioned information, and both times my friend the postal worker had said only, "Not now information." I interpreted this to mean that my password and login information were not yet ready.

On this fourth visit—after waiting in line and not letting anyone cut in—I got up to the counter. Before I could even get a word out, she handed me the information. I was so excited, as though I had just received the key to some great secret hiding place. "I have my information!" I felt like shouting it from the rooftops. Instead, I said, "Xie xie," and headed home to try it out. All I wanted to do was log on and send an email from the comfort of my own home.

汤

It didn't work. I tried again and again before calling the maintenance office.

"*Wei*," someone answered—the standard response when anyone picked up the phone.

"Uh, yes, hello. I need help with my internet connection," I stupidly said in English.

"*Wo bu dong. Ni shuo shenma?*"

"Uh. . . ." I didn't know where to go from here. I had only learned how to say hello and thank you so far. "I have *problema*." *Okay, why is Spanish coming out of my mouth?* I had managed to learn my numbers one through ten, so I decided to tell them my room number. "*Er . . . Ling . . . Yao.*"

I said this at least five times before the guy realized that I was indeed speaking Chinese and was telling him my room number. When he finally understood me, he said a bunch of things followed by an "okay," to which I responded, "Okay," and hung up.

I had no idea what we'd just agreed upon, but five minutes later there was a knock at my door.

I opened the door, revealing a very slight man with a boyish face on the other side. He gave a shy smile, took off his sandals, and came in, speaking Chinese to me. I smiled and pointed to the phone cord, then to the computer. I made some crazy gestures indicating that I could not connect the two, and miraculously, he understood. The problem was that I didn't understand his response.

After much back-and-forth, I managed to understand that I needed a different phone cord. The phone I had was quite antiquated and it looked like the attached cord would not allow for a modem connection. I could not believe it was this much trouble just to connect to the internet.

The maintenance guy left and came back a few minutes later with a paper that had "management office" written on it. He handed it to me and left again.

汤

Arriving at the management office the next day, I explained with pantomime more than language that I needed a cord. They nodded and gave me three forms to complete first. I paid two yuan at a different office and was told I could pick up the cord at a warehouse on the other side of town.

Later that night, I found the warehouse and showed my piece of paper with "phone cord" written in Chinese to every worker I saw. They didn't know what to think of me. Many of them looked at me as if they have never seen a foreigner in their lives, and I realized that they probably hadn't. Each person that I met guided me through a different part of the maze that was the warehouse until, finally, I found the right office.

"*Ni hao*," the older man in the office said.

"Ni hao," I said, and handed him the paper.

He came back with the cord in his hand.

My heart was filled with hope. I couldn't believe that after all this, I was finally going to get this phone cord. I couldn't wait to go back to my cozy little apartment, plug in the cord, and finally email my friends and family.

But then I looked more closely at the part the man was holding, and the wind was knocked out of me. It did not even resemble a phone cord. I wanted to cry or choke someone, but instead I took a deep breath. I tried once again to explain and show the man, pointing to his phone, exactly what it was that I needed.

They didn't have those here, the man finally explained. I would probably need to go to another city.

Although this was terrible news, I realized how happy I was to have actually understood what he'd said. I wondered how it was possible that in this humongous place, they had no phone cords. I thought about that the whole way to Siqao, a nearby city, where I got off the bus, walked into the first little store I saw, and found a phone cord.

chapter 9

As I hopped on the bus for Siqao, I had to remind myself that many of the people I encountered had never seen a foreigner before, and I should try not to be bothered by their open-mouthed stares. I was constantly reminded that while in China, I would never be anonymous.

Even when I was doing my grocery shopping in the market, people looked intently in my basket to see what I was buying. They watched to see if I would barter and whether or not I'd get a good price. I went to get my hair cut one day, and I was deeply relaxed, enjoying the head massage that is always a part of a haircut in China, when I casually looked out the window. At least ten people were leaning up against the glass, peering inside with open-mouthed stares. A smile and a wave on my part brought them out of their trance, but this is what I encountered when I ventured outside the gates of my little community.

As time went by, my list of cultural differences accumulated. I also realized, though, that in many ways people are much the same wherever we go. On the bus one day, among all the noise, cigarette smoke, and the huge variety of people—from farmers to businessmen—a woman with a baby got on, and it was suddenly as if nothing else mattered. All the talking came to a halt as we all took notice of the baby and became fascinated by everything he did. We all, vocally and otherwise, *oohed* and *aahed* at the way the baby moved his hands or pointed to the window. Everything was adorable, amazing, and for a few minutes, we were all enthralled. Then, the next stop came, the baby and mother got off, and everyone went back to their own worlds.

Scenes such as this probably occur everywhere in the world, but during moments like those it would hit me that I was really living in China, on the other side of the world, and that the world is not so big after all.

Today, as we drove along on the bumpy road (which seemed to be under permanent construction), I thought about where I was going. An orphanage. One of the American teachers had arranged for a few of us to volunteer every Sunday afternoon, and I was planning to meet some of the other teachers there. The woman who organized the visit, Julie, had already adopted a little Chinese girl, which was how she had been established a connection with the orphanage.

Prior to coming to China, I had developed an interest in the one-child policy and the reasons behind it. I'd always known I wanted to be a mother. Knowing about Chinese orphanages, or at least having read about them, I guess I'd also had thoughts about adopting a Chinese baby. Now that I was in China, it seemed like a real possibility.

The thing was, though, that I couldn't imagine being married. I suppose I had imagined it, but I'd never thought of it in a serious way. It's not that I was against marriage; on the contrary, I strongly believed in the notion of marriage. I guess that's why I didn't think it would happen for me. I knew what I wanted in a husband, and I had never met or dated anyone who had come close to being that person. Anything was possible. Still, I wasn't holding my breath. I was approaching thirty and living in the People's Republic of China, not exactly a dating haven.

The fact that I'd gone to college and even graduate school still shocked me once in awhile. I'd somehow figured out how to do these things, and fairly well. Now, here I was living in another country, with the chance to begin a promising career. So maybe not all my dreams of a nice husband and happy family would come true, but being a mother would be close. I could be a single parent. I could hire the help I needed, and eventually even my own mom could help out, which she would love. I knew I had a lot to give. I tried to tell myself this—that I was okay with being single, that I didn't wish to find actual enduring love and a beautiful relationship—but something about that story didn't ring true, and I knew it.

汤

As I rode the bus to the orphanage, I thought back to the stories I used to hear about China and their one-child policy. It was beyond my comprehension and sounded so oppressive. How could a government mandate how many children a family could have? And what about all those stories I'd heard about people abandoning baby girls? Was that why there were mostly girls in the orphanages?

As is usually the case, I would eventually discover that there was a nugget of truth to all the stories I'd heard, but the Chinese themselves painted a very different picture of this policy. In fact, the Chinese friends I later discussed it with said they were grateful for the policy. They acknowledged that there simply had been too many people in China, and since the government began to implement the policy, the economy had gotten better. Quite simply, there was more to go around.

As to the practice of abandoning babies, people acknowledged that, sadly, it did happen, and maybe to some extent continued to happen, in the countryside. People were scared of not being able to feed their baby, or were afraid that a girl wouldn't be able to contribute to the family in the same way that a boy would, so yes, sometimes they would leave the baby. Did some babies die this way? Perhaps so, but that isn't the case anymore.

The traditional belief that boys are more valuable than girls is still somewhat present in the countryside, which is why there are so many baby girls in the orphanages. People in more rural areas tend to believe that when a girl gets married, she joins the man's family—so when her parents get old, she will not be there to take care of them. In addition to that, they want a son so the family name will be carried on. So it's easy to see why, from their perspective, a son is very important.

The truth is that families in China can indeed have more than one child. The government in no way actually stops them from doing so; it does maintain, however, that the compulsory education of only one child per family will be supported by the system, as that's all they can afford. Despite this policy, some families choose to have more children. They simply pay the fine and shoulder the expense of their other children's education themselves. For most of the families at our school, for example, this was not an issue. They had as many kids as they wanted; they could afford to pay the fine. But even for the less affluent, the choice is there and many take advantage of it. If the family has a second child and doesn't have cash to pay the fine, the government will take furniture or anything else of value to exact its fee. Many people I know have chosen this route. Like many Westerners, they believe family is more important than possessions and they can always replace the furniture later.

汤

I was thrilled to have this chance to go to an orphanage and maybe learn a bit more about Chinese adoption in the process. The fact that my colleague had gotten us in was a major accomplishment in and of itself, because foreigners, even those who were adopting, weren't usually allowed inside.

When we arrived, Xiao Jiang, the woman my colleague knew, greeted us at the front door and guided us through the rooms where we'd be working. The orphanage was not what I expected, though I wasn't really sure what my expectations had been. It was very simple, with concrete walls and floors. There were two rooms: one with small cribs lined up in rows and another with a few toys. It was clean and organized, but very dull in appearance and limited in supplies. Xiao Jiang said that the main thing we could help with was holding the babies. The people taking care of them seemed to be gentle and to care about them, but there were only a few workers and so many babies. They simply didn't have time to cuddle every baby as much as a baby should be cuddled.

Most of the workers took several of the babies to the other room to feed them. Before leaving, though, they nodded toward the cribs, smiling, indicating that we should hold the babies. It was amazing to be trusted with all these precious little girls— and all we had to do was hold them? Heaven!

I walked to the crib closest to the window and looked down at the baby girl inside. She looked healthy—all bundled up in lots of clothes and then swaddled in a blanket. I picked her up and pulled her to my chest. She didn't show any reaction, but it was a wonderful moment for me. I felt so blessed and lucky to be there. It hit me what a rare chance I'd been given. I looked around the room at my colleagues, who were quietly doing the same thing, and tears came to my eyes.

I lowered the little girl from my chest and cradled her in my arms so I could look into her eyes. I wondered what would become of her. Would she stay in this orphanage until she became old enough to leave on her own? Would an American family come to

China and adopt her? Would I one day adopt a baby girl like her from this very orphanage? My thoughts were all over the place, yet filled with peaceful excitement about her life, as well as mine. I hoped we'd both get what we wanted.

As I looked at this innocent little girl, I thought of what kind of mother she might have. I thought about who would adopt her and what her life would look like. The role of a mother is so important, I thought. I guess I'd known that before, but holding her, looking into her eyes, a quiet and clear thought washed over me. Children need love, yes, but they need boundaries and clear expectations from their parents. This baby, this girl, would need a mother who wouldn't be afraid to say "no" at times. This girl would need to know that she was expected to work hard in school, to prepare for the future. I thought about my own life and my sweet parents. They had done their best, but I wished they had been more direct with me. When I became a mother, someday, I would tell my children things directly. I would teach them. I would tell them about my faith—why I chose to go to church, what I believed about God, how the spiritual aspects of my life were so important to me. I never doubted my parents' faith in God, though they lived their faith quietly. Their approach had its own beauty, but I wish they'd been more open, more direct. I felt peaceful thinking about how I might do things differently if I ever had the chance.

I put this little girl down, walked to the crib next to hers, and picked up another baby. Similar thoughts went through my mind about this little girl and what her future might hold. Suddenly the world didn't seem so big. I knew that I was in China and that it was the other side of the world from my home, but at that moment, I felt very connected to everything around me, including these little girls. I loved being there—in China, in the orphanage, all of it. My mind was wrapped up in their lives, in my life, and in how our lives could intertwine.

Before I knew it, it was four o'clock and our time was up. My heart hurt and I didn't want to leave. I felt bad for those babies and I felt a little bad for myself. I so wanted to be a mother. I had never been more sure.

chapter 10

I had decided immediately that I didn't want to be the kind of expat who lives in China but can't say anything other than "*ni hao*" and "*zai jian*" (hello and good-bye). I was loving China, and I wanted to make the most of my time there. Learning Mandarin was an obvious necessity to really learn the culture and be a part of things. To do this, I used a variety of methods, including informally learning phrases from Chinese friends and colleagues, studying characters from a textbook, and occasionally hiring tutors.

I'd never thought I would be able to make sense of this language, but as I studied and practiced, I began picking it up more easily. By the spring, I could go to the tailor and order clothes by myself. True, the girls who worked there and I always had a good laugh about my Mandarin, but I convinced myself that they were laughing with me rather than at me. Usually if I threw enough words out there and used some gestures, I got my point across. If nothing else, making these attempts forced me to get out there and at least hear the language. By accident, I began picking up a little Cantonese, too, since that was the local language. Sometimes I would get them mixed up and use parts of both in a sentence. People still managed to understand!

I had the chance to get a foot massage quite regularly here

since it was only about $5 US for an hour-long massage. This is a very popular thing in China, especially in the wealthier areas. It is not only relaxing, it is also considered a kind of preventative medicine. I usually went to the same person every time because the massage was just right, and I noticed improvement in my Chinese after talking with him.

My friend, Ryan and I would sometimes get foot massages together and it always ended up being a strange and fun combination of a party and language lesson. We often brought along treats like gummy bears or sodas and we would chat with each other and with our friends, the massage guys. We had our favorites and I like to think we were their favorites too.

My foot massage guy knew no English, so he taught me Chinese by using Chinese. I kept telling him that he was a brilliant teacher. It just came naturally to him, but as a teacher myself, I was amazed at how pedagogically sound it all was. He really used the available tangible contexts: he said things in many ways until I finally got the idea, then went back and explained all the other ways to say that one thing he had just taught me. Through this process I was getting a great deal more vocabulary and could repeat the things I knew, thus getting more oral practice. He always began with the same questions so I could practice answering them, and then he told me about his day, week, or whatever, and I got listening practice. I guess those who aren't linguists or teachers might not find this fascinating, but to me, this was sort of groundbreaking. I started thinking about writing something about it—"How I Learned Chinese at the Massage Place." Except I would have to come up with a much better title.

汤

On Saturdays, or even on some evenings, I liked to take the bus into Siqao, which was the closest city to the Estates. I just loved the ride itself and was fascinated by the people I encountered on these trips. They did things differently than what I was used to; even the way people dressed was so different from what I expected. I don't mean that in a cliché way, like everyone was walking around in traditional Chinese clothing. What I mean is, for example, that so many guys wear dress pants and suit jackets. It's kind of funny. The people who sell vegetables on the street, who work construction, who fix the sewer, who do your taxes—all of them wear dress pants. Siqao is just the dress suit capital of the world, I guess. Whether the fashion choices, food variety, or a host of other cultural differences, all I knew was that this place was growing on me.

Another thing I loved to observe was how everyone could sit all day in that squat position. It's normal in China, especially for men, to assume that position while waiting for the bus or while relaxing and talking to friends. I actually find the position quite comfortable and natural, but it's something you don't see in the States. Seeing groups of five on a motorcycle, everyone's making-up-the-rules-as-we-go-along driving, the buses that really didn't have any particular route and would stop anywhere and tell you to get on (doesn't matter where you're going; they're going your way), the fact that you'd sit with complete strangers at a restaurant if there were no other tables and they had room at theirs, and even, dare I say, the dirt and the grey buildings—it was all growing on me.

汤

At some point during this first year in China, I began to treasure my Sundays more deeply than I ever had before. Easter meant more to me. It seemed to me that my personal faith was growing. I found myself keenly aware of my own spirituality. I sat in my apartment one day, immersed in reading the scriptures—in this case the Old Testament—and I felt such happiness, like I was in exactly the right place doing exactly what I was supposed to be doing. I'd been preparing a lesson—a discourse on how trials and affliction can strengthen us—to teach in the women's group I belonged to the following Sunday, and rather than it being a task to complete, I felt joy in preparing it. After all, this women's organization wasn't just any group. The Relief Society of the Church of Jesus Christ of Latter-Day Saints is one of the oldest and largest women's organizations in the world. Somehow being in this small version of it, in China, made me feel part of the whole even more. Through these discussions on Sunday, I felt connected to women—my sisters—all over the world.

I felt nothing but gratitude during times like this—for my life and the beautiful experiences I was having in China, but also for the family I'd come from, the challenges I'd faced, and all I'd learned in the process. It was supposed to mean something—all of it was—and my time in China was giving me the clarity to finally get that.

chapter 11

Chinese people are very health-conscious, and older people in particular take great pride in their stamina and youthful abilities. There was a man-made mountain down the road from the teachers' apartments, and I often climbed it, usually early in the morning, just as the sun was coming up. It was a tough workout for me, despite my having gotten in much better shape since coming to China; I could run six miles three times a week, but climbing this mountain almost took more out of me. I always felt great afterwards, though, which was probably what kept me going.

The other thing that kept me going was the fact that these ninety-year-olds continued to pass me on the way up. They would bounce right by me and, noticing that I was struggling, give me a nod of encouragement and a "*zao shang hao*" (good morning).

I saw this again and again—the stamina of these older people. They were so incredibly fit and healthy, and I often wished all of America could live in China just long enough to let this lifestyle have an influence. We are so caught up with the latest diet and newest trick toward losing weight in the US, yet the answers are really so simple. Having struggled with trying to learn healthy eating habits myself, I knew how difficult it could be to establish and maintain healthy habits. But now, in China, I had finally internalized everything I'd been trying to learn and I felt healthier than ever. And it wasn't a quick fix that had gotten me there; it was a combination of modifying my diet (though not so much that I didn't still eat McDonald's or Pizza Hut once a week) along with the active lifestyle that in China was just so accessible, and inviting.

Not only did people climb the mountain in the morning, they also did tai chi in the park. It was a beautiful thing to watch. Tai chi is a series of fluid, smooth movements that flow together like a very slow dance. To do it well requires great balance and flexibility, and also great patience. When I first joined them in the park to try to learn, I wanted them to put it in fast-forward. *These movements are great*, I thought, *but can we speed it up a bit?* It was only after I let go of the time element and did as they said, thought about each and every movement, that I began to get it. It is about the process, about the journey from one movement to the other, rather than simply getting to the next move—much like life should be, I suppose.

Another thing that stood out to me was how comfortable people were with wearing their pajamas outside their houses. In the evening, this was a fascinating thing for an outsider to watch. After dinner, when the sun went down, couples, families, and individuals came outside for a walk. They walked through their neighborhoods, to the park, or around the lake. When it was hot, the women might carry a small fan. Sometimes they would walk backwards for a while, since that's good exercise for the bum muscles. And they did all of this in their pajamas.

When I first saw this, it seemed strange, since in America the most we'll venture outside for in our pajamas is to get the paper from the porch (actually, do people even do that anymore?)—and even then we put on a robe first. Not in China.

As time went on, I began to like this habit more and more. Now I find going out in my pajamas comfortable and a normal part of my routine. I never see any other Westerners doing this, and I guess that's not unusual. I love that I don't really care.

汤

It never occurred to me how unusual it was that I had adopted the wearing-pajamas-outside thing until I ran into two teachers from the school one night. They had just come from the Pink Chair, a popular make-shift bar outside a local restaurant. There was no actual furniture there, save a few plastic pink chairs, hence the name.

Now that I was here in China, being given this incredible chance to learn and grow, I didn't want to waste one moment. There was something to learn, either about China or about myself, all the time, and I just could not fathom giving up a Friday night to watch others get drunk and complain about school—which, according to the people who attended the Pink Chair get-togethers, was exactly what happened there.

I had also heard some of my colleagues more than once complaining about "the Chinese," and I definitely couldn't tolerate that kind of talk. So my Friday nights were filled with reading, yoga, arranging my pictures, and sometimes having dinner with friends.

When Tess and Becky rode up on their bikes that night, I got a strange vibe from Tess, who rolled her eyes when she saw me. These two women were people I considered to be friends, and I didn't know what to make of her gesture.

"Hey, guys," I said.

"Hey there, Lori. Nice pj's," Tess said with a stifled sneer.

"Thanks," I said, not offering an explanation.

Becky looked between us and said, "Well, we better get going. Enjoy your walk."

"I will," I said, and they rode off. As they pulled away on their bikes, I heard Tess say to Becky, "Seriously, did you see that? Does she think she's Chinese?"

The comment stung, just for a second. But I kept walking. It was an interesting question, actually. Obviously the answer was no, but it was telling that people were so quick to get uncomfortable when someone else stepped outside of their assumed category. No, I did not think that going for a walk in my pajamas made me Chinese; I did think I was in China, however, and that I would like to try on different cultural norms. Was I going to take up smoking because most men here smoked? No. Was I going pretend that chicken feet were my favorite food? No. I did not plan to do things in which I had no interest just to fit into the culture, and I had no intention of trying to be something I wasn't. But how could I know who that was if I wasn't open to new experiences? Going for an evening walk in nice clean pajamas after having washed for the day was an interesting concept, and one I was really growing to like.

Part of the reason I enjoyed it so much was that there was a connection among people as they did it. I really felt a part of the community during these walks in a way that I wouldn't have if I'd been walking with a specific destination in mind or was in a big hurry. Even though my neighbors and I weren't walking side by side, we were all outside, enjoying the night air, together. We said "ni hao" to each other or simply nodded as we passed one another. We were greeting our neighbors and taking advantage of the beautiful walkways and gardens that surrounded us. I was finding these evening walks to be one of the most peaceful, thought-provoking times of my day.

When I came back to the states years later, once in awhile I would revisit this tradition. When I did so, it was easy to mentally transport myself back to China, walking among all the families who were doing something good for their health and making a connection with the people and things around them. When I did so, it was easy to mentally transport myself back to China, walking among all the families who were doing something good for their health and making a connection with the people and things around them.

chapter 12

ne day, I took an early bus into work. The streets were
quieter than usual. One of the Chinese teachers I worked
with got on at the same stop and we exchanged pleasantries. He
was probably in his fifties and was very distinguished looking.
He was always kind to me and patiently listened and nodded as I
tried to crank out a few sentences in Mandarin.

On this particular morning, we were the only two people who
got off at 13th Street, which led to the back gate of the school.
The rain had started the night before and hadn't stopped. It was
doing that a lot during this time (hence the term "rainy season").

As we exited the bus, we realized that all the side streets were
flooded with at least a foot of water. We checked a few others
to see if there was less water there, but they were all just as bad.
Now, this man did not speak any English, and my Mandarin was
more limited than I realized. I didn't seem to have the vocabulary for this situation. He began talking super fast and making
all these gestures. Because I had no idea what he was trying to
communicate, I timidly began to just walk through the puddle.
I figured there was really no alternative and a little (or a foot of)
water wouldn't kill me.

He took me by both arms, looking straight into my eyes, and
said, "*Deng yi xia!*" (Wait a minute!). He took off his shoes and

59

socks, put his socks in his pocket, grabbed his shoes, and rolled up his pants. I started to do the same.

"*Bu! Bu! Wo bei ni.*"

I knew this literally meant "I back you." I was still doing this translation in my mind when he walked over to me and actually scooped me up onto his back. I fussed a little at this, because I was not exactly a lightweight, and he was not a young guy! I had these immediate and awful images of him falling down in the water because of me and I couldn't stand it, so I tried to refuse.

"*Bu xing!*" I cried. "*Wo tai zhong. Bu ke yi.*" (No way, I'm too heavy, you can't.)

Well, he insisted. He carried my gigantic backpack and I carried an umbrella, trying to protect both of us from the rain.

When we arrived at the school gate, I thanked him profusely as he gently let me down off his back. I felt so embarrassed, but I was incredibly moved by his gesture—not to mention impressed by his strength.

汤

All I could think about throughout the week was my colleague's poor back. I didn't see him for a couple of days and that made me very nervous. I kept wondering if I had misunderstood his offer. Maybe he hadn't intended to carry me at all. Maybe he was offering to carry my backpack, not me. Maybe when he bent down and said something about his back, maybe it was that his back really hurt, and then I jumped on! I had images of him talking to his colleagues about this: "What could I do? I offered to carry the foreigner's backpack and next thing I knew, she jumped on me!!"

Thoughts like this haunted me all week until I finally saw him, caught him alone, thanked him again, and asked him how his back was. He laughed and said it was no problem. Then again, I doubt he would have told me the truth if his back had been killing him all week. Regardless, long live true chivalry in China.

chapter 13

My friend Mike, his wife, Janice, and another friend Ryan decided to start a running club after school, and I could not have been more excited. As soon as Mike mentioned it, I jumped at the chance to join. For me, running had always been something of a dream—one of the end goals in my fitness quest process. To put on running shoes and step outside and simply run is something that successful, healthy, fit women do. I used to dream about it—of being that kind of confident, successful woman—and although I was not yet entirely there, I was closer than I had ever been, so this running club was a dream come true.

As I thought about the importance of the running club, it dawned on me that there were several goals along those lines that I was hoping to realize while I was there in China. I hadn't come with a plan to rid myself of old habits and finally create my true identity, but in some ways, that was exactly what I was doing. Being a respected teacher, one of the few there at that time who held a master's in applied linguistics, was a part of that. Nobody there knew that I'd had no role models when it came to higher education and that I'd had to figure it out on my own. I'd even flunked out of community college twice before finally getting my associate's degree and getting serious about my education— and none of that mattered now, anyway.

The same was true of my fitness. As far as my new friends knew, it was no big deal that I was going to join their running club. They had no idea that my family struggled with morbid obesity and that I had grown up not knowing what it meant to eat normally and have a healthy lifestyle. No one knew that this had been a difficult issue for me growing up and that I was just now beginning to figure it out. I'd worried too much about these things as a child and it had definitely impacted me. But I didn't want to dwell on that anymore. I was so genuinely happy that I'd finally moved beyond those worries and I was taking control of my health and my life. What mattered now was that I was putting on running shoes and going running with my friends three times a week.

Our school had a beautiful track, so when we finished our work for the day, about four of us headed out and warmed up. Mike's knees were bad, so he liked to take it slow. This was a huge relief to me, because anything but slow was not an option for me as I began my running journey.

That first day, we started our slow jog around the track, and I was already huffing and puffing before I had finished the first lap. But I made myself finish, and then I walked three more. Mike and Ryan continued running while Janice and I walked. It just kind of worked. Everyone was doing their own thing and I actually didn't feel one bit bad about the shape I was in. After all, I was out there. I was trying. I felt proud of myself.

汤

Every time we went out to the track, I added more running time. Mike was very encouraging. He simply loved running. He wasn't doing it to lose weight; he was just doing it for general health and the love of the sport. He may have even considered it an art, the way he talked about it. He was passionate, and his passion helped keep me motivated when I felt like I was going to die and could not possibly keep running.

Ryan made no pretense about liking running. In fact, he often said he hated it and that he only ran so he could continue to eat McDonald's without getting too fat. I loved that about him! I found myself feeling so comfortable with these people. They had no idea how much they were helping me.

Halfway through my first year in China, I was running six miles twice a week and ten miles every Friday. My self-confidence skyrocketed. For me, this was not only about running; it was about doing what I had always wanted to do but never had the support and the opportunity to make it a reality. In many ways, Mike, with his consistency and positive attitude about running, actually changed my life. Becoming a runner gave me confidence to do so many other things. It was a jumping-off point, and I was truly finding myself.

chapter 14

On the hour-long bus rides I took to church each Sunday, I often thought about the history of China and why religion hadn't played a bigger role there. To be honest, I didn't share the same feelings many people did about the lack of freedom of religion in China. I thought freedom was a good thing, of course, and I supposed it would be great for everyone to have a choice about what religion they practiced. But as I thought about it, I could sort of understand why China was not opening its doors to Western religions at this point. I wouldn't say that I feel that I'm living in a communist country, though, at least not usually.

The history of China and Western religion is long and complicated on both sides. Part of the reason is that the official political party of China is, of course, the Communist party, and organized religion does not coincide with the core philosophies of communism.

Living in China in the year 2000, I observe that China does seem to shelter is citizens. Certain books or media are off limits and it's true that people are not allowed to practice religion, outside of what is approved by the government. When it came to religion, it was a tough issue for the government. I was sure the leaders of the country did not believe every religion is inappropriate, but there was the fear that if they opened the door to what they deemed appropriate or "good" groups, China would become susceptible to every influence, good and bad—and they definitely didn't want that.

China has been victimized repeatedly by Western countries—countries claiming to be Christian and democratic. Other countries have thought they know what is best for China and, in a condescending and sometimes violent manner, have tried to change it accordingly. Other countries have outright attacked China, taking what they wanted. In fact, seven different Western countries have invaded China, tearing down their precious Summer Palace and destroying many valuable artifacts in the process. Is it any wonder that Chinese are skeptical of, if not cynical about, Christianity? After all, these were Christian countries!

When I shared what I had learned with another foreign teacher in China, Alisha, she expressed the idea that my view was too one-sided. Surely, she said, China was not an innocent victim in all that had taken place. She cited the Cultural Revolution and Tibet as examples. What I told her, and what I stand by, is that those were internal struggles and, complicated as they may be, are not the same thing. I had started to care deeply about China and its history. My perspective was changing, opening.

I was grateful that I could continue to practice my religion in the same way I'd done at home—through church attendance, honoring the Sabbath, praying, and reading scriptures. Some rituals we can take with us anywhere, as they are personal and quiet, but church attendance—having a group of people worshipping together, however modestly—now felt like a privilege.

It's always meaningful to go to church, but because of the special circumstances in China, my sense of spirituality seemed to deepen. In larger congregations back home, churchgoers could be kind of anonymous and participate only when keen to do so. But there in Guangzhou, with such a small group practicing together, everyone had a significant role to play and everyone had more than one responsibility, be it teaching, organizing service projects, playing the piano in sacrament meetings, or one of the countless other jobs that needed to be done in order to keep our little branch (as smaller congregations are called) going. Nobody could sit on the sidelines—everyone was noticed, and everyone was needed.

It is kind of ironic to me that I experienced such significant spiritual growth in China. I mean, after all, this was a country without freedom of religion. Chinese citizens could not legally come to church with me, even if they wanted to. We didn't even have a church; we held our meetings in Ted and Louisa's home. There were fewer than fifty of us altogether. And yet I felt my spirituality deepening with every passing Sunday, and really, with every passing day. Maybe it was because our little branch was without the big chapel and huge congregation that I felt more truly what religion and spiritual peace were all about. There, on the other side of the world, I had come to more fully understand the nature of my own faith.

chapter 15

Although work could be intense at times, it seemed that there was always another holiday just around the corner to look forward to. This sustained us, I think, as during regular weeks we had observations and parents' day and open day and every other extracurricular activity in between.

When the holidays rolled around, everyone started planning where they would go, and many of my colleagues often ended up going on trips together. I guess they wanted to save money—and it can be more fun to explore China with a group, of course. I, however, set a rule for myself that I would travel solo as often as I could.

There were a couple of reasons that I made this choice. For one, living in our gated community meant that not only did I see my coworkers at school, but I also lived in the same apartment complex as they did. We went to the same restaurants and stores, and we rode the same buses. I liked most everyone I worked with and had nothing against them, but when it came time to travel, I wanted to see not only different places but also different people. Otherwise, the conversation inevitably turned toward work, and then there wasn't much of a vacation, no matter where we traveled.

On one particular trip, I went to Beijing with a sweet Southern couple whom I'd met at an expat gathering the previous month.

"Are ya'll about done here?" Peggy asked twenty minutes after we entered the Forbidden City.

"Um, not really," I said. "There is still so much to see."

"Okay, well, I'm gonna scoot on over to that shopping center for a bit," she said. "How 'bout we meet back at that frozen yogurt place we walked by earlier?"

I had to smile. "Sure."

Off she and Drake went.

It seemed that the whole trip, I found myself wanting to quietly contemplate the history of my surroundings while Drake and Peggy wanted to look around for anything that reminded them of being back in the United States. They were fun, great people, but we had very different traveling styles.

Another reason I preferred traveling alone is that I thought it did my confidence good. Hopping on a plane, train, or bus by myself was absolutely exhilarating. Just that act reaffirmed to me how far I had come in my personal journey. I'd always known there was an adventurous girl inside me—not self-destructive, just bold and adventurous. It would have been impossible for me to break out of my mold while living in Chicago, but in China I didn't need to think about the past. I was shaping my identity, and I was discovering that I was a girl who was not afraid to travel all over China by herself. With every trip that I took, I solidified that part of my identity and my confidence soared.

汤

Half the school year had passed, and we were given a three-week holiday for Spring Festival, the Chinese New Year. I'd been looking forward to it for so long because this would be the first time I would travel alone in China. I bought my airline tickets and made hotel reservations. I didn't know exactly what I'd find when I got to these places, but my overarching goal was to find more than a travel destination. I counted down the days and was thrilled to watch other teachers book their group tours, knowing I would be traveling alone this time.

I chose two cities in Guangxi province. Guilin is that place in China the painters visit—or at least imagine—when they want to put beautiful landscapes in their artwork. It is believed to be one of the most picturesque places in the world because of the jagged mountains there, which seem so spring forth right out of the water. Yangshuo is a much smaller town and is known more for its ambience and beautiful hills for climbing. Both are usually tourist hotspots, but this was the off-season, so I was hoping not to run into too many tourists.

I got to the airport that morning in plenty of time, only to have my flight delayed. Twice. After waiting four hours in the airport, I was finally off to Guilin. I had made arrangements with a travel agent in Guangzhou to have someone meet me and take me to the places I wanted to see. Later, after I'd spent much more time in China, it would occur to me that I had wasted a lot of money this way. But at the moment, knowing that someone would be there to take care of me felt great.

I found the guide. She actually had a little sign that said, "Miss Lori." What was I, royalty? I hadn't expected this. She spoke fairly good English, and introduced herself as "Miss Mandy" as she led me to the car. The driver only spoke Mandarin, but as I listened to the two of them talk, I realized how far my language skills had come. Granted, I couldn't understand everything they were saying, but I did get the main idea and could speak enough Chinese to them that we didn't need to use much English.

I had left the plans up to the agency I'd booked the guide with, so I really had no idea where we were going. The first stop was a gigantic cave, which ended up being a gigantic bore. For whatever reason, caves are big tourist attractions in China, and

I can honestly say that the thrill was lost on me. Miss Mandy wanted to share every fact possible about each site we visited, and I found my patience wearing thin early on in her tour.

"Miss Lori, this limestone is very rare. Very special."

Hmm.

"Miss Lori, do you see these colors? This because weather change rock over time."

"I see. . . ."

"Miss Lori, now you will notice the shape of the formation. . . ."

Before she could begin her fourth Miss Lori, I interjected, "Miss Mandy, you can have a rest out on the bench. Please go relax and I will walk around by myself."

She looked partially worried, partially relieved, so I reassured her, "*Zhen de, ni ke yi xiu xi ba. Wo man man kan.*"

She let out a big smile and said, "*Hao de, hao de. Wo wai mien deng ni.* Xie xie, Miss Lori!"

And with that, I had a little peace.

汤

We then went to a site called Elephant Trunk Hill. It's a large park surrounding a stone hill that does indeed resemble an elephant trunk. Again, I wasn't as fascinated by it as the guide seemed to think I should be. What was more interesting was the park itself, in which a number of large stone tablets marking various historical events were on display. (For example, there were markers indicating where President Nixon and President Clinton had stood when they visited China.)

I sent the guide and the driver off to dinner so that I could have some time to myself. Miss Mandy didn't even try to protest this time. What I wanted to do was sit and look at the landscape and write in my journal. It was getting cold and dark and I planned to leave for Yangshuo that evening, so I didn't want to waste time. Miss Mandy agreed to come back in an hour and a half, which I thought would give me plenty of time for peaceful sitting and thinking.

I was glad I had come during the off-season, because the park wasn't crowded at all. I pulled my mittens and hat out of my backpack and made sure my jacket was zipped all the way up. Then I found a secluded bench near the lake and sat down, tucking my knees up under my chin. A vendor came by selling steamed bread—a little unusual for evening time, but since it was one of my favorites and I hadn't eaten much on the plane, I bought a few pieces of *mantou*.

The sun was setting and I realized that I could not have chosen a more beautiful time, or a more beautiful spot, to sit and look at the famous hills of Guilin. When we had driven here from the airport and I'd caught a first glance of the hills, I'd thought maybe they weren't as impressive as the guidebooks had indicated. Sitting here now, though, I saw them differently. It wasn't the same thing to glance at them from a car or admire them while walking along with a tour group. No, the beauty of these hills could only truly be felt when sitting at their base, without a crowd or noise to distract.

I decided to pull out my journal and write whatever came into my mind. What came out was: *I'm sitting here in China, in Guilin, a place I've traveled to alone. I'm comfortable with myself. I'm happy. I don't know when this calm feeling came upon me, but it has and for that, I'm grateful.*

汤

I heard footsteps behind me and saw that Miss Mandy had returned.

"*Ni zhuen bei hao le ma*, Miss Lori?" she asked with a smile.

I smiled back. "Yes, I'm ready." I gathered my journal and mittens and followed her toward the car.

Chinese girls are very comfortable holding hands with other

girls, and Miss Mandy was already doing that with me at this point. It felt a little unnatural, since we'd met only hours earlier and I was never going to see her again.

"Can we can be friends?" she asked me as we approached the car.

"Um . . . yes," I said, not really knowing what that meant in this context.

She opened the passenger door for me. "The driver will now take you to Yangshuo," she said, gesturing for me to step inside the vehicle.

I panicked inside, feeling suspicious of the situation.

Then again, what did I expect? That she would accompany us on the hour-long drive? No, of course not. I supposed I hadn't thought about it at all.

"Okay." I nodded and said a silent prayer as I slipped into the passenger seat.

I didn't have a creepy feeling about the driver, per se, but objectively this seemed like a stupid thing to do. I was a foreign woman, traveling alone. It was dark, and a man I'd met only hours earlier was now driving me down a deserted road. *Oh my gosh, if my mother only knew*, I thought, *she would have a heart attack.* I thought *I* might have one, just thinking about the possibilities.

At first the driver didn't talk besides asking me if I was comfortable and telling me to feel free to adjust the heat if I got cold. I was thinking of my money. I wasn't wearing my money belt. I had put it in my backpack, which was now behind his seat. I had more money in there than he would probably see in a year. I didn't know why I had brought so much cash. I also felt ashamed for being so suspicious. Yet I was completely uncomfortable.

The driver reached in front of me and opened the glove box. He fumbled around for a cassette tape and then put it in. English love songs. *Oh man, is he trying to seduce me?* I tried to plan an escape route in my head. What would I do if he pulled the car over and tried to attack me? *Hold on*, Lori, I thought. *It's probably just a coincidence that these are love songs. He might not even know that, since he doesn't speak English. He just knows they are English songs and he is being polite by offering me some music he thinks I'll like. Okay, breathe, relax.*

He began to make conversation, asking me what I thought of China and how I liked Guangzhou. I began to relax a little, and before I knew it, we were in Yangshuo.

汤

When we pulled up to my hotel, the girl who would be my guide there came out to greet me. She spoke a little English and welcomed me, calling me "Miss Lori," just as the other guide had. The driver put my bags inside and I thanked him. I knew the cost of the taxi was included in what I had already paid the agent, but I gave him a tip anyway. I actually don't like the concept of tipping anymore, but at that time, I didn't know any better.

My guide showed me to my room. The hotel was nice. It had a ski-lodge kind of feel about it, and had clearly been made with foreign tourists in mind. I hadn't even paid attention to what anything cost, including the hotel; looking back, I'm sure it was way overpriced.

The girl asked me if I wanted pizza for dinner. I was so excited at this prospect that I readily agreed. She left my room and said she would bring the pizza up when it was ready.

I was freezing, and dying for a hot shower—but when I checked out the bathroom, I didn't see one. I finally looked up above me and did see a shower head, but there was nothing I would call a shower.

When the girl came back with my pizza, I asked her to explain how to use the shower. She looked at me with a strange look and indicated that I should simply stand below the shower head, just near the toilet, and have my shower. There was a drain on the floor.

Okay, I thought. *Whatever. As long as the water is hot.*

I didn't know where she'd gotten the pizza but that, along with a can of Coca-Cola, hit the spot on my first night traveling alone.

She had supposedly fixed the heat before she left, but I was still cold. I went downstairs to ask for another blanket but was told they didn't have any. Interesting. I was sure I was almost the only guest in this deserted hotel, and I found it hard to believe they couldn't round up another blanket—but again, whatever. I wouldn't let this dampen my spirits. I had made it to Guilin and Yangshuo, and tomorrow I would see the sights. I felt excited and relaxed at the same time. It was great to not have to run my travel plans by anyone or do things I didn't want to do. This trip was all about what *I* wanted to experience. I planned to relax, get some exercise by bicycling and climbing, and write in my journal.

汤

I loved my time in Yangshuo. The guide was a little less than honest, I realized later—for instance, I wanted to buy a painting in a secluded little shop at edge of the river, and she convinced me to give her my money, saying that she could get a better deal for me. I pointed out what I wanted, slyly handed her the money, and waited outside. She came back with the painting and no change, when there should have been at least twenty yuan left over. She said the shop owner had cheated her and seemed in a hurry to get away. She literally grabbed my arm to try to pull me away when I suggested we go back to the shop and straighten things out. As soon as I said that, I saw the panic in her eyes and knew that it was she who had been dishonest.

I didn't care that much about the money but I felt sad that

this girl would lie to me. I knew she had been paid by my travel agent in Guangzhou for accompanying me, and I really regretted signing up for this. Once again, though, it was another lesson learned. Next time, I would simply buy the airplane ticket on my own and not book the tours and hotel with an agency. Yes, I felt more independent this time than I had in Beijing and Xian, but this still was a far cry from true adventure.

汤

Things were uncomfortable with the guide after that, as it was clear that she knew that I knew what she had done. For the rest of the trip, I did as many things on my own as I could.

I spent the next two days bicycling all over the place. I rented a bike and bought a warm pair of gloves and a hat and took off, hoping I wouldn't get lost.

I was happy to be in the countryside. I didn't know how rural this was compared with other parts of China, but I knew it was a far cry from Guangzhou and my gated community at the school. It was at once beautiful and depressing. To me, the conditions seemed very poor, but as I spent more time looking at the people, I began to feel different. I even took the chance to talk with some of the people in a village I rode through. I started talking to one girl and before I knew it, it seemed the whole village had gathered around. One family invited me in their home and showed me that they had a television. It wasn't plugged in and it actually looked like there was no electricity, but it was important to them to show me that they had a TV.

My first impression was that this village was cold, dirty, and very, very poor. What I realized, though, is that different people are used to different things. When I saw a concrete house with a dirt floor, my first reaction was, "This house is unfinished," when in fact it was considered by its owners to be a perfectly good house. They were proud of it. I thought it unbearable that there was no heat, but nobody else was shivering. I thought it was depressing, yet people around me were smiling and going about their business. Nobody, except me, considered these conditions depressing, and after a couple hours among the people who lived there, I felt different.

chapter 16

After returning from my holiday, I still had a couple of days before the other teachers returned and the new semester would begin. My mood was sort of melancholy when I returned to the Estates. The weather was much colder, and the skies were gray all day, every day. As I unpacked my bags and straightened up my apartment, it hit me that I still didn't know why I was in China. This bothered me. Almost haunted me. I had left Chicago in August and now it was February. Things were going well at work. I loved my church congregation, the branch, and my chance to teach the women's group one Sunday each month as a part of our church program. I felt good about the fact that I was gaining some independence. Although I missed my family, we emailed or talked on the phone almost weekly, and they were fine. So why was I sad?

I spent the rest of the day in Siqao walking around markets and alleys. What was I looking for? What was it I was craving to see in China? What was missing from my experience?

Well, whatever I was looking for, what I found were sweatshirts. I spotted a small shop with a sign advertising zip-up, hooded sweatshirts for thirty yuan. Since that was only about four dollars, it got my attention and I peeked in. I felt intimidated at first to try one on, knowing that usually all things off the rack in China were still too small for me. But something prompted me to try, and I felt absolutely exhilarated when I zipped it up comfortably. I couldn't believe it. I knew that I was getting more fit, but it had been months since I'd tried on new clothes, and I was astounded at the difference. I was so excited that I bought four, one in each color they had.

汤

As May holiday approached, I wasn't sure where I might explore next. One of the teaching assistants, Jonny, had asked me if I'd like to travel with him to Hunan province. He was extremely outgoing, and we had gotten to know each other through the Chinese class he taught for the foreign teachers.

Although I thought it would be fun, I also thought it a bit awkward that he and I would go together, just the two of us. I decided to bring it up with him one day after class.

"So, Lori," he said as he erased the board. "Have you decided about Hunan? Do you want to go with me?"

I knew he wasn't asking in a romantic way and that to him this was completely fine and innocent. In some ways, it was stupid of me to think otherwise, but I just didn't know how it would look—the two of us taking off for Hunan together.

"Well, it sounds fun . . . but do you think it's better if we invite some others to go too?"

He looked at me with an exaggerated puzzled expression. "Hmm?" he said. "You want more people to come?"

"Well, it's just that in Western culture, usually if a guy and girl travel together, just the two of them, people might think there's something romantic going on."

He laughed out loud. "Really?"

I found it kind of strange that he'd never thought of this before, since it seemed that Chinese were really into their social rules. Then again, Jonny didn't quite fit into that category. He was a bit naïve but very confident. He didn't care too much what other people thought of him. He was goofy and seemed to simply enjoy life. It was obvious he had never thought that it might be awkward for just the two of us to travel together.

I told him I would love to go as long as there was someone else going along. The next day, he found me after Chinese class and said that Sally, another teaching assistant I knew, would join us.

I decided I could live with that, and we made plans to go to Hunan.

汤

I was a little thrown off when I approached Jonny and Sally at the bus stop on the morning of our departure and noticed that neither was carrying more than a small backpack. Where were their changes of clothes? After all, we planned to travel for at least three or four days. And what about their journals? I was wearing my backpack, which was totally full, and also carrying a duffel bag. All I could guess was that they planned to wear the same clothes the entire time.

When we got to the train station, I really regretted bringing so much. As soon as we got out of the taxi, we entered a huge mass of people, all pushing and shoving and trying to get inside the station. It was hard to carry that heavy duffel bag and to maneuver it through the massive crowds of people. But the three of us linked arms and went for it, with Jonny leading the way.

Sally was a very quiet girl, but I knew there was more to her than met the eye and I looked forward to getting on that train, finding our seats, and getting to know each other. At the same time I felt very claustrophobic pushing through the crowds and was angry at people who were stepping on my feet and shoving me. People stared and commented about my being a foreigner, but it didn't stop them from pushing me just as they were pushing everyone else.

I didn't quite understand the system and why all these people were here. *We can't all possibly fit in this train station*, I thought.

After what seemed like an eternity of pushing, we finally got to the train station entrance. The guards who checked tickets looked so calm. They stood on platforms, a little above the madness, and didn't seem to be at all worried about the pushing and shoving in which we were so engrossed. We flashed our tickets and were allowed inside. I felt like I needed to sleep for a week, I was so exhausted from fighting and pushing.

Inside, it was better but still crowded. We decided to keep going rather than take a rest, and forged our way through the crowds again in order to enter the train platforms. An hour later, we finally got on our train. We fought our way down the aisle, stepping over people on occasion, and found our seats.

So this is traveling Chinese style, I thought. Maybe my adventurous side had been a bit overly optimistic. I thought back to my Beijing trip with Drake and Peggy, who wanted to shop, and then to my Guilin trip alone in February. I had been so pampered, even on my attempt for adventure in Yangshuo. I'd never dealt with such crowds and I'd taken planes, not trains. I felt a little overwhelmed and more than a little disappointed with myself that I already missed some of the comforts I was used to while traveling. It sort of bothered me that I hadn't been comfortable traveling Drake and Peggy style, and yet here I was, getting the real Chinese treatment, and I wasn't entirely comfortable here either. *Oh well*, I thought. *We're on the train now, and I need to have a positive attitude.*

Jonny was a lot of fun and Sally seemed like an interesting girl. We were headed toward an entirely new province, just north of Guangdong, and I was away from all other foreigners. This part I liked.

The three of us were seated at a table, with Jonny on one side and me and Sally on the other. The train filled up and I noticed that there were people standing in the aisle.

"Jonny," I said. "Why are these people standing up?"

He looked at me with an expression that said the answer should be obvious. "They don't have seats."

"So . . . they're just going to stand there the whole time?"

He shrugged. "I guess so."

He began speaking in Chinese to a young man standing next to us and then turned back to me. "He said they paid the same price we did but they were told they would have to stand."

Wow. This felt very strange to me—and I guess I felt sort of guilty. I mean, this was a sixteen-hour trip, and we were going to sit here the entire time while they stood? A moment before we learned this, I'd been on the verge of mentioning how the seats weren't so comfortable. Now, suddenly, they seemed fine.

汤

As the hours passed, Jonny, Sally, and I chatted about our plans for the future. Neither of them wanted to stay at the school much longer, but they both felt the experience had been good overall. Compared with other schools, the salary was high, and they felt their English had improved tremendously through working with the foreign teachers. On the other hand, there was no room for promotion, and they felt that they were overworked and under-respected on the Chinese administration side. Jonny wasn't sure of his future plans but wasn't too worried about them, either. Sally, on the other hand, was very interested in going to America. In fact, Peggy, with whom I had traveled the previous year, was in the process of helping her get a tourist visa to go to the States.

As the hours passed, we got into more personal topics, such as romance. They both wanted to know how old I was and whether or not I had a boyfriend in Chicago. I think they wondered why I wasn't married, since in Chinese culture, women tended to marry a bit earlier. I told them that in America, it was considered perfectly fine to be single into one's late twenties or even thirties. The truth, though, was that I felt a lot more like they did than I let on. I did wonder why it was that I was twenty-eight years old and unmarried. Was I in denial about how old I really was? Was I going to be single forever? Would I be okay with that?

I hated myself for having these thoughts. After all, I had come so far in so many ways. Here it was, May; I had been in China for ten months, and my life was drastically different now. So why was this self-doubt creeping up on me again?

Actually, it had been creeping up for a while. Not only the self-doubt but the guilt. I often thought about how I'd left Mom and Chrissy with all the problems at home. Every time I talked to them, I ached with sadness and shame. I knew what life was there. It was still trips to the Veterans Hospital, getting Dad to take his pills, helping him do basic things, and constantly worrying about him falling or wandering off. It was obvious how incredibly wonderful my life was and how their lives really hadn't changed that much. There were times that I almost forgot where I came from and what I'd left behind. I would get caught up in my career, my fitness, my friends, my travel, my Chinese lessons, my massages, my manicures, my facials . . . It hit me hard, right in the gut, that only a year ago I'd been immersed in that life back in Chicago—and that they still were.

汤

The train ride came to an end just as we were on what seemed like our fiftieth round of "Yesterday Once More." It had been a very surreal experience: A group of university students had begun making conversation with us—some of the passengers who had paid for their tickets but were stuck in the aisle. They were medical students from Hunan, and all of them had studied English. Only one was confident enough to converse with me, and he also managed a rendition of "Yesterday Once More"—and before long, it was a grand sing-along on the hard seat train to Hunan.

Before we got off the train, we exchanged email addresses with the English-speaking student, and with a couple of his classmates as well. I sincerely hoped we would keep in touch. Sally thought he was incredibly handsome, so she especially hoped to hear from him.

汤

As soon as we arrived in the dusty outskirts of Zhang Jia Jie, we wanted to get away from the city.

"We need to get up to the mountains," Jonny said, gesturing toward the peaks above us. We had heard how beautiful it was up there.

"Okay, what's the plan?" I asked.

"We should catch a bus and just go up as far as we can," he said. "Maybe we can find a place to stay."

We hopped on a rickety old bus and headed up. *It's fun to travel this way*, I thought, *with absolutely no plans*. We didn't really know where we were going or where we would sleep that night. This felt very adventurous, and I was really enjoying the company of Jonny and Sally. They were both very fun and interesting people who had no agenda except to relax and have a nice time.

That bus ride, though, was anything but relaxing. It had rained a lot, and the mountain roads were extremely muddy. It seemed that the whole way up, we were moving at a snail's pace, and several times we got stuck. When this happened, we all had to get off the bus while the driver tried to get out of the mud. People would help push, and mud would splatter everywhere as the tires just spun around—until, finally, the bus got unstuck and we were all allowed to hop back in and continue up the road . . . until we got stuck again.

As we got higher up, the road seemed to get better and we could relax a little and enjoy the scenery, rather than having to worry about the next time we'd need to hop out. We stopped every so often to let people on and off, and I kept noticing all the kids who were taking the bus to school. I thought it would be really interesting to see what their schools were like; I mentioned the idea to Sally and Jonny, and they agreed it would be great.

A few stops later, an old man and his grandson got on. The little boy sat close to his grandfather and held his little school bag tightly in his hands. Jonny began making conversation with the man, and before we knew it, we had been invited to visit a school.

In the end, this old man completely changed the course of our trip. Not only did he help us find a school to visit, he also found us a place to stay and showed us around. He'd been a teacher as a younger man, but because of his family name he'd been blacklisted during the Cultural Revolution and hadn't been allowed to teach after that. I could not believe we actually were talking to someone who'd gone through that.

He told us he had been on his way to sell vegetables, which was how he earned his living, when he met us. I was touched that he put that off for us. Later, we found a way to give him a little money to compensate for what he'd missed out on.

One always has to be careful about giving money in China. Sometimes it's appreciated, but nobody will ever accept it the first time it's offered. Also, it's very difficult to give money without upsetting the delicate balance of friendship. To have just handed this man money would have made him lose face and would have sent him the message that he was not our friend. In some ways, that was true, but in China everyone always tries to maintain the premise that we are all friends and equals.

That afternoon, we visited the local school. One of the old man's former students was now the assistant principal at another school, and he took us there. I'd always known that the school where I was teaching was truly the exception in China, but now I knew to what degree that was true. Plain and simple, this school was very poor. They had one overhead projector; they had saved the money for it themselves, and they were incredibly proud of that. Old desks, old books, no supplies, broken windows—the whole thing made me feel like I was in a different time period, maybe even a different world. However, despite these conditions and the fact that there were fifty kids to a classroom, the atmosphere was extremely positive and the kids worked so hard. I watched a few classes and talked with the kids and the teachers afterwards. I kept thinking that I wished I could bring my students there so they could see how the rest of China attended school each day. I know there were schools in between—not as poor as this one but not as rich as ours—but it was really good for me to see the other end of the spectrum.

We ended up staying there, rather than in a hotel. We slept in a couple of rooms behind the school. No running water, no heater, just a very simple existence. Our hosts were the kindest people. They took us in, opened up their school and their homes to us, and even cooked for us on the last night. They prepared some of their hometown specialties for us as well—one of which I had to pray to God He would help me choke down without getting sick right then and there. The woman had gone to so much trouble to make it, using bark and syrup from a tree and some other things that were special to her but definitely not so special to me. Somehow, though, I finished it off with a smile. After dinner, as a special treat on the last night, this family also went and got us hot water so we could soak our feet.

This was the travel experience I'd been yearning for.

chapter 17

For my final trip of the year, I went to Sichuan province for one week. I'd heard about the pandas there and figured I couldn't say I'd really seen China if I didn't see its pandas. I flew into Chengdu and went to a biological preservation place where they bred pandas and had an area where visitors could watch the pandas in an environment almost identical to their natural one. It was refreshing, and not like a zoo at all. I was only about ten feet away from the pandas and really got to watch them play and eat—which was very cute, of course.

I spent the rest of the day walking around the city. After seeing a tea house and some temples, I sat in a bamboo forest and wrote in my journal. I ended the evening by eating some wonderfully spicy Sichuan food (still definitely the spiciest I've had to date!).

The next morning, I took a bus ten hours north to a place called Song Pan. The people of Song Pan represent one of China's fifty minority groups. They look very different from Han Chinese and are Muslim by religion, which makes the cultural feeling there quite different from other parts of China. The town is very poor, and their major source of income seems to be from tourists. People go there on their way to Jiuzhaigou, which is supposed to be one of the most beautiful spots in China. I didn't go quite that far north.

The reason I went so Song Pan was because I'd read about the horse treks offered there. They give you a horse and you ride up in the mountains until you get to the top. You camp for a day or two, and then you come back. They provide the tents, the food, and everything else. I couldn't wait.

汤

The horse trek proved to be a very interesting few days. The scenery defied description. The whole time, I kept thinking, *This can't be earth*, because it was just too beautiful. Blue skies that seemed close enough to touch, green mountains that stretched farther than I could see, hills, and valleys . . . and everything was so quiet. The trails we were on could not have been more than two feet wide, and we just kept going up and up. *If my horse takes one tiny step to the left*, I kept thinking, *we'll fall right off the cliff!* It was horribly terrifying and exhilarating at the same time.

One thing I had not prepared for before this adventure was how freezing it would be in the mountains. The first night I couldn't find a hotel, but luckily I met two girls from Korea in the same boat, and together we found someone who let us stay with them. We paid them fifteen RMB each (about two dollars) for the night. For this, we got a bed and use of a public toilet—two things, mind you, that were nowhere near each other in proximity. That made late-night bathroom trips a joy.

The second night I spent in the area was actually in the mountains in a tent, which of course was freezing again. So, after all this freezing, I decided when I got back to Song Pan the next night I would really live it up and stay in the best hotel in town.

"Best," of course, is a relative term.

The hotel I chose was "best" because it was the only one that had bathtubs and, during certain hours, hot water. Hardly any place in China has heat, and this place was no exception. So once

I checked into the room, I decided I would take a bath so I could get warmer.

It took forever for the water to get hot and the tub never did accumulate more than an inch of water—it didn't have a plug to hold the water in—but I have never been so happy and grateful for hot water in my life. So I just sat in the tub for about an hour and a half letting the hot water pour out of the faucet. With the bathroom door closed, I was actually warm. It was amazing. Honestly, I will never forget it.

Later that night I was even more freezing, so I decided to take another bath to warm up. According to the schedule they'd given me, I knew they should have hot water for another three hours.

I was so overjoyed at the thought of another hot bath that I didn't actually wait for the water to get hot before I jumped in the tub; I just jumped in and turned on the faucet, anticipating that nice, hot water pouring out and warming me up.

I waited. It was cold. I thought that was strange, but figured it would take a few minutes to warm up. It never got warm. So, I was freezing before, and now I was sitting in a freezing cold bathtub whose faucet is pouring out freezing cold water and I was *really* freezing. At that point, the thought of moving and even getting out of that tub and facing a whole night like this, knowing it was only going to get colder, made me want to cry.

I had bought some long underwear and undershirts two days before, and after getting out of the tub I put both pairs on, along with two pairs of pants, my sweater, my scarf (which I wrapped around my head), and two pairs of socks. Then I jumped around my room, trying to get warm, but because I had such a terrible headache due to the cold, altitude, and general exhaustion, with every jump I felt even worse. Great. My options were to freeze or aggravate an already splitting headache.

I decided to try to sleep. I was a bit paranoid because several thefts had been reported at local hotels while I'd been in town, and foreigners are, of course, the target since they are presumed to be rich (which, comparatively, we are). The town was so poor, I almost wouldn't have blamed them if they had robbed me—but with a bad headache and freezing body, I wasn't up for a room break-in on that particular night. So, to feel more secure, I moved my bed against the door and tried to move the chair in front of the window that wouldn't close, which meant an unsecured room and a freezing draft as well. I knew the chair in front of the window wouldn't actually keep anybody out, but I thought it would at least make a noise if someone stepped or tripped on it while trying to break in, and I'd have time to get out.

Am I crazy? Am I the only person who does things like this? Do other people, even subconsciously, make escape plans when feeling frightened? I can't be the only person who does this—and if I am, then I guess this admission can be evidence for the commitment hearings.

That night as I lay there saying my prayers—eyes closed, hands folded, silently reaching out to God—I asked for three things: please let my head stop pounding, because this pain is terrible; please let my body stop shaking from cold so that I can feel just warm enough to sleep; and please keep me safe. Then it occurred to me that I had just prayed for three things that I had taken for granted every day of my life. True enough, I had had real problems before, but I could not remember a time when my immediate needs were health, safety, and warmth. *Who thinks about these things?* I thought. *They are the givens.*

Well, for me they were; but for so many others, they were not. It was a humbling thought.

The happy ending to my little trauma was that I got to sleep, my headache went away, and I woke up with my money belt still intact.

汤

I got up at five thirty the next morning so I could catch a six o'clock bus back to Chengdu. As I woke up, I noticed my stomach hurt a bit and I felt sort of sick, but I didn't think much of it. It's sort of par for the course when traveling.

Well, about fifteen minutes into my ten-hour bus ride, I started to feel really, really sick, like I was going to vomit at any second. So, I kindly (in broken Mandarin, of course) asked the driver to pull over. He refused. "We're on a schedule," he said. I begged him to pull over but he wouldn't. His answer to the problem was to give me a bag. *Thanks*, I thought. *This tiny little bag will really help a lot . . . not.*

I returned to my seat, which was in the very back row. The roads we were using were not paved and were very, very bumpy. For an already upset stomach, this was not good. Because I was in the last row, I was higher up than everyone else and was not level with the window. So in order to lean out the window to vomit, I had to bend way down and get in a really awkward position. While my head was out the window, it banged against the window ledge with every bump in the road. Ouch.

Now, our bus wasn't exactly going slowly and it was a cold, windy day. As I began to vomit, I realized that this was going to be a problem. Since the wind was blowing in my face, as I vomited the vomit itself was also blowing right back in my face. However, I was very sick so I absolutely had to get it out.

The one benefit to the fact that we were on a very windy road going down the mountain was that the driver had to slow down frequently. Also, when he slowed down, my head hurt less because the bang on the window ledge was not quite as sharp. So I started trying to time my vomiting with the slowing down of the bus and the bumps in the road. After five hours or so, I had this down to a science.

Five hours after our departure from Song Pan, we stopped for a bathroom break. The driver pointed to the bathroom as if he were helping.

Yeah, thanks, I thought, internally rolling my eyes. I really didn't have a need for the bathroom at that point. A nice older lady gave me some medicine to settle my stomach during the break, however, and I was able to sleep for the next few hours. I still don't know what was wrong with me that day, but I had never felt that sick in my life.

When I finally got back to Chengdu, I did go to a very nice hotel, and the first thing I did was take a hot bath—simply because I could!

chapter 18

I decided to stay in China for another year. It was the easiest and most natural decision I'd made in a long time. When the option presented itself, I could not even think of leaving. Funny, because I wouldn't have taken the job if I'd had to commit to two years at the outset. I was only planning to go away for a year, and was not sure I'd even last that long. The job really had surpassed my expectations, and I'd even been offered a promotion—director of the English Language Center—for the next school year. Although I missed my family, I knew I could help them more from here and I didn't see a good reason to leave.

Beyond that, though, there was also this sense that I wasn't finished there, that there was something else I was supposed to do, or find, or become. I still hadn't found out why I'd really come to China. Sometimes I felt okay that I didn't know; other times, I felt anxious about it. I knew it was more than the job. Over the past year, I'd had so many growing experiences—spiritually, personally, and socially. These things had meant a lot, but I had a strong feeling that these were not the core reasons I was here. I couldn't leave yet. *Maybe next year,* I thought, *I'll discover what it was that really brought me eight thousand miles from home.* And even if I didn't find it, something told me things would still be good things in the process.

Coming to China had turned out to be one of the best decisions I'd ever made. I now looked back on the process of making that decision as nothing short of a miracle. So many things had to fall into place for this experience to happen, and I was grateful they had. I'd been there less than a year and already I felt that so many changes had taken place in me. I was more comfortable with myself than I'd ever been, and I'd begun to really love the learning process, whether it was learning about China or about myself. I couldn't remember a time in my life when I'd felt this much peace and had been this happy just to be alive. From where I was sitting right now, life was good.

chapter 19

Going home was hard. I knew that once I was there and around my family, I'd remember what I was missing, and it would hurt to know I'd be leaving them again in a matter of weeks.

This summer's visit would be my second trip home; I'd taken the first at Christmastime. During that visit, I remembered thinking how comforting it was to be with my family again, to see the snow, and to be in a place where I didn't have to stutter and whip out my dictionary every time I wanted to order food, go to the bathroom, or take a cab. Even after having lived in China for only a few months, it was shocking to be back in the States. It was a positive shock, I guess, as I marveled at the cleanliness and the endless choices available—but it was definitely a shock.

This visit would be different, though, I was sure. My plane would be touching down in Chicago in less than an hour, and suddenly I was nervous. My nightmare had come true. The thing I'd always been afraid of had happened. Why was I not falling apart?

I'd always thought I would be fine living in China, knowing Dad was at home and still coping. It seemed it would be the end of the world if he got so bad that he had to live in a nursing home. Well, when I landed in Chicago, a nursing home was the first place I'd be going to—Meadowbrook Manor.

Mom had talked to me about it several months earlier, after she and Chrissy had discussed it. They really hadn't found another solution. Mom still had to work full time at this point, and it was impossible for her to leave Dad home alone. I knew it was an extremely hard decision for her, but I stood by her choice. She really had no other. She said it wasn't too far from home, the care was pretty good, and Dad's medical card covered the expenses. Logically, it all made sense—but now, as I was about to go visit my dad in a nursing home, I felt sick.

汤

My first impression was that it was far better than the Veterans Hospital, and I was thankful for that. I was also grateful that it was in a nice neighborhood. It struck me as odd, suddenly, that I would notice such a thing and that it would matter so much. Most people, at least the people I associated with in China now, wouldn't understand why that was important to me. But I remembered almost holding my breath for the last few miles, just praying we would make it through the dangerous neighborhoods, when I'd visited Dad at the Veterans Hospital in the past. I suppose it's up to a sociologist to explain why, but here in the States we associate poor, inner-city neighborhoods with crime. In China, in contrast, there is absolutely no link between poverty and crime. I don't worry for my safety when visiting the poorest areas in China—it's not an issue.

As my mind was exploring the sociological reasons behind this difference, I heard Chrissy's voice ask me, "Are you ready? His room is just down this hall."

Am I ready? That was a good question, and maybe the answer was *no*, but not seeing my dad was not an option.

I shrugged. "I'm as ready as I'm going to be."

In the car on the way there, Chrissy and Mom had filled me in on the place and on Dad's condition. They told me not to be surprised if he didn't recognize me—and I told myself I wouldn't be, but I secretly hoped he would.

The first thing I saw was a little TV, which Dad clearly had set on the highest possible volume. With *Jerry Springer* blaring in the background, I caught my first glimpse of my father. He was sitting up in his bed, drinking Coke through a straw and not even looking at that obnoxious TV.

"Hi, Daddy," I said, giving him a hug and kissing his head.

He was surprised to see me. I couldn't tell if it registered right away who I was, but he knew he hadn't seen me in a while and that I had come a long distance to see him. He just stared at me.

Please, Daddy, I thought. *Some recognition.*

He reached for my hand and gave a little laugh.

That's good enough for me. I didn't need him to say my name, which surprised me. Just having him hold my hand and give some different expressions made me happy.

"What are you watching?" I asked.

"It's trash," he said. "You should turn it off."

No problem.

"But Dad, you always have that show on at this time when we come," Chrissy said in a teasing voice. She whispered to me that Dad seems to have gotten interested in talk shows since coming there and that sometimes in the day room, she saw him and the other patients all blankly staring at the likes of Jerry Springer and Jenny Jones.

汤

Dad was still somewhat himself on most days, but the Alzheimer's was clearly in high gear at other times. It was odd how in one moment he would know who I was and that I was visiting from China, and in the next breath, he'd ask me to go to Zink's Grocery to get him a candy bar. We'd decided to stop trying to explain that Zink's was a store in Starbuck, Washington, where he'd lived seventy years earlier. When he made his candy bar requests, I just went down to the machine and got him his candy bar, and when I returned we continued our conversation. For him, both things could be true—that is, he could sit there with his grown daughter who was home from China and eat a candy bar from Starbuck at the same time.

On some days, I was glad he wasn't too clear, because when his mind was clearer, he got depressed. He knew, for example, that he was wearing diapers and could not use the bathroom by himself. I felt his humiliation when the attendant came in to change him and he waved me out of the room. He knew he wasn't at home—but he also knew, I believed, how loved he was, particularly by Mom.

My mom and dad had always had an interesting relationship. I had never seen them kiss or hold hands. Theirs was a different kind of marriage, but there was love there—humor and love.

I saw them hug exactly once. I'll never forget it. I was nine years old, and it was in the house in Wisconsin. I remember Dad's soft, baby blue shirt and Mom's tan wool coat. She was heading out the door to the hospital for some kind of minor surgery. I don't remember why he wasn't taking her to the hospital himself, but it seems her friend Joanne was driving her instead. Mom was getting ready to walk out the door, and I remember that she turned and looked at him as he held the door for her.

"Well," she said. And they smiled at each other. And then they hugged. Chrissy and I looked at each other, surprised and happy.

Even working ten hours a day babysitting, Mom was at the rest home every possible minute she could spare. She took Dad to Bingo and encouraged him to play. She brought him hamburgers and Cokes from McDonald's. On her days off, she was there all day. She joked with him and tried to make light of things. I had never realized before leaving for China just how deep their love ran. I watched him look at her as she fixed his bib, saying, "There ya go, Louie. Here, looks like they gave you a good meal tonight"—and his eyes didn't leave her. The love they had for each other was beyond the physical. They'd endured so much hardship together and this, in some ways, was just another phase of their lives. They were taking it in stride.

While I was there, though, Mom did take a little break, which she needed. She didn't need to keep Dad company every minute while I was there, and I actually appreciated the time with just him. I tried to spend as much time at the home as I could listening to Dad talk about the past, which sometimes he believed he was still in. I found myself actually encouraging that belief so I could learn more about him. While he was sleeping, I read about Alzheimer's—the professional medical articles as well as case studies and personal stories. Most of them agreed that we should try not to be freaked out when the patient thinks he's somewhere else. I was trying not to let it scare me or make me sad when he was confused, and he seemed more at ease if I just let him be wherever he wanted to be.

It was depressing and wonderful at the same time. Part of me loved sitting there in a chair next to his bed, sipping my Diet Coke while he munched away on his candy bar "from Starbuck." He was genuinely happy as we chatted and even laughed about old times. Some of his memories were from before my time, but I tried to go with the flow and just imagine. He asked me a lot of questions about China, and this got him talking about World War Two and the time he spent in the CCC (Civilian Conservation Corps). This got him back on to history and it just cycled from there . . . but it was wonderful. Sometimes I almost forgot where we were and just how sick he was.

Then, suddenly, I could not feel much of anything except helpless and rotten. What kind of daughter was I, anyway? Five minutes earlier, Dad had been fine—and then something changed. He started talking about "the sheriff" and began to cry. He begged me not to leave, saying someone was going to get him. When I tried to comfort him, he began using odd phrases that had never come out of his mouth before. He swore. He was not himself. For a full ten minutes he was extremely sad and worried.

I gently caressed his head and arm. "It's okay, Dad. There is no sheriff. This is a good place and even if there was a sheriff, he'd be a good sheriff. You'd like him."

"Okay," he said. His eyes didn't even blink. He was in some kind of trance, and I was helpless to get him out of it. I didn't get it. Minutes earlier we'd been talking about the skating pond he'd made for us when we were kids and then he'd started ranting about the sheriff.

"Close your eyes and lie back, Dad," I said. I adjusted his pillows and dimmed the lights. He was tired. He was like a baby now, my strong daddy.

I stared at his face. His face was precious and told so much about him. It was a kind face, a humble face. It was a face that had seen a lot and withstood great trials. He was a good man, my dad. Tender. Loving. Sensitive. I thought about the fact that I hadn't seen him in a long time, and I began to comprehend the great burden my family had been carrying since I'd left. I'd gone to China and left the stress of this behind. It was no longer in my face every day; my immediate world no longer consisted of Dad's sickness, Mom's financial problems, and tensions with other family members. My world was a good job, a beautiful place to live, running club, tai chi in the park, and journal writing. I had escaped to the wonderful world of China, but while I'd been off discovering myself, these problems had continued to exist. They had not gone away simply because I had.

汤

On the night before I was to return to Guangzhou, Mom and I sat at the table doing a puzzle. I didn't like puzzles at all, but she did, and putting the pieces together seemed to give us both something we needed.

"Mom, I feel awful about leaving tomorrow." I couldn't even get the words out without the tears coming. "It's not fair that I left you to deal with all this. I don't know how I justified this. . . ." I couldn't talk. The sobs were in my chest, coming more quickly by the second.

"Lori, don't you do that." Mom's mouth was trembling, but she kept going. "Don't do that. You have a chance and you are where you need to be." She was holding a puzzle piece, moving it around between her fingers as she spoke.

"But I'm off having this great life and you're here, just . . . holding it all together."

"Lori, the problems would be here whether you were here or not. Now, Dad is doing okay. They take good care of him there, and we get to see him every day. I'm okay. We're all okay." She put the puzzle piece in its place and looked at me. We'd never been good at the eye-to-eye thing, Mom and me, but she looked right at me. She took a breath. "You had such a hard past. I remember so often thinking you would die young, that you'd put yourself in a situation you wouldn't be able to get out of. You've had such good luck at times, but also such bad luck in your life." Now her tears came.

She was talking about things neither of us wanted to remember, things we wouldn't verbalize. Insecurities I'd had as an adolescent surrounding self-image. Choices I'd made as a teenager, mistakes that had brought incredible pain. There were things a mother should have overtly warned me about, talked to me about, and times she should have put limits on me, limits that would have kept me safe. But we both knew my mom never could. I knew in that moment she was thinking about the car accident I'd been in at sixteen—which hadn't taken my life, but had destroyed my chances of becoming a professional dancer, something that had given us both hope for so many years. She was talking about my high school boyfriend, who'd started off charming, but by the end of our relationship, had become violent. I'm sure Mom wondered why I'd allowed it. I still didn't know, but it had to do with self-worth, I guess, and those critical teenage lessons that I hadn't really learned. Years where young girls can be vulnerable if they don't have a strong sense of who they are and what their standards are.

I remember going to church and every Sunday reciting the Young Women Theme in our class. This was meant to remind us that we are all children of God, but it especially emphasized knowing our individual worth, and having self-love and self-respect. I'd known it, but I guess I hadn't always internalized it. It was something I so wished my mom had talked with me about. I wish those ideas and values had been more present in my everyday life. I learned valuable lessons on Sunday, but then I went to junior high, and high school, and was hit with different messages, different temptations. I'd made mistakes, painful mistakes which brought regret.

That was a turning point, though. I was always, always able to start over. To pick myself up, to carve out something new. Always. My mom was talking about all of it—the ups, the downs, the extremes, a life that seemed like several lives, and how I'd managed to pull it all together, to finish college, to finish graduate school, to find peace. And that I'd grabbed on to this precious opportunity to go to China.

Somehow that night we finished the puzzle, and our conversation. I boarded that flight for Guangzhou the next morning feeling a mix of emotions, but mostly feeling peaceful and ready to return to my life.

Part Two

chapter 20

The new school year was off to a good start. I was walking around the school and the city with a new level of confidence. First, I was in incredible shape and I felt fantastic. I had become a runner, yes, but I'd also discovered several types of exercise that I genuinely loved. I'd found some great deals on stylish clothes while I was home over the summer, and I now found that local Chinese sizes were flattering as well. This was a huge deal to me, to say the least. Beyond that, I was now the director of the English Language Center—an administrator in charge of my own department. My Chinese was coming along, and I'd developed a very good reputation at the school with everyone from the maintenance people to the Chinese administration. Life was good.

Getting the ELC in the shape I wanted it to be in was challenging but also a thrill. I was already noticing some success with decisions I'd made, and I had a good group of teachers who were willing to work hard with me to make the ELC the best it could be. This center had always been the "underdog" department of the school, but every year it had gotten a little bit better—and I was determined to continue that trend. I had so many ideas that I found myself there until nine o'clock most nights. I usually went out and ran from five to six and then came back up to my office and worked. I liked it, though. I'd turn on my CD, kick my shoes off, and just write policies, make plans, and think. I truly loved my job.

"Goodnight, Lori," I heard one night as I sat engrossed in typing the latest class schedule.

I looked up to see Qian Zhi Ming, whose English name was William. "Oh, William, goodnight. See you tomorrow." He was one of the new teaching assistants in our department, and lately, I'd found myself thinking about him a lot more than I probably should. After all, I was his boss. He was from an entirely different culture and probably would never consider dating a Western woman. Actually, he probably had a girlfriend. Why wouldn't he? He was incredibly good looking and was a true gentleman.

Still, there did seem to be a connection between us of some type. He always said good morning and goodnight to me, and I know he had smiled at me in the past.

Oh stop it, Lori. Get a life and quit fantasizing. As if it would be that easy. "Hey William, I know I'm your boss, and American, but hey—how 'bout going out to dinner with me?" There are not too many things less likely than for me and William to start up a romance. I'm sure he has never even thought twice about me.

Okay, back to work, Lori, I tell myself. But I can't. I'm looking at my computer screen and I'm thinking of him.

What is it about this guy? It's been years since I've been interested in anyone romantically. I haven't always made the best choices when it came to relationships. In the years leading up to my coming to China, I'd taken the dating equation out. I was logical enough to know that it wasn't likely I would find someone to spend my life with, and it was better to just keep that part of my life untouched. In truth, it had been several years since I'd even had the slightest interest in someone. I hadn't thought about the idea of love or romance in years. Until now.

I'd been watching William, taking notice of him, for the last few months, and there was something completely special about him. I felt a strong desire to know him better, to have him know me. Assuming for a moment that he didn't have a girlfriend and had even an ounce of interest in me, I wondered if he could ever see past our differences. The cultural divide was so great—and at school, everyone was in everyone else's business, thinking it was their own. Still, I'm a strong person, and I knew I could handle that. Something about the dignified way he carried himself suggested to me that he could handle such a situation too. The question was, would he would want to?

I had met him before going home for the summer, in the two weeks in July I'd stayed at school to prepare for my new position. He'd been interviewing for a teaching assistant position, and since there was no one else around to interview him, I had agreed to do it. It was only the second such interview I had done, but it went well. Irene, our secretary, brought him to my office and introduced him by his English name, William.

I thought he was handsome and dignified; if I had to describe my first impression, that was it. My second impression was that he was a strange combination of nerves and confidence. He asked good questions and spoke eloquently about teaching methodologies and his experience with teaching adults and children. I guess it wasn't nerves I noticed as much as caution. He chose his words carefully and sat rather stiffly. He thought before he spoke and wasn't concerned with making small talk. He wasn't trying to put on a façade, a rare trait in any culture, and perhaps that's one of the things that impressed me most.

After we'd spoken, I had led him downstairs to Irene and waited for him to leave. He thanked me for my time and we said good-bye. It wasn't love at first sight; actually, the only feelings I had for him at that time were that he would be a wonderful teaching assistant to have in the ELC. He was capable and serious, and I needed that in my department. I told Irene so, and made her promise that when they made TA placements in the fall, Qian Zhi Ming—that, I learned, was William's Chinese name—would be placed in the ELC. She said she'd do her best.

Despite that promise, things changed when I got back. When we returned in August, I learned that the elementary principal had made other plans. I looked at the list of my new TAs, and William's name was nowhere to be found. I went to Irene to see what the situation was and she shrank into her desk. I guess I looked intimidating, as I was mad. I had gotten a reputation among the Chinese staff as being very *li hai*—which, loosely translated, means someone with whom others don't mess. It was a title I didn't mind having. I think I was known as a nice girl as well, but when it came to work and the ELC, which had become my "baby," it was known that I would speak my mind.

I had many friends in the school and I dealt directly with people. I never played the games or had the same frustrations other Westerners did about "the Chinese," because I knew them as individuals. If I needed something fixed in my department, I did not take the thirty-two steps through the various departments; I had had the head of maintenance over for dinner before with a group of teachers, and since that day I simply went to him directly if I needed something. Some people may have said this wasn't fair, but it was perfectly sensible to me. While everyone else filled out forms and complained about the inefficiency of the Chinese system, I made friends and learned just how swift the system could be. Now, in all fairness, I have been on the other side of the system at times, and it can be a nightmare—but that shouldn't stop people from trying to know others as individuals. It makes life so much easier, not to mention interesting.

So, with my "li hai" reputation, it was no wonder Irene didn't know what to do that day. I wasn't mad at her, of course, but how was she to know that? She just saw me storming into her office, asking where Qian Zhi Ming was!

Irene explained that Shelly, the elementary principal, had placed him with a fifth grade teacher. Her words continued, like a bubble hanging in the air—but I was already walking forcefully toward Shelly's office. There, I put on my best assertive face and explained that I had interviewed William that summer and had been promised he would be placed in the ELC.

"Well, I know," she began, "but I really think that Kathy needs a strong TA, and his credentials are quite impressive."

"I know they're impressive," I said. "I interviewed him. That is why I want him in the ELC. We are short on TAs as it is, and I think it's only fair that because of that, we're allowed to have some of the stronger ones. He is an experienced teacher, and I need his experience in my department."

"Well, let's talk about it and see what Ginny thinks," she said. She called Ginny, the TA coordinator, over and explained the situation to her.

"I'll be honest, Shelly," I said after Ginny joined us. "I feel strongly about this. I would like Qian Zhi Ming in my department, where he was originally placed. I stayed here for two weeks of my vacation interviewing these TAs, and I feel that I should have a choice in the matter." Because I was starting to get more confrontational, my mouth was starting to do that weird twitching thing it does when I get nervous. I hate that, but I have yet to learn how to control it.

"Well, okay," Shelly said, "that actually sounds fair. Maybe we can put another guy in with Kathy. I just really feel that she needs a male TA to help her with discipline."

"Fine with me, but I'd like William in the ELC."

"Okay, Lori, let me think about who we could put there, but that should be fine."

"Thanks," I said. I was smiling as I walked back to my office.

汤

Since the day I discussed William's placement in the ELC with Shelly, I've thought about how I was able to make that change happen. Because my mom had some deep insecurities, I'd taken some of those on as well, especially as a teenager. My core, though, had always been tough. I was the advocate for our family from a very young age.

As young as eight years old, I would stand up for Chrissy if she were teased or not included with friends. At age nine, I took it upon myself to arrange a meeting for my family with our bishop at church. I was concerned that Chrissy was not being reverent and that she was running around playing instead. I felt my parents needed some tips for how to keep her quiet. I remember arranging the time and Mom, Dad, Chrissy, and I going into the bishop's office after church to discuss strategies. If memory serves, I believe I kept a file on their progress in following through.

I often felt that people didn't give my dad the respect he deserved. Perhaps because of his humility, people may have assumed he was beneath them. It bothered me because I knew how smart and wonderful he was. At the same time, I know there were times I felt embarrassed by his appearance, but it never stopped me from standing up for him when I felt it was needed.

When I was 15, my dad had been pulled over by a police officer when I was with him. Like many people from a lower socioeconomic level, my dad was scared of the police. Anytime he would see a police officer, he'd get very tense. "Uh-oh, cops! Wonder what they want," he would say, even if the officers were nowhere near him. On this day, though, we'd been pulled over, and this particular officer was pretty condescending—the worst stereotype of a police officer. I didn't like the way he was talking to my dad.

"Sir, your registration sticker is expired," he'd said. I watched how nervous my dad was.

"Yes, sir. I'm sorry about that. I don't have it."

The officer smirked. "Well, you can't just drive around without the proper registration. You can't just get it when you feel like it. You're supposed to get the sticker first, then drive the car," he said, chuckling at his own attempted joke.

I started to say something and my dad gently put his hand toward me and gave me a "shh, I've got it honey" look.

"Yes, sir. I didn't have the money and I'm driving my daughter to her physical therapy appointment. I'll get it tomorrow, sir, I promise you that. My daughter was in a car accident and she needs her therapy and. . . .

The cop interrupted, talking right over my dad.

"Well, I can't just accept that. There are laws. . . .

I couldn't listen anymore. Who did this guy think he was talking to my dad that way?

"Excuse me, but maybe not everyone has the money to get a stupid sticker on their car. My dad was driving safely and has every intention of getting the sticker as soon as he can. And by the way, there are people out there doing way worse stuff. My dad was obeying the laws, and he's doing this for me, and I don't think you have the right to just. . . ."

The absolute panic in my dad's eyes and his gesturing me to be quiet happened at the same time the officer bent down, put his head in the window, and shook his finger at me, inches from my face, his arm reaching right in front of Dad.

"Young lady, one more word out of you and I'll have your dad arrested right here. I'll slap those handcuffs right on the old man! You want that? I'll do it right now."

I saw his anger and sick pride right alongside my dad's fear and panic. I wanted to talk back to him and tell him to stop using his power to intimidate an old man and teenage girl, but I knew it would get worse. I knew what to do. Do as my dad was doing, do as he always did.

"No, I don't want that. I just don't want my dad in trouble when he's only trying to help me." I could feel tears coming, as suddenly I worried I'd just made this so much worse for my dad.

The officer looked at me, looked at my dad, and wrote a ticket.

"Sir, you'll need to appear in court on this date. Bring the proof of registration and you shouldn't need to pay the fine. But do not drive this vehicle until you get the proper registration. Do you understand me, sir?"

I was fuming at the way he continued to talk to Dad, like Dad was stupid or something. But I kept quiet.

"Yes, Officer. Thank you, Officer. I'm very sorry, Officer."

I felt so bad for my dad, and I felt so bad for my whole family. Why didn't we have any power? Why did people feel they could talk to my parents like they were nothing? I'd guessed it was because we didn't have money. I told myself then, as I'd told myself as a ten-year old researching career options, that I would never be poor.

The more I considered it, I'd always been one to advocate for others and for myself. Sometimes there had been periods of insecurity, but I'd always managed to get past them, and even when I was intimidated or downright scared, I could usually muster the strength to fake enough confidence to get through a given situation.

Maybe my faith had been part of my confidence. My level of spirituality had deepened recently, at least in the area of understanding the importance of my body. The application of all those gospel principles was finally taking shape. I had always believed that my body was a gift from God, but I don't think I'd really internalized all the beautiful teachings about my body being a temple"—something holy—and that it was a privilege to care for it. After all, I had spent a lot of my youth feeling confused about what a normal body size was, and why my mom looked so strikingly different from my friends' moms. I'd felt embarrassed by her size and then I'd felt shame for feeling that embarrassment. It was a lot for a teenage girl to deal with.

During my ninth grade year, we had a family therapy session with a child psychologist. The school counselor had referred our family to a counselor because she and my parents were concerned about my rapid weight loss. No one was really saying that I had a specific eating disorder. I probably didn't, but I certainly had an unhealthy obsession with losing weight. Part of it was pressures from the ballet world in which I was so immersed, and part of it certainly had to do with being afraid, perhaps irrationally, that I was destined to be obese like the other women in my family. My parents were at a loss, and this was an incredibly difficult time for my family.

This was the first family therapy session we'd had—I actually think it was the first and last. Mom, Dad, Chrissy, and I were gathered together in a small room with Dr. Krane, the psychologist I'd been working with individually at the suggestion of my school counselor. None of us knew how to "do" therapy—this was so far outside the norm for us. I know that my parents were desperate to help me.

Early on in the conversation, Dr. Krane had said the purpose of this meeting was just to try and help me and to help our whole family as we were all dealing with this sickness—and of course my being sick affected the entire family. I didn't like being referred to as "sick" but I also knew something was wrong and that I worried about this way too much. I did feel that talking with Dr. Krane helped me. I could share how I felt different from my family, although I loved them. And that I felt guilt for feeling different. That I wished my parents were younger, healthier, and that we had a nicer house and a car that didn't often break down. I told him how I longed to just feel normal and to not have so many worries.

As Dr. Krane shared the goal of the session, my mom inched forward on her chair. I looked at her with her tan polyester pants, her blousy blue-and-green shirt, flowing down past her stomach. She'd done her hair, used the curlers, I'd guessed. Almost immediately after Dr. Krane had finished his introductory comments, Mom began. Lip trembling, voice soft, hands folded, my mom said that she'd like to say something. She said that her childhood had been difficult and there had been some abuse in her family, that she was not well-cared for. She gathered her strength to go on: "I just think it's why Lori is sick. Maybe it's my fault." she said through her tears. I winced as she spoke. I felt sorry for her but I wanted to tell her to pull herself together. This was so awkward and I wanted to run out of the room but I knew I should show compassion. She never expressed these kinds of emotions and I wasn't ready for this. I felt extremely uncomfortable, followed by guilty for feeling uncomfortable rather than compassionate.

In hindsight, I know she thought it would help to say aloud that she'd had bad experiences in her childhood which made her parenting harder, making it hard for her to set boundaries and teach us important things we needed. But none of that was clear then, and it would be years before we would talk about it any further. They just knew I wasn't eating enough, I was sick, and that I had a lot of worries. They all just wanted to know why. I guess I did too.

I wondered if it really was possible to be different, and to not have so many worries, to just let things go, but I could never do that. My worries translated into the need to take control in order to fight off insecurity. I put a great deal of effort into always being ready and willing to stand up for my family—to make sure nobody teased Chrissy or mistreated my parents. At fifteen, it just seemed that was my place. No one asked me to take it on. I just did.

chapter 21

As I sat in my office on a Monday evening, I should have been planning for the next day, but instead I was trying to think of an excuse to talk to William. It certainly hadn't been conscious, but looking back, I wondered if on some level I'd known I had better keep him up there with me in the ELC so I could become his friend and fall in love with him. As strange as it sounded, even to me, I felt like I was heading in that direction. I had never really been in love, true love, before, so I wasn't sure how to identify this feeling. We had never even had a real conversation; he knew nothing about me; and yet there was something about this man that both comforted and excited me. Just thinking about him simply made me smile.

Mike came in to tell me a parent was waiting to talk to me. Jia Jin had been my student the previous year and was now in Mike's class. She was struggling with her literacy skills and was exhibiting some behavioral problems, so Mike had called a parent conference and asked me to be present for it.

I walked in to the meeting to discover that William was there, too, so he could translate for Jia Jin's mother. She talked for what seemed like forever, but she was a good woman and was concerned about Jia Jin. We talked out some possible plans for working with Jia Jin and before I knew it, it was already seven o'clock. We thanked her for coming and Mike ran out behind her, already late for a date with his wife. William and I were left sitting at the kiddy table in the ELC lobby.

"Sorry you had to miss your dinner, William," I said, knowing the school cafeteria where he usually ate was now closed.

"No problem," he said, looking at me and, I thought, hoping I would continue the conversation. I wanted to, but I didn't know what to say.

Luckily, he thought of something to say first. "What will you do for dinner?"

Okay, do I say I'll go out? That I'll go home? I told him the truth: "I'll probably just go home."

Okay, was I really thinking he would take this cue to ask me out? That would have been too bold, so I wasn't surprised when he said, "Oh, well, you'd better get going. It's late."

"Yes, you too," I said as we both stood up and pushed in our chairs.

I gathered my stuff and heard him say goodnight. *He's probably got a date with his girlfriend. Duh, Lori! What are you thinking?* I walked down to the bus . . . and there he was.

"Oh, hi again," I said. "Aren't you heading back to your dorm?" This bus only went up to the front of the Estates.

"No," he said, "I think I will go to a restaurant and get something to eat.

The seconds between this statement and the next were an eternity in my mind. *Please, just ask me. Ask me and I'll say yes.*

He did, thank God.

"Would you like to join me?"

Bless this man!! That was a very bold move, especially for a Chinese man talking to a Western woman. But right now, he obviously wasn't letting that stop him. We were just two people waiting for the same bus, both of whom were hungry. He'd done the natural thing, and I was so thrilled that he had.

"Sure," I said, grinning, "that sounds much better than going home and eating a sandwich."

The bus came and he motioned for me to get on first. Ever the gentleman.

汤

Dinner was wonderful. William told me of his hometown and his life before coming to Guangzhou. He was not overly talkative but was careful not to let the conversation lull, either. When it did, though, it wasn't uncomfortable. We kept seeing people from school passing by, and I wished they'd all go away; we lived in such a bubble existence there, and it was almost impossible to separate work from life. Still, William and I had a wonderful dinner, and I was so happy to be with him.

When it came time to pay, he went to take care of the bill but I suggested we go Dutch. He didn't argue, which I appreciated. I made about a zillion times the amount he did, and I didn't want to put him on the spot.

It was so lovely simply to walk next to him, to be with him. He was kind and smart. I enjoyed his company. The walk back to the bus went quickly and suddenly we were walking toward my apartment, and it was time to say goodnight.

"Thank you so much, William," I said. "What a nice dinner."

"Thank you, Lori," he said. "I'm so happy to have dinner with you."

We said our "see you tomorrows" and went our separate ways. Back in my apartment, I rehearsed the evening over and over in my mind. What had just happened here? Had we had a date? What was he thinking? Was I his boss? His colleague? Or was there a chance that I was a pretty girl whom a handsome guy wanted to get to know? Was it possible?

I fell asleep hoping that it was.

chapter 22

William and I spent the next month finding excuses to spend time with one another. At least I knew *I* was doing that, and I was almost positive he had been doing the same thing. My ayi had made a special dish for me the previous week, and I'd brought it to work to share on a Friday before I left for Hong Kong. We didn't finish the dish that afternoon, so I left it for everyone to enjoy.

I had gotten very used to having household help, and my ayi, Asim, had quickly figured out how to make my life easier. She did the cleaning, the laundry, and the shopping, and helped me handle any maintenance tasks that came up. No more traipsing around with my broken Chinese, trying to get repairs done; she simply took care of things. I also no longer felt guilt or weirdness about having a maid. It was completely normal in China, and the cost was well worth it. I had felt a little strange when I told my mom, but she had been nothing but happy for me and had actually been quite fascinated by the whole concept.

When I got back from Hong Kong on Saturday, I had a text message from William asking if it would be convenient for him to return my bowl to me. I literally jumped up and down after receiving this request because it was clear he had gone to some trouble; there were several people who could have taken the bowl and washed it, but he'd made sure he was the one to do that. Also, it would have been easy to leave the bowl at work and I could have gotten it on Monday. But no, Qian Zhi Ming had managed to get that bowl and take it to his dorm Friday night so he would have a reason to call me on Saturday.

I told him to bring it around six and then added, "Maybe we could have dinner together." I quickly sent the message before I lost my nerve, and then waited for his response, my stomach in knots. He wrote back with, "Great, see you at six."

汤

That night we walked around Siqao, looking in shops and talking for hours. The week before, we had also come to Siqao together—I had asked him to help me buy a mobile phone. There were countless other people who could have helped me buy a phone, but I'd wanted William to be the one to accompany me.

Almost every day that month, there was something like this; whether it was a conversation or a bus ride to Siqao, we were finding excuses to be together.

All of that passed through my mind as I stood at the base of the mountain, waiting for William to arrive. Tonight, there was no excuse to meet. Neither of us needed any help of any type. We knew we were meeting simply because we wanted to spend time together. My stomach was doing leaps. I felt sick, but in a good way. "Nervous" did not begin to cover it.

We had decided to climb a TV tower that was at the top of a very large hill, right down the road from our apartments. People usually climbed this hill for exercise, but William had pointed out to me that if you climbed a little higher, there was a tower at the very top. He was curious about it, and when he'd invited me, I'd told him I was game. Now, though, my heart felt different— more than just racing, it was beating so hard I assumed passersby could hear it.

Up until tonight I'd had doubts about whether William could be truly interested in me. At one point in my life, I would have attributed his possible lack of interest to my own inadequacies. My insecurity at this point, though, had more to do with all our differences. After all, he was a quiet, dignified Chinese man, and I was an outspoken, American woman who just happened to be his boss.

There had been moments when I was almost positive he saw more in me. The way his eyes seem to look right through me, and how a smile always began to emerge on his lips when my eyes met his. He could not walk into my office and say anything without smiling, and I could never help but smile back. We could be talking about a student's assignment or paperwork, or any other mundane thing, yet we both constantly had these gigantic grins whenever we spoke.

William walked toward me, waving. I waved back and it occurred to me that I had never seen him looking so handsome—which is saying something, because I always thought he was extremely good looking. His white shirt was untucked, and he was wearing khakis and tennis shoes. I had only seen him in formal slacks and dress shirts, and he always wore formal black shoes. He looked so casual and sort of rugged, and I suddenly had the overwhelming urge to kiss him and scream to the stars, "I love you, William!"

Instead I said, "Hi," and we started walking toward the steps leading up the mountain. I sensed that he was as nervous as I was. We had spent so much time together lately, but this felt different. This was the first time there wasn't an excuse to be together. We were doing something together because we were interested in each other. I wanted to spend time with him and he wanted to spend time with me—simple as that.

As we climbed the mountain together, it was as if we were climbing into another dimension. With every step we took we arrived one step farther away from the walls of the community in which we lived. We were leaving behind our labels, our categories, our worries. It was no longer about our differences. There was nothing physical or material to define us, because those were not the things that had drawn us to each other in the first place. Sure, we were attracted to each other, but there was more than that to this, and suddenly I could feel it. There was an unspoken goal between us of getting to the top of the mountain and looking at each other in a way we'd never done before. It was as if we had known for forever that we were meant to be together, but we needed to get away from it all in order to say so.

As we sneaked by the guard toward the tower, William touched my back, guiding me toward the ladder.

"Ladies first," he said.

I began to climb the ladder, aware of him climbing behind me. When we got to the top of the ladder, we took a few steps only to find another one. There were three ladders in all, in fact, and each step I took made me feel more exhilarated. Granted, what we were doing wasn't truly dangerous, but it was just risky and surreal enough to feel like nothing short of magic. After all, there we were, at nine thirty on a Thursday night, sneaking up a TV tower in a posh community in the People's Republic of China.

When we finally got to the top, I was super sweaty. I felt self-conscious about it and thanked God for providing a cool breeze that helped to dry my sweaty face and neck.

The top of the tower was no more than eight feet in diameter, but the view was more than I'd imagined it would be. We stood there for a few minutes, catching our breath and looking out at the Estates and the stores. In one direction, we pointed out our school, the grocery store, and the tennis courts. Behind us, though, was what I referred to as the "real" China: housing for the workers—temporary shacks that look like a small breeze would destroy them. Farther on the horizon, rice fields and open space. Another world.

We stood still for a while, both our hands visibly shaking. Finally, we began to talk. We talked openly and honestly. The topics flowed naturally and freely—unfulfilled dreams and regrets, as well as hopes and ideas for the future. We talked about our families and our responsibilities toward them and the love we had for them. We talked about the past and the future and as he talked to me, I had a kind of epiphany. I could see everything. I could see our pasts and our futures, and I could see them intertwined. I knew that as a child I had lived in America and he had lived in China, but I could see us together. All of a sudden I was aware that when I was ten years old and Jake Marley was taunting me on the playground, William was there. When I was in high school, thinking there must be more to life than cheerleading, Friday night dances, and superficial boys, William was there telling me I was right. When I couldn't sleep due to anger at things that had hurt me, or a society that wasn't fair, or a dying father, or a struggling mother, William was there singing me to sleep. When I forgot about the beauty of life, William was there telling me to wait, that there might be a reason to hold on. When I accepted a job in China and then promptly wondered what on earth I was thinking, William was there to assure me it was the right thing to do.

I hadn't known his name was William at the time and I hadn't known that the encouragement I'd gotten my whole life was tied to him. But at that moment, as I stood there listening to this man, something in his voice and his eyes and the way he carried himself told me I knew him. I saw his past and I really saw *him*. I saw our future and our children and grandchildren. I saw the life we could have together, and it was as real as anything I had ever known.

I recognized him. There is no doubt about it. I knew this man before me, and I prayed to God that he knew me too.

He told me that he'd come to Guangzhou from his hometown in the hopes of finding a good job. He hadn't wanted to teach English, but there hadn't been any positions available in the business fields he was interested in.

"When I came to Guangzhou," he said, "I got confused." He said this as though he were still trying to figure it out. He'd come in search of any job other than teaching English, and he'd ended up doing just what he didn't want to do.

Something about the way he said this made me love him. It was in his honesty and humility; it was as if he were saying it to the stars, admitting that he was still confused about how he ended up here. Even after he'd had the interview at my school, he hadn't been sure he'd stay in Guangzhou. Yet he had.

As William looked straight ahead, seemingly still thinking about why he'd become so confused when he came to Guangzhou, I wanted to say something kind of bold. I didn't know how he would react, but I suddenly I knew I needed to say it aloud.

"Maybe you came here for a reason," I said.

At that, he smiled. He smiled a big, genuine smile, as if he already knew this and was glad I had caught on. He looked down as if to gather courage and said, "Maybe now I have a reason to stay."

Now we both smiled. There were those uncontrollable grins again. I wondered where the conversation would go next. I was filled with questions.

He answered before I could even ask the question.

"Do you know what I'm thinking right now?" he asked.

"No, what?" I asked.

He took a slow, long breath and said, "I love you." As soon as the words left his lips, his smile became even bigger. He stood up taller and said it again, as if to be sure I had heard him: "I love you."

For me the world and more specifically the tower was

spinning. I was so glad he'd said it twice because if he hadn't, I might not have believed it. I just stared at him. His gigantic smile seemed to get bigger and brighter with every second.

"William," I began, "I . . . I'm so happy you told me that because . . . because I feel the same way. I love you too."

I didn't know if that was adequate. I didn't know what to say. I couldn't believe any of this was happening, but it was.

"May I embrace you?"

William's English was good—maybe too good, as he hadn't thought of saying "hold" or even "hug." Nevertheless, I said "okay," and he did in fact embrace me. He touched my shoulders, then my face. A wisp of hair blew across my mouth and he gently pushed it aside, staring into my eyes. He leaned toward me and said, less formally this time, "Kiss you?"—and then he did.

chapter 23

Over the next two months, William and I didn't leave each other's side. We began to hold hands in our little community, letting people know that we were indeed a couple. This was quite a shock to everyone around us. At that time, it was very unusual for a Western woman and a Chinese man to be romantically involved—one simply didn't see that very often. The response was mostly positive; there were a few exceptions, but we didn't let those get to us.

I think at first people weren't sure what to think of us. It wasn't as if we announced to any of our friends that we were a couple. Rather, when someone invited me somewhere, William came too—his hand in mine. It was the same with his friends. I liked that we made this decision to let people figure it out for themselves. Of course, our closer friends knew the bits of our love story we'd chosen to share with them, but all the other curious people were left to wonder—and, of course, gossip.

We could tell certain people were jealous of him or resentful of me. Other people raised issues that didn't need to be raised, such as how a couple could possibly work together without there being a conflict of interest, but we didn't let it bother us. We were so on cloud nine that nothing much else mattered.

We talked late into the night almost every night. I asked

William if he had any interest in going to America and he replied that he had never thought about it.

"I know many Chinese are crazy about America and can't wait to visit there or study there," he said. "To tell you the truth, I never thought about that."

"Is that because you don't want to go to America or just that you never thought it was possible?" I asked.

"Maybe both. It's just not an option. I have, well, I *had* no reason to care much about America." He looked up at me and smiled. "Do you want to live in China forever or would you want to live in America again?"

I considered the question. "Well, I could see myself living here forever, but at the same time I would want to keep living in America as an option."

The truth was, I really could see myself living in China until the day I died. I don't know when that became true but at the moment, it was. I'd recently spoken with Chrissy about it during one of our phone conversations. She asked how long I thought I would stay, since initially I'd only planned to be there one year. I guess it was then that I first said I didn't necessarily see an end in sight. I hadn't thought it through, but I knew I was in no hurry to leave.

汤

One Saturday morning, William and I met for breakfast at the local *jiaozi* restaurant. The conversation turned to religion. He asked me about my church.

"So every Sunday you go to the church. What do you do there?"

He had no concept of church. It was completely foreign to him, and I suddenly found myself at a loss for words, but I tried to put something coherent together that would explain why I spent three hours there every Sunday.

"Well," I said slowly, "we basically learn. We have lessons and learn about, well, about the teachings of Jesus Christ, about serving others, about . . . about how to be happy." How could I explain taking the sacrament without going into the atonement of Christ? How could I explain Sunday school without explaining the scriptures? This was harder than I'd thought it would be. I'd had people ask me about my religion before, of course, and I'd always been very comfortable talking about it. However, those who had asked me in the past had some frame of reference, or some comparison to other Christian religions or Judaism, Islam, whatever. William had none of that. He was simply interested in what I did every Sunday.

I didn't know where to start. After some deliberation, I decided to start more generally.

I began by sharing some of my basic beliefs about the importance of family, service, and having an eternal perspective. This led into interesting discussions on culture, particularly about how Chinese culture also placed great emphasis on family, honor, and education. I had mentioned the fact that in my religion, we believed marriages and families last forever, even beyond death. I told him that although I had not had good experiences with romantic relationships, I still believed that marriage was sacred.

I realized I had probably been rambling a bit, though I hadn't meant to. I decided to eat for a minute and let him talk. He had been listening so intently.

I had just bitten into a jiaozi when he said it.

"Lori." He paused and looked at me very seriously. "Do you think we should talk about marriage?"

I was stunned and thrilled; I felt like I was floating above my chair. For the first time in my life, I did indeed want to talk about marriage—and it was with a man I'd been dating less than a month. Had he only brought it up because I had mentioned it? No, I already knew him well enough to know that he didn't say anything that he had not already thought about. He took everything seriously. But how could this be real? This was the first time in my life I had wanted to have this conversation, but I had only been dating William for a few weeks. *Is this crazy?* I wondered.

Still, this conversation felt so natural. His approach was honest and straightforward. He was matter-of-factly stating that since we loved each other, wasn't marriage the next step?

So I responded, "I would love to talk about that."

And we did. We talked about what we wanted in the future and how happy, how ecstatic, we were to have found each other. He talked about the fact that it would be hard because he didn't have much right now, but he knew we would be happy.

I had no doubt about that.

汤

As the days and weeks went on, I observed William carefully and completely. I watched the way he lived his life—so thoughtfully. He was confident but in the most humble of ways. He was one of the few people I had ever met who honestly did not care what other people thought of him.

I noticed that when we attended functions together, he never seemed to feel pressure to make small talk with people. I was not embarrassed by it, but at first I felt a little awkward, as if I had to take up the slack to keep the conversation going. I wondered if he was just plain nervous or insecure about his English, but as I watched further, I noticed that it was just the opposite: He was definitely not arrogant, but he also had this tremendous sense of self-confidence. If he didn't want to talk, he didn't, and he didn't feel pressure to make idle conversation. When he spoke, it was because he had something to say.

I came to wish that I had that ability. I was a master of superficial conversation and could chat with anyone at any time. I didn't necessarily enjoy that, but since I was good at it, I'd always found myself playing that role. I think growing up I'd taken on that role in my family, as well. I was concerned with what others thought of us, afraid they would think we weren't good enough. I so often felt ashamed of our home, of our car, and sometimes, of my parents. I wished they were younger, that my mom were fit and fashionable, that my dad could hang out with the other dads. It was never the case, so I tried to represent the family in the best way I knew how, talking—filling any awkward silences. Desperately wanting to take the focus off what our home looked like or whatever else might seem wrong with my family. I hated that I felt that way sometimes.

Through our conversations, I realized how very little I knew about the world. Here was this guy from inner China, and he knew American history better than I did. It seemed to me that there wasn't a single subject he couldn't discuss, and it impressed me so much. In those early days, it was fun to ask him all the questions I had ever wanted to ask about China but had been told never to voice aloud. One night, when we went for a walk near the lake, I brought up the "three Ts."

"So, William, someone once told me that in China there are some things that I should never talk about with a Chinese person," I began.

He smiled and seemed surprised. "Really? Why? What kinds of things?"

"Well, I didn't hear it directly, but Kassie told me that someone told her that there are three "Ts": Tiananmen, Tibet, and Taiwan. Supposedly, these are really emotional issues for Chinese. Do you think so?"

He liked the question, I could tell. He loved to think and loved to share ideas.

"Yeah," he said, "that's interesting. Those are important issues. Tibet, um, not so important really, but Tiananmen and Taiwan are major issues."

As I listened to William talking, it occurred to me how much his English was already getting less formal, less textbook-like. I supposed we had been spending most waking moments together lately, so it made sense.

"Well, I know when I asked Hong An about Tiananmen last year, I got a really weird response," I said. "She was very defensive, and I really didn't say much about it. I just told her that it was powerful to visit there because of what happened. Her response was shocking. Her whole demeanor immediately changed and she kind of freaked out."

"Yeah, that's not unusual. It's a sensitive issue." William went on to explain the politics behind Taiwan—the history and different perspectives.

He was like a walking history book.

汤

Things moved quickly for us. Once we told one another how we felt, it was as if we skipped a lot of the superficial stages that many relationships must go through. We knew we were each other's reason for coming to Guangzhou. Everything clicked in a million ways and on every conceivable level. Even things that could have been obstacles, such as having completely different religious belief systems, were not obstacles for us. We knew that everything, every single thing, would work out.

I wanted to tell my family about William. He was, really, my first true boyfriend, and I knew in my heart that he was the man I would marry. I called them up early one morning before work, since that was evening their time.

"Hello?" my sister's voice answered.

"Hey Chrissy, it's Lori."

"Hi! What's up? Mom was just talking about you."

"Oh really?"

"Yeah, some visitors from church just left and she spent

the whole time they were here bragging about you. Nothing's changed, Lori, you're still the golden child."

She tried to sound annoyed but I knew she was glad to hear from me. It was kind of an ongoing joke with Barb and Chrissy that I could do no wrong in Mom's eyes and I was the favored one. Chrissy especially felt this way. It bothered me, yes, but at least we'd gotten to a point where we could joke about it. The truth was that any objective observer could see they were right. I think Mom loved us all equally, but she did talk a lot about my accomplishments. She always had.

"So, what's up?" Chrissy asked. "How's life over there?"

"It's really, really great. Hey, how's Dad?"

"He's the same, Lori." She had a little edge in her voice, and I could understand why. I didn't want to get into that right now, though.

"Yeah, how 'bout Mom? Is she driving you nuts or are things okay?"

I asked this because Mom and Chrissy had an interesting relationship. They were very alike in some ways—loved the same movies and books and enjoyed each other's company—but at the same time, Chrissy had always felt invisible next to me and resented Mom's focus on me. So there was tension sometimes. Also, Mom was just a character—increasingly so as she was getting older. I'm sure it was hard for Chrissy to live there and hear about Mom's aching back, sore feet, and hemorrhoids.

"It's pretty good," Chrissy said. "We're just hanging out tonight watching movies. We ordered pizza."

It was funny to hear that they'd ordered pizza. I remembered when that was a regular occurrence for us. There was a period of time in which this was how we spent our Friday nights, or even weeknights if nobody had to work. We'd get movies from Blockbuster with money we didn't really have and order pizza, also with money we didn't really have. I don't recall us going out for a walk, or interacting much with other families. We just sort of hunkered down and almost hid ourselves away most of the weekend, going out only to go to church on Sundays. It wasn't always like that for us, I knew, but in the recent years leading up to my moving to China, I remembered so many weekends like that. I think we were kind of depressed, really, and that was our escape.

I contrasted this with the meals William and I ate together. He came over for dinner almost every night these days, but there was always planning beforehand. We would go to the vegetable market together, think about what we were going to cook, and buy the veggies and herbs. Then we'd go buy the meat. Then we'd bring the items back to my apartment and start the process. Often we'd listen to music in the background and talk as we washed, chopped, and cooked.

I had never spent so much time preparing a meal in my life as that first home-cooked meal with William, yet this had now become my norm. Even after this short time dating, on nights that we didn't have dinner together, I still followed this pattern on my own. I liked it. A lot. It felt good. It felt healthy and positive, and it was fun. So much care and preparation went into the shopping, washing, chopping, and thinking about the meal. William was very concerned about preparing things that were "good for health." My whole perspective about food and what it meant to eat a meal had changed in a short time. I felt normal, and I wondered if this was what most families did.

"Anyway." Chrissy sighed. "I'll put Mom on with us."

"Hi there, China girl," Mom said in her overexcited voice.

She was so precious, but at the same time it was hard to know to what extent she lived through me. She had experienced so many challenges in her life, and during these telephone conversations I always realized just how proud of me she really was.

We started out by talking about Dad, the nursing home, and plans for his care. In retrospect, it was sort of odd to go from that topic to my romance, but at the time I just couldn't wait to tell them and really, there would never be a time when things were going great there. I knew I would always feel that it wasn't the right time. So as talk about my dad petered out, I just went for it.

"Well, I have some news for you guys."

"Oh, what is it? What's going on?" Mom asked excitedly.

"Yeah, what's up?" Chrissy chimed in, her voice perking up.

"Well, I think I told you a little about William, one of the guys I work with. We're actually seeing each other now." It didn't sound adequate. I felt like there should be some special word for what we were experiencing. "Seeing each other" didn't seem to cut it.

"Oh," Mom said, her tone less excited this time. "And is he Chinese?"

"He is," I said. "He's from Hubei province, which is a bit north, and he's just . . . amazing, Mom."

"Uh-huh," she said. I could tell she was trying to sound positive, but was a little overwhelmed at this news. Nothing, however, could have prepared me for her next question. I could understand her asking if he was Mormon, what kind of family background he had, or even what sort of income he had, but what she asked instead was, "So, is he a communist?"

"Mom!" Chrissy shouted, half laughing.

I just started laughing—half out of shock at first, but before I knew it I was full-on belly laughing, and suddenly my mom and Chrissy were, too. The three of us couldn't stop.

Finally, after I'd laughed so much my stomach hurt, I answered her. "No, Mom, he's not. He was raised with that background but he doesn't consider himself a communist." I knew it would take me a while before I would be able to think about her question without laughing. "Mom, he's just . . . I've never known a better person than William. It's as if words to describe him haven't yet been invented. He is humble without being weak and strong without being macho. He is sweet without being sappy and optimistic without being naïve. He is a gentleman in every sense of that word—thoughtful, respectful, and gentle. He does things because he loves me and not because he wants recognition."

"Okay, so you like the guy!" Chrissy said in a teasing tone. "We get it already."

I hadn't even realized I'd gone on and on. It was hard to describe William because I knew no words would do him justice.

We finished our conversation and then I called Barb to tell her the same things. It was fun to say this out loud. It was real. When Barb used the term "boyfriend" about him, I had to laugh, but then I realized that indeed, that was what he was. I had a boyfriend named William.

chapter 24

*B*efore I knew it, it was December. My family had been updating me on Dad's condition and I had planned to come home for Christmas. On an early December morning when Barb called and told me how bad he was, though, I knew I needed to go right then.

"Hello?"

"Lori, it's Barb. I know it's the middle of the night there but . . ."

"Never mind that, how is Dad? Did . . . did something happen?"

"Lori, you need to get home. His body is just shutting down so fast. He . . ."

Barb's voice broke after that and I could hear her sobs as if she were right next to me.

"Don't worry, Barbie, I'll get there. Tell him to hold on, Please. I love you."

I hung up.

It was four o'clock in the morning and a group of friends were on a weekend getaway a couple of hours outside of Guangzhou. Along with William and I, there were 4 other couples and we'd all had a great day exploring the area and enjoying some nature. Barb's call shook me. I couldn't do a thing for the moment. So I paced back and forth, and, as an attempt to gain a small degree of clarity and peace, I prayed.

A few hours later, William and I finally caught the first bus we could to Guangzhou. As we set off, I called Kassie and my family while William called the airlines. Of course, it was complicated to get my flight changed and we spent a lot of time on the phone. Incidentally, I had never been as grateful for technology as I was at that moment. I didn't realize it at the time, but it later dawned on me that I had called Chicago from the countryside of China on a mobile phone (in 2001 this was something)!

Once we'd made the necessary arrangements, William and I rode along in silence for a while, both of us reflecting on the events to come. I was thinking about what I'd been taught my whole life at Sunday school—the afterlife, heaven, God, all of it. It occurred to me that I had no idea what William thought about all of this.

"William, I'm just wondering. What do you think happens when we die?"

"What do you mean? You mean like funerals and traditions?"

"No, I mean like our spirits. Like heaven, an afterlife. Do you believe in any of that?"

He thought for a minute, then said, "To tell you the truth, I think death is the end. That's it."

I nodded, taking it in, thinking it through. I could see why people thought that. I never had, but only because I'd been taught otherwise.

"What about you?" he asked. "What do you believe?"

"Well, I hope that there is life after death. I feel like there is because I believe there is a God. I don't know exactly how it all works, and I don't need to. But for me, I need to believe that. I guess I have faith that our spirits live on somehow."

He listened carefully, studying my face as I spoke.

"It's interesting," he said.

We went on to talk about God, life, death, my dad, and both of our families. I understood why William felt the way he did. If I hadn't been brought up in my faith, it would have been natural to believe that death was absolutely final. Talking with William reminded me of all that I did believe and hope—and explaining it to him, while listening to his ideas as well, made me feel these things on a deeper level.

汤

When we arrived in Guangzhou, I went to my office to take care of a few things. William packed my bags for me and managed to get my ticket changed. Before I knew it, I was off to the airport and off to America.

Twenty hours later I landed at O'Hare International Airport. I grabbed my luggage, and raced out the door to where my brother-in-law, Bill, was waiting in his truck. We said our hellos as he sped away.

I couldn't believe I was actually just forty minutes away from the hospital. Bill couldn't drive fast enough for me. I wanted nothing more than to see my dad and have him see me. I wanted him to know I had come home before he left this earth.

I tore through the hospital and straight to my dad's room when we got there. Out of the corner of my eye, I saw my family as I burst in, but my focus was on my dad. I walked straight to his bed, grabbed his hand, kissed his forehead, and looked into his eyes. He looked back. He really looked. He saw me. I breathed. I breathed in a way I hadn't in a long time, and suddenly everything was okay.

汤

I had a chance to catch up with my family. My niece, Shaleen, was curled up on a chair next to Barb with Chrissy and Mom close by. I looked at the four of them and realized how much I'd missed these women. I loved listening to their stories and reliving the memories they shared about Dad. Barb's husband chimed in with hilarious stories he recalled and before we knew it, it was after midnight. I sent them all home for a well-deserved night's rest." They had been at his bedside around the clock for days, and I wanted some time alone with my dad.

On this night, I lay next to Dad in my chair, telling him all I'd learned from him from the time I was a little girl.

"Daddy, I loved when you would take me fishing, ice-skating, sledding, or swimming," I said. "You played with us kids so much! How lucky we were! Even more, I loved when we would go for walks, or sit outside after dinner and have our chats. I remember you taking the time to do that from the time I was three years old. I remember you reading your scriptures, again and again and again. How the pages were marked up with questions you had, or passages that meant something to you. You never missed a Sunday at church, or a chance to go to the temple. You were so strong in your beliefs. I never once doubted your faith. I'll never forget, Daddy, how you told me I should go to China. I wonder if you remember that?"

As I talked, I looked at his face, or at the ceiling, or out the window just beyond his bed. The room was dim. It felt like there was nobody else in that hospital except the two of us. I had dragged the chair in the room right next to his bed so I could hold his hand. I thanked him. I reassured him. I looked at his body and thought of the millions of things wrong with it. I saw all the tubes in him, all the machines surrounding him. I thought of the last two times I'd come home and how each time he had gotten weaker and weaker and had suffered more and more pain. It was time for him to go. I knew that. His tired and worn body needed rest.

汤

The next night we were all in the hospital room together. It seemed we each had a continual prayer in our hearts—a conversation with God that was meant for Dad's heart as well: "God, please let him rest. Help him to know we will be okay and that he can let go. Please don't let him forget all he has done for us. Remind him of this now so that he can be comforted. Please, God, take away his pain."

We all joined hands and looked at Dad. We didn't speak. It was nothing we'd planned. It was just what we did, and we knew when to do it. We listened to his breathing and noticed that with each successive breath, he was struggling a bit more. The spaces between the breaths became longer and longer. Our conversation was quiet and hardly real, none of us truly involved in our words, just very aware of Dad. The talk lulled and we squeezed each other's hands, knowing it would come soon. There were tears on my sisters' faces, and on my mom's as well. There was an overwhelming sense of quiet in that room. I think those last few breaths my dad took were his attempts to stay a bit longer with us, to feel the love we had for him and for each other—to soak it all up and take that warmth with him.

It was Barb who finally spoke: "Should we say a prayer?" Her voice was soft, her eyes were wide.

We all nodded and Mom, through her tears, said, "You say it."

In this moment, we all really looked at Dad. He took one last, rattling breath, let it out, and then didn't breathe again. Neither did we for a moment. We were all waiting to see if it was real. And it was.

汤

We spent the next week planning for the service, having the funeral, the burial, all of it. There were moments when everything seemed almost normal. We would be sitting around the table, sharing a memory, laughing. Then we'd stop and wonder if it was appropriate. Should we be laughing? Was it okay to smile?

We made it through those days, hard as it was. I think what kept me from breaking down was knowing that William was waiting for me on the other side of the world, and that I had a life, my new life, to go home to. My home was there now.

A week after my dad died, I was on a plane bound for Guangzhou.

汤

I couldn't wait to see William. The hours on each flight back passed so slowly—which, in many ways, was good, because I had a lot to think about. My father had died and my heart was broken. At the same time, I was on the verge of something wonderful with William. I was also truly happy about me—just myself. I liked the life I'd made in Guangzhou. I liked my yoga, my running, my friends. I liked learning Chinese. I liked my apartment, feeling independent. I loved China, and yes, I believed I loved William, too. As I sat on the plane, I thought about all this and marveled at how extreme grief and extreme hope don't feel all that different sometimes.

chapter 25

I was only fifteen minutes away from landing in Guangzhou, and I could not stop smiling. I knew William would be there waiting for me when I arrived, and my heart was beating so hard I thought it might be visible to the other passengers.

As I turned the corner near the luggage carousel after going through customs, I saw him. He saw me too and waved. His smile was gigantic and it didn't leave his face until I kissed him. Well, even then it didn't leave. We were finally face to face. I could finally touch him.

"Hi, my sweetheart," he said with such excitement in his voice. He extended his arms and I fell right into them.

"Hi" was all I could get out before the tears came. I buried my face in his chest and breathed a big sigh of relief. I was so happy to be with him again. He held me tightly and stroked my hair. This was pure joy. I looked up at his face and was reminded of the first night we kissed, for now, as he had then, he brushed the hair away from my face, leaned in, and kissed me. I knew that was a big deal for him because Chinese people rarely show affection in public. Still, he didn't care. He had missed me just as much as I had missed him, and he couldn't wait to give me a kiss.

It seemed we'd stood there hugging for a long time when he finally said, "Let's get in line for a taxi."

I had thought a lot while being away from him. I'd thought about marriage, the future, and all the events in my life that had brought me to China. I had even prayed about him—not asking God if he was the one, just expressing how I felt. I felt peace as I thought about a future with William. And when I prayed, I felt even more peace. I never doubted he was a good person, and that we connected on a deep level. I wanted nothing more than to marry him and to spend the rest of my life learning and growing with him. I had found a man so wise, pure, gentle, intelligent, and just plain good to his very core that I knew I would be an absolute fool to not make our relationship the first priority in my life.

汤

After Christmas break, I threw myself into work and spending time with William. I was also running and doing yoga regularly. I was in the best shape of my life, it seemed, and everything was suddenly . . . good. I had this wonderful man in my life, I loved my job and was well-respected at work, and I was happy and fit. All of these things were dreams that had come true.

chapter 26

efore I knew it, it was time for Spring Festival. We had decided to go to William's hometown so I could meet his family and see where he was from, and we could try to get our marriage certificate. We told nobody but our families that we would attempt this. We knew it would be difficult, and we also thought it was nobody else's business.

The system of selling tickets in China never ceased to amaze me. During Chinese New Year, the train station chooses the strangest blocks of time to sell tickets, like five to seven in the morning. They'll sell tickets for a couple of hours and then just stop, informing all those waiting that they'll start again at, say, four that afternoon. So all those people have to either stay in line, for fear they'll lose their place, or take a chance and come back later. William left early one morning, well before five, and after standing in line for hours, he managed to get us two hard seat tickets to Hubei.

It really is all relative, and this train ride wasn't so bad. I guess I had become used to certain aspects of life China, because someone unfamiliar with the culture might not have described the journey that way. Because we could only get tickets for the hard seats, our travel companions weren't the classiest folks. Most men in China smoke, so everyone around us was smoking at one time or another. Also, it's perfectly acceptable on buses and trains to throw garbage on the floor; people figure that it's not their home and someone will clean it up eventually, so why not just toss it where they're sitting? So, rather than putting peanut shells or orange peels in a bag, they just throw them on the floor. A year earlier these things would have shocked me, but by this point I saw spitting on the floor, chain smoking, and bodies packed on top of one another without enough fresh air as par for the course when taking a train ride in China.

I read more than half of my book, a novel about Abraham's wife, Sarah, and played thumb wrestling and "try to open my hand," some silly games from my childhood, with William. Our total time on the train was about twenty hours.

When we finally made it to Wuhan, the capital city of William's home province, his best friend, Zhang Jin, picked us up. He had booked a very comfortable place for us to stay at William's former college; the rooms actually had heat! He took us out to dinner, and then I went back and slept while William went to Zhang Jin's room to chat.

My first impression of Zhang Jin was that he was sort of shady. William had told me a lot about him, and I knew he was involved in some illegal, or at least less-than-honest, dealings. He drank, smoked, and just seemed so different from William. I didn't get an especially good vibe from him that first night. However, the next day he joined us for lunch and my image of him softened a bit. He seemed like someone with really good intentions but who was sort of trapped in a certain lifestyle.

On our first day in Wuhan, we made a list of what we needed to accomplish in the next twenty-four hours. We only had so much time before we needed to take a bus to Huang Mei to meet William's family. There were a lot of sights we had planned to visit around Wuhan, but we decided they would have to wait. The first thing we would do the next morning was to visit the marriage certificate office to see what the application procedures and costs were. We had tried as best we could to prepare all the necessary documents beforehand, but all the government workers we'd spoken with had been so evasive, and nobody seemed to agree on exactly what it would take for an American woman to marry a Chinese man.

We were about to find out that evasive replies and misinformation would be the least of our frustrations.

汤

First thing the next morning, we went to the government office to apply for our marriage certificate. Even though William had tried to prepare me that this process wouldn't be easy, in my heart and mind, I really thought it would be. I didn't fully understand that getting married in China is nothing like what we're used to in the West, and that for a foreign woman to marry a Chinese man was highly complicated at best and nearly impossible at worst.

When a couple is married in China, there is nobody to "pronounce" them husband and wife. Although we did eventually have a ceremony, this is not a necessary part of becoming legally bound in China. There is no ritual exchanging of rings and no walking down the aisle; rather, a couple is married once they have obtained a marriage certificate. That may sound simple, but every requirement in the process of getting this certificate seems to have at least one hundred sub-requirements, and, depending on the mood of the officials, these requirements can change at any given moment. We learned and relearned this a million times over the next couple of weeks, but it all began in Wuhan, the capital of Hubei province.

We arrived at the office about one minute after it opened. We walked into a fairly small, older room. It wasn't what I had expected at all. I had pictured something bigger and more official looking. After all, this was the place that issued a most important document: a marriage certificate. The tattered appearance of the walls and furniture didn't strike me as particularly odd, though; after all, this was China. Most things there were not as modern, new, or well-maintained as we're used to in the West. What did strike me as odd, however, were the three workers sitting behind the counter. They looked like high school students, especially the man seated in the middle. There was a girl on either side of him and none of them looked a day over nineteen. *These are the people who will decide whether or not we can get married?* I thought. *These are the government officials?*

It turned out that the man (or should I say "boy"?) was the official in charge of issuing marriage certificates. My first impression of him is hard to describe because it was neither positive nor negative. He did look young, but because I knew he was the one who could help us, I didn't hold that against him.

William and I walked up to the desk hand in hand, smiling confidently.

"Ni hao," William said politely.

"Ni hao," the man replied.

William then began to ask a series of questions regarding this procedure. The man asked to take a look at my documents and I confidently took out my passport, work permit, birth certificate, other forms of identification, and the all-important non-marriage certificate, which I had gotten in Chicago a few weeks before. This is not a document we routinely use in the States, if ever at all, but my research had shown that I needed a notarized document saying I was single. Although it sounded strange, I'd had this document drawn up when I was home and brought it back.

I laid all these documents in front of the official and waited for him to say "okay" or some Chinese equivalent. But "okay" was not what I heard.

The official began to talk . . . a lot. He pointed to this document and that paper, but he pointed mostly at my non-marriage certificate. My Chinese is limited, clearly, but I heard a lot of "*bu xin*" (not okay) and "*bu keyi*" (cannot do). Basically, I heard a lot of "bu." Even if I hadn't understood a word, I would have been able tell just by looking at how William's smile had disappeared and feeling how he was squeezing my hand that things weren't going well. He looked at me with eyes that said, "This is going to hurt, and I don't want to translate it."

Apparently, my non-marriage certificate was bu xin. The form they needed was one to be obtained from the American embassy. The one I had was not official enough.

I asked William to explain to this man that my form was notarized, and that in the States this was considered highly official and should be completely valid. He gave me an "Okay, I'll translate it, but it isn't going to make a difference" look.

To every one of William's attempts, the man gave a rebuttal.

"William, tell him that this stamp is official," I said.

"Sweetheart," William said softly and gently, "I told him that."

"Well, tell him he should accept this. It's just as valid as anything I'd get from the embassy."

"Sweetie, I told him, but he said they have to have that certain form."

"But we can't possibly get that form now. We're in Wuhan. The embassy is in Guangzhou." My voice began to quiver and tears began to well up. *Don't cry, Lori*, I told myself. *This official is not going to be moved by tears and will probably be more amused than anything.* Don't *cry.*

As I stood beside William in the marriage certificate office, I couldn't help but feel sick at the amount of power this government official held in his hands. As I looked at him across the desk, I tried to look deeply enough into his eyes to reach his soul. I wanted him to look into *my* eyes and stop being the world's biggest jerk. I wanted him to look in William's eyes and feel his sincerity. And I wanted him to just give us our marriage certificate.

I don't know why I was so naïve going into that office. I actually thought we could just go in, give the official our documents, and become man and wife. After having lived in China for a year and half, I should have known that would not be the case.

William could see I was about to lose it. He put a strong arm gently around my shoulders—partly to be sweet, partly to keep me from falling over. I was so sad. I didn't understand all of the official's rebuttals. In fact, I hardly understood a word. I only knew that as I stood there with the man I loved, knowing that what we both wanted more than anything was to become husband and wife, we were being told "no." And that word has the same impact in any language.

We turned away from the desk and walked to the elevator. It couldn't have been more than ten feet away from the office door, but I felt like we walked for an hour. Every step was hard to take; I felt like I was going to pass out. We had come to Wuhan with all our documents in hand. We had a few precious days in Wuhan and a few precious weeks to get things accomplished. This was our window of opportunity to become husband and wife—and we weren't going to be allowed to do it. With every step I took away from that door, I was taking one step away from what I wanted most—my William.

As we got in that elevator, went downstairs, and headed toward the exit, I realized that this truly was our chance. *We cannot take no for an answer*, I thought. So we stood in the lobby and talked for a long time, sorting out all the possibilities and trying desperately to think of a way to get the document we needed from the American embassy in Guangzhou without having to go to Guangzhou ourselves.

"What if we fax the certificate to the embassy and ask them to confirm that it is valid?" I suggested. "Then they can pass on that confirmation to this office and maybe they'll accept it." The more I talked, the more excited I got. "Yeah, that's it—this guy just needs proof that it's valid, and I'm sure the embassy can confirm that!"

William grabbed both my hands in his and smiled the biggest smile. "Yes," he said in an excited whisper. "Let's go."

We walked back toward the elevator with some hope.

But when we got back upstairs and William explained our solution to the official, excitement evident in his voice even though I didn't understand all of the language he was using, the official once again replied with his familiar "bu keyi" and "bu xin." He didn't think it was likely that the embassy would accept anything by fax, and even if they did confirm that the notarized signature we had was valid, it still wasn't the correct form.

汤

When we returned to the hotel, we called the embassy on my mobile phone. They confirmed that they couldn't do anything by fax and that we did indeed need to have the appropriate form.

"Well, you'll need to go to Guangzhou," William said matter-of-factly after I hung up the phone.

My eyes widened. "Sweetie, what do you mean? Go to Guangzhou, get the form, and come back here? This is crazy. It's totally expensive, and we're so short on money now!"

"What other choice do we have?" he asked. "This is our only chance to get that form."

I knew he was right. I couldn't believe we were going to do this, but what choice did we have?

Throughout the day we tried to focus on what we could do—which wasn't much. However, we were required to get a medical exam, so we figured this was the best time to do it. We had gotten the form for the medical exam from the official and took that with us to the hospital.

We had to pay almost five hundred kuai (yuan) right off the bat—another expense we hadn't planned for. The irony is, money was not usually an issue for me in China. I made an American salary, and when we converted that to yuan, we multiplied by eight! This generally equaled me not having to worry too much about lack of money.

These circumstances, however, were quite different. I had gone home just one month earlier, and the expense of that trip and my dad's funeral costs had all but wiped me out financially. As we forked over the five hundred yuan to get our medical tests, we began to be conscious of how little money we really had—especially since we'd just learned that we needed to buy me a plane ticket to Guangzhou so I could get that precious piece of paper from the embassy.

All the plans William and I had about giving his family lots of money and buying them a new washing machine and water heater went right out the window as these marriage certificate expenses continued to add up.

chapter 27

The medical exam was fairly routine. We each had to uri-
nate in a cup, give some blood, and have a chest X-ray.
Everything was going along fine until William stepped in front
of the X-ray machine. He stepped off the platform and the doctor asked him to get back up. Confused, he complied, assuming
they'd made some mistake and just needed to take the picture
again. Next thing we knew, the doctor came out from the next
room and asked him to come into her office.

I anxiously waited outside. When William walked out,
there was a look in his eyes I'd never seen before. A million
things went through my mind: *What did she tell him? It must
be bad. Is it about me? Maybe she told him the bad news because
she can't speak English and couldn't tell me directly. Do I have some
serious problem? Or does he? What could be wrong? What does a
chest X-ray show?"*

As I was mentally going through the list of possibilities, William was leading me out into the hall. He took my hands in his
and spoke slowly, seeming as though he were trying to sound
much calmer than he felt.

"Sweetheart," he said. "There is some problem in my lungs."

In his lungs, I thought. *What kind of problem? Cancer? Pneumonia? Yes, actually of course, that must be it! He's had a cough for*

quite some time. I've been wondering if maybe he has a touch of bronchitis. Okay, that we can handle. I breathed a sigh of relief.

But William was still talking. "She says I have . . . how do you say it? . . . tuberculosis."

I couldn't talk. I didn't even comprehend what he'd just said. *That disease doesn't exist anymore,* I thought. I mean, hadn't they found a cure for that a long time ago? Didn't we vaccinate for that? *People don't actually get TB,* I thought. *William doesn't have that! That's a fatal disease. William doesn't have that. William does not have TB. I'm sure the doctor didn't say that—he's probably translating it incorrectly, or maybe the doctor is just inept. This is impossible.*

He obviously saw the horror and mass of confusion on my face. All he did was hug me very tightly; he didn't say anything. Because of the way the morning had gone, I was stuck in a practical rather than emotional frame of mind at this point. That's why, rather than asking about the disease or treatment or his feelings or anything normal, I said, "What about the form? This means she won't sign the form."

We needed that form in order to get married. Even if we managed to get the form from Guangzhou and every stamp and certificate we needed from William's hometown, without this medical form, none of the rest of it was any good. This diagnosis was one more thing to stop us from getting married. I couldn't even begin to think about the disease and what it meant because of the urgency I felt about getting the form signed. How sickening, actually, that having just learned that my husband had a deadly disease, my first question was about the stupid form.

William looked at me as if my words had hurt him more than the news of having this awful disease had. He told me to wait a minute and went back in to talk to the doctor. I didn't find out until several months later what actually took place behind that door—but when he came out, he had both our forms signed, indicating that we were both in good health and had passed the medical exam.

"Well, if she signed it, she must not be sure it's TB," I said. "I mean, she wouldn't sign it otherwise, right?"

"Hmmm. Mmm," he said, trying to smile.

"So, I'm sure she's just wrong, sweetie, I'm sure it's not really that," I said, hoping he would agree.

"Well, I think she's right," he said with a slight shake of his head. "I think I do have it but she knows we can get treatment."

"And I guess she figured, what's the point in denying us our marriage certificate, right?"

"That's right," he said, still trying to smile.

汤

A month later, William and I were sitting on the couch in our living room, chatting about work, funny things students had said that day, and the gossip from the secondary school where he taught at the time. I talked about the frustrations I was having in the ELC and the ideas I had to fix it. His wallet was on the coffee table and for some reason, I picked it up and started playing with it as we talked. Maybe I was curious about it, or maybe it was a mindless action—it wasn't something I normally did—but I started looking at his identification cards, and I noticed that his $20 US bill was gone. He'd enjoyed having this American money in his wallet, and obviously there hadn't been a chance to spend it in China, so I asked him about it.

William got a weird look on his face, and I didn't know if he was going to cry or throw up—that's how weird this look was.

"I need to tell you this," he said.

I was curious about what he was going to say, but I wasn't really worried. I just figured he'd had to spend it on something and felt guilty for not telling me, and now he wanted to "confess." If it hadn't been for the strange look on his face, I would have thought it was cute. Looking at him, though, I didn't know what was about to come out of his mouth.

He sat for a long time, his face sort of twisted. There seemed to be a bit of fear in his eyes. Fear of me? Fear of something he'd done? I didn't get it. *Tell me already!* I thought anxiously.

"Do you remember when we went to that doctor in Wuhan?" he finally asked me.

"Of course," I said. "How could I forget?"

As I waited for him to go on, it hit me. I didn't need him to tell me. I knew what he was going to say. Suddenly, it was obvious. I'd known at the time it was strange that the doctor had signed the form. I mean, why would she give him a clean bill of health when she'd just told him he had TB? Why hadn't he invited me back into that room with him? It was so clear now.

"You gave the doctor the money," I said as it all sank in.

I didn't care about the bribery so much. We were in China, and unfortunately that was how things worked there. What hurt was the realization that any hope I had of William not actually being so sick was gone. I had held out hope that she'd signed the form because his case was mild and he was going to be fine. Now I knew that she'd signed it for twenty dollars—a lot of money to her.

汤

After leaving the doctor's office that day, we walked back to the marriage certificate office. As we went, I thought out loud about the possibility that he actually had tuberculosis:

"I mean, I guess it's not so impossible. I just have never heard of it as being something people still get. I thought the disease didn't even exist anymore, or if it did, only in remote places." I paused. "Then again, you are from a remote part of a third world country. You've spent your whole life being exposed to things that I haven't. Some of the diseases rampant in China are those that Western countries automatically vaccinate for. In America, I think they just automatically do certain vaccinations when you're a baby or when you enter kindergarten."

He looked so surprised. "Wow! They just do that automatically in America? So people are protected from those diseases?" It was as if the thought had never occurred to him—like it was a novel concept. I didn't realize that to him and many people in China, it *was* a novel concept.

At that moment I wanted nothing more than to give William a magical shrinking potion, stick him in my pocket, and take him to America. He would go to a clean hospital with carpet on the floors and paintings on the wall. There would be magazines on the table for him to read while he waited, and maybe soft music playing in the waiting room. He'd sip on a soda and look out the window at a well-manicured lawn. All of the things that had never mattered to me before suddenly took on significant meaning. I thought of the dingy grey hospital we'd just visited and the filthy air and surroundings outside of it. How different from home. I'd been in poor hospitals in the States, like the Veterans Hospital in Chicago; I was painfully aware of how bad things could be there. But even compared to some of the best hospitals in China, that place was paradise.

All the love I'd had for China disappeared. I felt intensely angry. I don't know whom my anger was really directed at, but I was mad that William had this awful disease. I was mad that this country was so dirty and that people's lungs got so dirty as a result. Why hadn't anyone thought of this?

I suddenly felt very grateful to have been born in America. There are so many things I had taken for granted. But so many things that were just automatic in America were unheard of in China. I was mad, overwhelmed, and just very, very sad.

William was dispassionate about the whole thing. I think he was more worried than he let on, but he also didn't know much about the disease. And according to him, many people in China had tuberculosis.

I couldn't help thinking how unfair this was. William, of all people, did not deserve this. I thought back upon all the stories he'd told me about his childhood and I marveled at what he had survived and how extraordinary he was. He grew up never being full. He and his friends once gathered together all the money they could find in order to buy one small piece of steamed bread to share among the four of them. When his father was little, his parents both worked about six hours away. They, like many people of the time, earned their daily rice by working on a reservoir. For a day's work, his mother and father each got a small amount of rice, of which they would eat only what was necessary to maintain their strength. The rest they would put aside in a small bottle and save for their son. They would let the rice accumulate for about a week and then William's grandfather would make the six-hour journey back to his son to give him the rice. William carried his father's memories, and his own childhood memories, of hunger with him, and I could see the hurt in his eyes when I threw away food or balked at accepting anything used. It physically hurt him to be wasteful.

汤

We had plans to see lots of William's friends and former classmates that day, and I wanted William to have a good time with them and to be happy, so I tried hard to put thoughts of his illness out of my mind. It was hard, though. Between my worries about his sickness and our marriage certificate, I was emotionally exhausted.

William was so kind, attentive, and good to me and to his friends that day, and I was basically kind of a jerk. He didn't often get to see his classmates, and I should have been more patient. The day started out okay. We had lunch with Zheng Jin and a few other friends and then we went to see the Yangtze River. We walked across a really long bridge, one that had been started by the Russians and finished much later by the Chinese. We went to a temple and then to dinner.

Later that evening, we visited another friend, and when his girlfriend joined us, I felt my "wench" button switch on. She was a sweet girl, but I was not in the mood for sweet. It was as if she had just studied a long list of English vocabulary words—all related to sports—and was dying to practice them. I thought her questions would never end.

"Do you like tennis?" she asked.

I thought it was an odd question, since it came out of nowhere, but I figured maybe she liked tennis and wanted to talk about it, so I said, "Yes, I do."

"Do you like baseball?"

"Um . . . sure, yeah, I like baseball." *Where is this going?*

"Do you like football? Do you like swimming? Do you like. . . ."

I squeezed William's hand under the table, begging him to save me before I asked her if she would like to shut up. It wasn't her fault. She had never met a foreigner before and was excited to use her English. Another time, I might have been more patient, but right then I felt worlds away from this girl. She wanted to do karaoke and party down and I was praying for William's life.

We then went to visit another of William's former classmates in her dormitory. The room held two sets of bunk beds and four desks. It was long and narrow and there was hardly enough room for an aisle between the beds. This girl was nice, and very quiet, which was a welcome change after Little Miss Sports Authority. It was an interesting experience to meet her because I could tell that she had once had feelings—perhaps serious ones—for William.

The emotion I felt upon realizing this wasn't jealousy, because I knew William's heart, and I didn't feel insecure about his love for me. However, I did think she might be the kind of girl he would have ended up with had he not met me. She was sweet, beautiful, smart, and classy. I was very glad to meet her. It occurred to me later what a tremendous blessing it was to have no jealousy in my heart. In past relationships, I'd often experienced that emotion. Not with William. I never doubted his feelings for me or his commitment to our relationship. I promised myself that this was something I would never take for granted.

We finally said goodnight to everyone and went back to the place Zheng Jin had arranged for us to stay. Once we were alone, we had a really good talk. I told William how worried I was about his health and how I didn't want him to wait until we got back to Guangzhou before seeing a doctor. He talked to me about his fears too, and we agreed that we would get through Spring Festival and then begin treatment in Guangzhou. I knew that night, as I had known before, that this wonderful man would be my everything. I felt incredibly lucky.

chapter 28

It seemed like just days before that I'd lost my dad. Time wasn't making sense, and all the scenes in my life were running together. As I was about to land in Wuhan on the flight back from Guangzhou, it hit me just how exhausted I was—not just physically but also emotionally. This process of getting our marriage certificate had been so much harder than I had anticipated, and it had really just begun.

It was only that morning that I'd left William, but I was thrilled to know that in just a few minutes I would see him. I had the precious paper from the consulate safely tucked inside my backpack (on which I had a death grip, knowing the consequences if I were to misplace it). So many documents were in my backpack now—there were so many pieces of paper to keep track of—all with the purpose of proving we were who we said we were so that we might get approval to get our marriage certificate. Tomorrow we would be off to William's hometown, but for tonight I just wanted to see my husband-to-be and get some sleep.

The next morning, after a breakfast of mantou and porridge, we boarded the bus for Huang Mei. We had a mile-long list of documents that we needed to retrieve from William's hometown, all of which we hoped to bring back to Wuhan before the officials took their Spring Festival vacation. We knew if we didn't get our marriage certificate before that day, there would be not be enough time to get it before our return to Guangzhou the following week.

I took a deep breath and was grateful for William's squeeze of my hand. He seemed to know what I was thinking and was calmly reassuring me that we were in this together. I laid my head on his shoulder and thought about what lay ahead. I was actually getting nervous, as well as excited. With all that had gone on, those intense but depressing days in Wuhan, I hadn't even had time to think about the fact that I was about to meet William's family.

What would they be like? He'd said they were poor, but what did that mean? Would his mom like me? Would it matter if she didn't? Would I be able to understand two words they were saying? Would I do something to offend them? Would they look at me and feel sad that their son hadn't fallen in love with a Chinese girl?

Countless scenarios ran through my mind as I looked out the window. It was a sunny day and for that I was grateful, because my heart felt anything but. I had begged William to stay one more day in Wuhan so he could see a doctor. Having learned that he had tuberculosis had changed everything. I wanted to drop all our plans and focus on getting him better. In his mind, however, it was Spring Festival, a time of happiness and family, and he didn't seem nearly as worried as I was about having received this news. He also felt strongly that it was better to wait until we got back to Guangzhou, since that's where he would begin his treatment.

It seemed insane to me that, although we had just learned that he had a life-threatening illness, we were not going to do anything about it. We were just going to go to Huang Mei as planned and pretend we had a reason to smile, to think about the future. I could barely find the strength to breathe, let alone muster the energy to act happy and make good first impressions. All that kept going through my mind was that I'd found him—I'd found the one, my soul mate—and before I could even become his wife, I'd learned I could lose him.

汤

We arrived in Huang Mei before dinnertime, just as the sun was beginning to set. As we got off the bus, I had such a feeling of excitement, and it was clear that William did too. It was also clear as we rounded up our luggage that we had stepped into a different world. A crowd was already beginning to gather; people were catching their first glimpses of blond hair. William had warned me that he didn't think a foreigner had ever been to this county, and based on everyone's reaction, it was obvious he'd been right.

William took my hand with his right hand and waved the crowd aside with his left, leading me toward a taxi. Everything seemed very loud and rushed. The bus station was a sea of people, all of them returning home for Spring Festival, and I marveled at William's ability to maneuver his way through the throngs of people. I kept my head down and maintained a tight grip on his hand, just hoping to get to the security of a taxi, where I could finally breathe.

As William told the driver where to go, it occurred to me that he was no longer speaking Chinese, or at least what *I* knew as Chinese. He'd told me that people in his hometown spoke another language, and sure enough, there it was. It was so different from Mandarin! I couldn't understand a word. Suddenly, I felt like I was in a foreign country within a foreign country. William kept squeezing my hand, smiling, and looking as though he might jump out of his seat. He was genuinely happy. He was home for Spring Festival.

I'm not even sure what was so different about William's hometown to me—it's not as if we were in the countryside, and even if we had been, I'd certainly experienced China's countryside before. But my stomach was doing flips as I looked around and tried to take in as much as I could. I was looking at everything and thinking about him coming from this and how strange it was that he'd ended up in Guangzhou.

The sunset that evening was beautiful; the pink of the sky looked almost red when compared with the brown of the buildings. I decided I liked this town. It was dirty, yes. It was run-down, yes. But there was something about it that I liked.

I think I saw William when I looked around. I imagined him as a child in the faces of the kids I saw. I thought about him carrying his books and lunch to school, sometimes walking barefoot or carrying his own chair. I remembered him telling me that the students from his village who wanted to attend elementary school were required to bring their own chairs. The school provided the tables but they couldn't afford chairs. He'd said that if the ones they brought were kitchen chairs, they carried them home every night so the family could use them for dinner and then carried them back to school the next morning. Whenever the school decided it was time to ask for money from the students, most of them silently took their chairs and went home, knowing their families couldn't afford to pay.

My first reaction upon hearing such stories was to feel pity. That always faded, however, as William saw only the joy in his childhood stories. When he talked about the fact that his whole village needed to share one cow, I couldn't help but feel sorry for them, but William didn't see it that way. They were so poor, yes, but so was everyone else, so it didn't occur to him to feel bad about it. To him, it was normal to carry his chair to school, to share a cow with the entire village, and to wash your clothes by hand in the pond outside.

汤

Since it was early evening when we arrived, his family was still at the little shop they owned, so we met them there. At the city limits, we had transferred from a taxi to a *mao mo*, which was a little contraption consisting of a box attached to the back of a moped. It had woven its way through the narrow streets of this small town and then dropped us off at the store. When we arrived, William's brother let off a few small fireworks to welcome us.

There they are, I thought, catching my first glimpse of them. Here was my new family. William had told me they were not "huggers," or even hand-shakers. When I first met them, I drew the conclusion that they were not "talkers" either. I said "ni hao" to each of them and they just smiled and nodded.

I looked around their little shop. This was how they earned their living—selling basic necessities like soap and light bulbs. The store was part wood, part tin, and looked like a strong wind might blow it right over. There were pictures of the family on the wall—mostly of me and William, pictures we had sent them from Guangzhou. I could feel their eyes on me as I walked around, trying to show interest in everything.

After we chatted for a few minutes, William's dad and brother grabbed our suitcases and we all began walking home. His mom stayed behind for a minute to close the store. My new sister-in-law carried our niece and we headed home for dinner.

Home turned out to be right down the street and up seven floors. William's family had just bought this apartment, and it was very nice. Although they were from the countryside, now that they had an apartment in town, they had running water and electricity—luxuries unheard of by some of their relatives. His dad was very proud to show me the hot water heater. When I asked William why he was so proud of it, he told me they had bought it for me, so that I would be able to have hot water for bathing while I was there.

It occurred to me that it was strange they'd gone all these years without such a luxury and suddenly could afford to buy the heater.

"Hmm. . . ." I whispered teasingly. "Did you maybe send them the money for that?"

"Maybe," William said with a smile. Of course he had. I knew that it was not an insignificant purchase for him, either, since his teacher's salary wasn't much. I loved the gesture. The more time I spent with this man, the more I truly loved him.

汤

That night, after the sun went down and the frigid evening temperatures emerged, I became very grateful for the water heater. William had told me his province was much colder than Guangdong and I'd known we would have no heat, but I'd had no idea how cold it would be.

As the days progressed, I noticed that William's family didn't always use the hot water heater. They were accustomed to using cold water and if they did want warmer water, they heated it up on the stove first and then poured it into a big washbasin. However, I used that water heater like nobody's business, and I was profoundly grateful for every drop of hot water that flowed from the sink. After being in Huang Mei for several days, I looked forward to my bathing rituals more than anything else. It was the one and only chance I got to warm up each day.

Bathing in Huang Mei was unlike any other bathing experience. First of all, there was no tub, and secondly, there was no shower. What I did have were a few plastic basins, and I made the best use of those that I possibly could. It was the same routine each time I bathed, and I quickly got my method down to a science.

The first part of my ritual was to get three of the basins ready. One was bigger than the others—perhaps two feet in diameter—and the other two were quite a bit smaller. I began by filling one basin with hot water and dumping that into the big basin. Next I carefully took my clothes off, being cautious not to get anything wet, and then stepped into the larger basin. There was enough room in the basin to sit down cross-legged, and that's what I did. The hot water felt wonderful—and if there was no breeze coming through the window that never quite closed, the bathroom eventually began to get warm.

As the water began to cool, I filled up the second small bin with hot water. While that was filling up, I used the first small bin to scoop out some of the cooler water and dump that down the toilet drain (which was level with where I was sitting, since China has "squatters" rather than Western-style toilets). Then I added more hot water from the sink, and began to feel warm again.

This bathing ritual went on for a while. I could have let it go on all night; it was paradise. It had to end eventually, though, so right before I wanted to get out, I filled the basin with hot water one more time and then stood up. I dried off as best I could and then stepped into my slippers. Then I began to get dressed—a long process, given how many layers I had to pile on. If I could do all of this quickly, before any heat escaped from the bathroom, I felt wonderful.

I appreciated those baths so much. They gave me strength to face more cold.

In this part of China, most homes and businesses didn't have heating. People seemed to just manage during the cold months. During Spring Festival it was about twenty-five degrees Fahrenheit most days, which is cold for most of us, yet people routinely went about their business despite the frigid temperature. William had tried to prepare me for this change, and we had brought lots of sweaters and long underwear, but there really are no words to describe the ever-present chill.

汤

After almost a week of constant cold, I became crabby, to say the least. One day, after having had diarrhea for three days, my body aching with cold, and going through withdrawal from my Diet Coke, which could be found nowhere in the entire province, I lost it.

I had said nothing when a live chicken was walking around the house hours before it was served up for dinner. Nothing when William's mom put huge chunks of frog and eel in my bowl at dinnertime. Nothing when his niece pooped on the floor with no one but me thinking it was disgusting. Nothing when we spent hours upon hours visiting relatives who spoke a language I could not understand, and nothing about how freezing I was. But enough was enough, and I finally snapped.

"Are people here just crazy, William?" I demanded. "I mean, does it bother nobody else that we're sitting in here with six layers of clothing and I'm still freezing!? I'm so cold my body aches and my toes are numb. We are inside the house and I can see my breath. This is not normal! I cannot get warm no matter how much I jump up and down. I am miserable and I want a freaking heater!"

I wasn't proud of my outburst but I wanted someone to give me credit, to recognize that I was existing in an alternate universe, experiencing things that other foreigners—and even many Chinese, in fact—would never believe.

William didn't seem to know what had hit him. He listened to my outburst, my ranting and raving, without uttering a word. Then he pulled me toward him and hugged me. I hid my face in his chest and took deep breaths, trying not to cry. As he stroked my hair, he whispered, "Do you remember that day in Siqao when we tasted the bitter soup?"

How could I forget?

"Yes," I whispered, not getting the connection.

William continued to hold me, squeezing me even tighter, probably hoping I would figure it out for myself. Finally, feeling the security of his hug and the humility in my own tears, I remembered the bitter soup. I remembered everything.

It was shortly after we had started dating. The concept itself wasn't particularly new to me, but the way William shared it had touched my heart. And now, here, in this moment in Huang Mei, it was really sinking in. The bitter soup is about bad days making us appreciate the good days, the idea that there simply must be opposition in all things if we are to ever learn anything.

On that particular afternoon, we had been running errands and decided to eat lunch in between stops. He'd suggested that we have a particular kind of soup, and he'd asked me if I was up for trying something new.

"Sure, why not?" I said.

Well, when I tasted the thick, black soup, I had my answer as to why not. It tasted positively awful!

"What is this?" I asked, making a face. "It is the most bitter stuff I've ever tasted."

"That's kind of the idea, sweetheart," William said, chuckling. "It's *ku tang*. It's supposed to be very bitter and kind of hard to swallow."

"Well, mission accomplished," I said. "Why on earth did you purposely order disgusting soup for our lunch, babe? I mean, of all the things we could have eaten?"

"No problem," he said. "If you want to order something else, we can, but I wanted you to try this. Sometimes we have to have the bitter so that we better understand the sweet."

I just sat there for a moment. Clearly, this was not about lunch. He was trying to share something with me—something that was important to him. Although I was familiar with this idea of bitter and sweet, as it is central to my own religion as well as so many others, I had never brought this concept to life in such a tangible sense. I had thought about it before. I'd studied it before. But never before in my life had I tasted it. I had never tasted the bitter soup.

"So, what is this?" I asked. "A sort of reminder that you think I need?"

"We all need it. Look at how sweet our life is, Lori. Think of the amazing things that had to happen in order for you and me to find each other. I believe that if we volunteer to swallow bitterness sometimes, even when things are good and we don't need to, we'll be more prepared for the true bitterness that always comes, usually when you least expect it. Also, by tasting the bitter we are reminded of the sweet and won't take the good things for granted. And besides, this soup is very good for your health."

This man. He was always teaching me something. Even when he taught me something I already knew, he did it in a way that was new to me. I was grateful for the lesson and for all the good conversations between us that flowed from that soup.

We'd shared that moment more than two months earlier but now, on this day in Huang Mei, I was finally beginning to really get it. No more ranting about the temperature, the food, the toilet, and the fact that there was no Diet Coke in the entire province; I needed to swallow this bitterness. I needed to remember that a lot of people—my soon-to-be in-laws, in fact—lived like that every day. Nothing was easy and not too many things were pleasant. Everything was about work, about necessity, and about surviving. They were doing all they could to make me comfortable, showing love to me before I even deserved it. It was a really good thing they didn't understand English, because I would have been even more embarrassed, even ashamed, at my outburst if they did. His loving family was doing so much to make me comfortable and happy.

How sweet the bitter soup. With that, I went to my suitcase and grabbed another sweater.

chapter 21

The importance of stamps—rubber ink stamps—in China cannot be overstated. Surely, there must be some folklore from the Tang dynasty having to do with the reverence and awe of the beloved stamp, stories that have found their way into present discourse.

Despite my initial resistance to recognizing the validity of a little red stamp, by the end of my time in Huang Mei, I, too, was in awe of its power. After all, I had seen firsthand that a stamp is a passport to almost anything—in particular, a marriage certificate.

On a cold February morning, we began the process of getting our stamps. When I saw William's uncle Shi Mu ("mother's younger brother," in the local dialect) approaching us, I knew I liked him right away. Wearing a suit and tennis shoes, he was full of purpose. Against the dirty streets and rundown buildings, his suit and tie made him stand out. He was walking quickly, taking gigantic steps, and when he saw us he flashed a huge and genuine smile. He had his mobile phone in one hand and was motioning toward the cigarettes on the shelf of William's parents' small store with the other. William took the cue and began packing cartons of cigarettes into his backpack.

The cigarettes were for the purpose of *guang xi*. It's a little Chinese word that has huge implications. It literally means "relationship," but anyone who has ever tried to do anything in China knows it's much more than that. It exists at every level of Chinese culture and is used in every context imaginable. Among other things, it can mean offering a cigarette while you're asking a favor—or even asking someone to do his job! The unspoken rule seems to be that a person needs just a little extra incentive to get the job done.

This is most definitely the case when dealing with government officials, although it wouldn't be fair to say that all who use it are dishonest. It is simply how things get done in China. Knowing someone in a powerful position makes getting anything accomplished much easier. If that's not an option, offering a cigarette and displaying the right amount of respect is a start.

In order to get our stamps, we needed to engage in a little guang xi. Shi Mu knew this and, fortunately for us, he knew a few people. This didn't guarantee an easy time, but it meant a foot in the door.

Our first stop would be the school where William used to teach. They had his *hu kou*, residence book—something that's very important in China. This is the government's way of keeping track of its citizens. In the days before the Cultural Revolution, a person's work unit would hold the card, thereby giving the unit the power to decide if and when a person could move to another location. To some extent, this was still the case today, although William had gone to Guangzhou without getting his. In order to get married, though, it was absolutely necessary to have his hu kou in hand.

In addition to this, we needed the first stamp on our marriage application form, and this stamp could only be given by the principal of the school where William had worked. So much was riding on this.

When we pulled up to the school, the gate was locked. Shi Mu and William got out and went in while uncle number two and I waited in the car. He was friendly and tried to chat with me, but he was using Huang Mei Hua rather than Mandarin and I couldn't understand enough of what he was saying to hold a conversation. Besides, I was too busy praying in my head that we could accomplish what we needed to with these stamps to think about chatting with this guy.

Finally the gate opened, and we went in.

The first order of business was to find the principal, who was in a meeting. Did we let that stop us? No. Uncle one got a cigarette ready, and we all walked over to where the meeting was being held. Sure enough, a bunch of teachers were sitting around a makeshift table when Shi Mu walked right in and asked to speak to the principal.

When the principal walked out, I immediately tried to size him up. Would he help us? Would he try to make things difficult for us? Going through this process had taught me to do this—to judge people in an instant. It was so crucial to know what sort of person everyone was so that we knew how to proceed. Would he require extensive flattery and deference? Would he make us sweat it out? Initially I wasn't sure about the principal, but I soon realized he would help.

He led us to his office, where he got the stamp out of his desk. There was some discussion about which stamp to use and where to use it, but finally he finished the task. Then he took another cigarette and went back to his meeting.

汤

Our next step was to get William's hu kou, but the man who had it wasn't there. We waited a while, until we realized we were wasting precious time. The problem was that every other step depended on this one, so it wasn't as if we could work on another part of the process and then come back. However, we decided to try.

We left our phone number with the man's wife, hoping he would call us soon—and as we drove out of the gate and turned onto the dirt road, who should approach on his bicycle but the very man we needed. What timing! It was wonderful for me to watch William through all this. He was nervous but was handling the stress of the situation so well. There was so much hope in his eyes and he was trying to play the game, yet in his own honest way. He just wanted people to do the right thing and give us the stamps and information we needed. He was just so purely good—I saw that again and again, and with each time I just loved him that much more.

William and Shi Mu jumped out of the car and walked with the man back toward the school. Uncle one and I reversed the car and followed them. This man kept all the official documents for teachers, both past and present. We followed him to his office and William gave him a cigarette. The man looked in his desk, in the cupboard, under piles. I was not exactly confident in his filing system. As he looked here and there, he chatted casually with William and his uncles, as if it didn't matter much whether he found the residence book or not.

After exhausting the search in his office, the man got his keys and went to another room, which he searched in the same manner as he had the first. Finally, he returned to his office, got his bamboo ladder, and climbed up to a little makeshift attic above his office. We paced and prayed and waited until finally we heard him shout, *"Zhao dao le!"* (I found it!)

Shi Mu and I smiled in relief, and William practically skipped into the room to get it. This was his official ticket to a marriage certificate, and we now had it in our hands.

The four of us piled back into the car after having given this man a whole pack of cigarettes. William was absolutely beaming.

"Getting that card and the first stamp were the hardest steps," he said, "and now they are behind us."

Feeling completely exhilarated, we went in search of stamp number two.

汤

We sat at the security bureau, watching several government officials argue back and forth about which stamp was needed as the second stamp. When that argument was settled, they began to argue about whose responsibility it was to give William the stamp. None of them wanted to risk being the one to give the wrong stamp, and although they clearly resented us for imposing on their newspaper reading and tea drinking—the activities to which they seemed accustomed—they also seemed to want to make the most of this unusual situation. After all, they had never seen a foreigner before, and the fact that I wanted to marry a Chinese man from their hometown was causing quite a stir.

Shi Mu, uncle two, William, and I sat there, helpless, as eight officials gathered around one desk and shouted back and forth, pointing at the paper on which we needed to put the three precious stamps in order to obtain permission to get married. Even the man who appeared to be the janitor was in on the discussion at one point.

Finally, when it was clear these eight men would never agree, someone decided to call the man whom we would forever call "Second Stamp Man."

As we were waiting for that man to come, one of the officials noticed a problem with one of William's documents. The third character in his name was written incorrectly on his hu kou. The official informed us that without the two names being consistent, it was impossible for us to get the second stamp. Just when I thought things could not possibly get more complicated, they were getting ridiculously muddled.

Knowing that every second was precious, we quickly piled into the car and sped off toward the civil service office. The fact that we had use of a car for the day put us into a different category completely. In this small town, only people with very high government positions had cars, and even then they shared them. It was virtually unheard of for someone there to have his own car.

Earlier that morning, we'd wondered how we were going to accomplish the task of getting to and from all these places in order to get the stamps. Taxis weren't a possibility, since the security bureau was outside the city limits. We were almost at the point of jumping on the back of a tractor when Shi Mu was struck by an epiphany. How would it look if we pulled up to the security bureau in a tractor? How seriously would they take the three of us dusting hayseed off our clothes and smelling of the animals with whom we had shared the ride? And if we took buses or taxis or walked, we wouldn't have enough time to get everything done and nobody would take us seriously. With this in mind, Shi Mu got on the phone and called another uncle of William's who just happened to work as a driver. Fifteen minutes later, uncle two sped around the corner and we jumped in the car. He had somehow gotten use of a car, and we didn't bother to ask how—we were just grateful that he had.

Like Shi Mu, uncle two was clearly doing his best to help us by looking the part. He had a tie dangling around his neck and was shaving his face with an electric razor as he drove.

汤

When we arrived at the office, which was a one-room building, I noticed that the official was a woman. In the past, this would have caused me immediate relief—I would have thought that a woman would always be more cooperative in matters of the heart. After all, we were trying to get married. Now, however, after having dealt with both male and female officials in China, I had learned that in general, the attitude of a government official transcended gender.

William explained our situation to her, and I silently prayed that she wouldn't make this difficult. We were incredibly short on time. If we didn't get those stamps today, we would have to wait until after the Chinese New Year, at which time William and I would be back in Guangzhou, and all of this would be for nothing.

The official listened to William and then, without changing her expression in the slightest, walked to a shelf behind her and pulled down a huge book. There were about one hundred of these books, each containing registration information for the local residents. She told him matter-of-factly that he would need to find his page in order to prove that the name on the registration card was wrong.

As she handed the book across the counter, William and his uncle both grabbed it and began flipping through the pages as quickly as possible. We needed to find this page, have the official change the name on his registration card, and get back to the security bureau before Second Stamp Man left for lunch. I felt helpless as I watched them flip through the pages looking for William's information. Shi Mu would begin to turn the page, at least separating it from the one below it, and William would then actually turn it. This is how much of a hurry we were in— they were actually helping each other turn the pages.

The tension during this process was so strong that it seemed the four of us could barely breathe. When they finally found William's page, Shi Mu and I exchanged huge smiles. We were bonding over this, even though we couldn't say two words to each other due to the language barrier. I thought William might begin to weep on the spot—we were all absolutely overjoyed.

He showed his page to the official and she slowly took his registration card and walked toward the computer. William squeezed my hand. She wouldn't have taken the card in her hand if she weren't going to do anything with it. She was going to help us. We breathed a collective sigh of relief.

汤

We arrived back at the security bureau to find that Second Stamp Man had indeed arrived. William gave him a cigarette and Shi Mu apologized profusely for having made him wait those ten minutes. After making us sweat and grovel a bit, he gave us the second stamp. We felt as if we were holding solid gold as we left the security bureau. We had gotten our precious second stamp and were on our way to get the third and final stamp—or so we thought.

Shi Mu knew a guy who knew a girl who worked with the official who had access to the third stamp. It was Saturday afternoon at three o'clock—not usual business hours—but thanks to Shi Mu's connection, we were in.

William carefully gave the woman his paper that already had the first two stamps on it, handing to her with both hands—a sign of politeness in China. She looked it over and made what sounded like a casual comment, as if she were commenting on the weather. What she had actually said, though, was that the second stamp was wrong.

It was the scene at the security bureau all over again. Everyone was arguing, even though we were all on the same side. We simply could not believe this was happening. William and the girl were passing the paper back and forth, pointing to this and that. Finally, the girl got a book out, found what she was looking for, and read it to them. Shi Mu grabbed the book and read it for himself. He looked at William, who then looked at me.

We had no choice but to return once again to the security bureau and hope that Second Stamp Man would get it right this time.

Of course, when we arrived, Second Stamp Man was nowhere to be found. This time, his colleagues told us, he was getting his hair cut.

At this news, we didn't know whether to scream or cry—or just lie down in defeat. We'd had it. We were physically exhausted and mentally drained, and I felt just plain sad at how bleak our chances of getting our marriage certificate seemed to be. We had done the thing, we had played along with the ever-changing rules, and all we wanted was the stupid stamp! We were trying to get married, for Heaven's sake. Why on earth did it have to be so complicated? It was as if the universe were testing us, even taunting us, to see just how much two people would tolerate in order to get married.

Shi Mu looked around as if searching in the air for answers. Finally he looked forcefully at the janitor, who was quietly reading his newspaper, and said, "Take me to him."

Off they went to the barber.

汤

Not thirty minutes had passed when Shi Mu and the janitor returned, not with Second Stamp Man himself but with the key to the cabinet where the second stamp was kept. For a split second after we got our beloved second stamp, I began to wonder if perhaps those Tang dynasty legacies should have focused on the key rather than the stamp—but then I realized I didn't care. I was just happy that we had completed step one in the process of getting our marriage certificate.

As William, Shi Mu, uncle two, and I jumped into our semi-stolen car, I smiled and thought to myself, *Only nine hundred and ninety-nine more steps to go.*

William squeezed my hand as if to say, "My thoughts exactly."

chapter 30

*O*ther than working on getting these precious stamps, we spent Spring Festival getting to know William's family. Some of his aunts and uncles lived in the town where his parents, brother, and sister-in-law lived, while others lived in the countryside.

Spring Festival is the time of year when all Chinese go out and visit one another. Every morning, each family has goodies set out on their table so that when visitors come, they are prepared. It is actually a nice concept but like many things in China, it is rather intense. In all fairness, my own exhaustion with the tradition was probably due, at least in part, to the fact that I couldn't understand the language well enough at that time to truly participate. Also, no matter how hard William's family tried to include me, I just wasn't used to being around this many strangers, and for so long a time.

I wanted days of sitting around the house relaxing, but during Spring Festival this seemed to be impossible. I longed for holidays like Christmas, where my family stays in pajamas all morning, where there's no agenda, where everything is slow-moving and low-key. Here in Huang Mei, the expectation was that we would visit three or four families a day! And it wasn't as if we jumped in the car to do this; it involved bus rides full of cigarette smoke

if we were in town, and lots of walking if we were in the countryside. It was exhausting, to say the least. Nothing like what I
considered a "holiday."

And all the while, of course, we were trying to get our marriage certificate, *and* we were both painfully aware of William's
sickness and the fact that we had done nothing about it. We were
stressed about money and how we were going to complete the
other steps that needed to be completed in Wuhan.

How were we going to manage everything?

汤

We took the bus to Wuhan later that week. We needed to get
everything translated and then hand all of the paperwork from
William's hometown over to the government official. I was so
afraid of him, of the power he had. I hoped to God that he would
be fair and just do his job.

I don't know what was going through my head as we entered
that government building and took the elevator upstairs to the
office where we had received such bad news before. It had been
less than a week since we had seen this official, but it felt like at
least a year. So much had happened since those first few days
in Wuhan. For one thing, I had been to Guangzhou and back
and had gotten the non-marriage certificate. We had traipsed
through the countryside getting our three stamps, and we had
"celebrated" Spring Festival in the midst of all these uncer-
tainties about the certificate, our lack of money, and of course,
William's illness. So much was out of our control, and so much
was unknown.

Our documents were deemed acceptable; we were issued the
marriage certificate that day!

The final step was to get it officially notarized, which would
cost several hundred yuan. We had no choice but to use the last
of our money on the notarization, which meant that we would

not have enough money for a hotel that night—but we knew that would be fine, as long as we could get a bus back that night.

We raced over to the notarization office, handed them our certificate, and asked them what time it would be finished.

"The earliest you can get it is tomorrow afternoon," the girl behind the desk said.

We were in no way prepared to stay another night in Wuhan.

"What are we going to do?" I asked William. "This is so stupid. "When did we become so poor? We have actually made it this far, gotten our certificate. We are on the last step and now we don't have enough money to finish it!"

"It will be okay, sweetie," he said. "Okay, what's our money situation right now? We have about six hundred kuai, right?"

"Yeah," I said, "but this will cost almost four hundred, so that leaves two hundred to get bus tickets, then we'll have about fifty left over. Fifty is not enough to get a hotel tonight, and what about food?"

"Okay, what if I can find us a room for less than one hundred, and what if we take a different kind of bus to get back to Huang Mei? There must be a cheaper way."

I frowned. "I seriously doubt there could be anything cheaper than what we've taken, William; that bus is pretty basic."

"Trust me," he said. "It won't be pleasant, but there are much cheaper ways to travel."

汤

William managed to get us space in a dormitory at his former college for that night. It wasn't fancy, of course, but all we needed was a place to sleep and wash. It had both, and that was great. For dinner that night, we wanted to really celebrate. After all, we had gotten our certificate; by all legal definitions, we were married! Being on the filthy streets of Wuhan with a budget of one hundred yuan wasn't exactly what we had envisioned for our honeymoon, but we had each other, so we made the best of it.

William wanted to take me to a place that he said made the best soup. He said he used to get it all the time back in his college days. It wasn't so much a *place* we were looking for as it was a *guy*—the soup guy. His location changed from time to time, as most of his supplies were in a little wagon. He would find a little shanty and set up shop for a bit, until the police booted him out.

We walked around for a while and finally found him—right down the street from the government office, actually. He rounded up a couple of stools for us and turned a box upside down for our table. We sat right off the sidewalk near his little shanty, and he heated our soup over an open fire.

The soup was actually the best soup I'd ever had, and it filled me up. As we ate, we sat there looking around and looking at each other. Despite everything, despite all the stress that the last two weeks had brought, we actually had our marriage certificate in hand. William and I were married. With this realization, the soup tasted even better.

He reached across our makeshift table and took my hand. "I love you so much, Lori. You are my whole world."

"I love you too, William. I'm so happy to be your wife."

With that, I got my first kiss as a married woman.

汤

William tends to get pretty analytical, and that night, after dinner, we talked about what was most important to us. He said that we should have three principles by which to measure if we were doing the right things.

"I think it all comes down to three things," he said seriously. "First, we are together. Second, we are happy. Third, we are working on our future. If anything conflicts with these principles, it's not good. If it is in harmony with these principles, it is good, or at least is something to consider."

He said this so thoughtfully, and it made sense to me. I didn't know where he came up with this stuff, but I loved how his mind worked. I felt such gratitude that I'd met him, and that I felt like myself—the best version of myself I could imagine. Would I have found this best version of me back in Chicago? I didn't think so. I loved William with my whole heart, and I believed finding him was an answer to a prayer and hope I had never dared to verbalize, even to myself.

chapter 31

The bus home was one of the illegal ones. These buses are not registered with the local government, so they can charge the passengers less. They are only supposed to take a certain number of people; however, it is in the driver's best interest to get as many passengers as possible because, of course, the more people he gets, the more worthwhile the trip is. These buses will not depart until they are full, so they drive around recruiting others who want to go in the same direction. Usually their cost is about half that of the nicer buses, and if you can stand the waiting as the bus fills up, the filth, the cigarette smoke, the spitting, and the danger of getting caught by the police, this is the way to go.

We had gotten all our notarizations that morning and then called Mom. I said a quick "hi" and then put William on with her.

"Hi, Mom," he said. "We are going to tell you some good news. Lori and I got married yesterday."

She knew, of course, that we were working on it. They went on to talk for a few more minutes and I felt intense gratitude. I knew that if she could hear his voice, she would somehow be able to feel that he loved me and that her daughter had married the right man. I knew that happened as they talked. I talked with her after he did, and she was truly happy for me. I could also hear the sadness in her voice, though, about being away from me during the most important event in my life. I felt sad about that too. I never thought I'd be planning my wedding without my sisters. Then again, I never really thought I'd experience something so momentous without Dad there, either, and it made me realize just how much I missed him.

When we got home that night it was almost nine thirty but the family had waited, and when we arrived they held dinner for us. That is a very Chinese thing to do and is one way the Chinese show their love for one another. They hadn't snacked on anything as they waited. They'd simply waited. They would eat when the whole family was home.

This really touched me. As much as I'd loved my family growing up, we wouldn't ever have sat and waited like that when it came to eating. It almost made me laugh to think about it. Perhaps we would have waited on the formal meal, but we certainly would have eaten a peanut butter sandwich or something to "tide us over." No, discipline wasn't really a concept in our home. It was a happy home, for certain, and there were many great and fun things about my parents, but they did not set limits on us, particularly about what and when we ate. I think that is a big part of why my sisters and I struggled so much with weight, and really, why all of us struggled with limits of one kind or another.

As we ate with his family that night, William told them about our adventures in Wuhan and everyone was all smiles. They were so engaged and wanted to hear every detail of our experience. I don't think I'd ever seen them all smile that much. After we ate, we showed them the certificates and notarizations saying that we were, in fact, now legally married. His mother's next question was, "When shall we have the dinner?"

"Dinner" in this case meant *wedding* dinner.

We liked the idea but knew it was impossible. We didn't have the money for something like that anymore.

汤

That night, William's mom—now "Mama" to me—gave me a present: a beautiful diamond ring that had cost her almost two thousand yuan, an amount that would have taken her nearly a year to save. She had gone down to the jewelry store herself and picked it out. It was clear that she had used some of the money we had given her to buy it; we had given her and William's dad a few thousand yuan and had planned to give them at least that much more during our visit, but now we had only three hundred yuan.

This was so hard. It was hard for William to tell his parents we wouldn't be able to help them after all—that in fact, we would need their help to get back to Guangzhou.

William and I thought of the price of the ring, and how much that money would mean to his family. We decided to ask his mom to try to return it. The idea just about killed us. His sweet, humble mother had picked out a beautiful ring for her daughter-in-law, thinking she had the luxury to do so, and we didn't want to hurt her.

William felt so awful for his mom and for me. I told him not to worry about me and I meant it. The fact that he was now my husband made me the happiest girl in the world. Nothing could take the place of that, not even a thousand diamond rings. All of it would mean nothing without him, so if we needed to return the ring, then that was fine with me.

When he talked to his mom about it, though, she wouldn't hear of it. She was so upset. William tried to convince her but she adamantly refused to even consider it. "It's her wedding ring," she yelled, her voice quivering with sadness.

We all went to bed and decided to talk about it in the morning.

汤

I was so sick that night. I had sharp stomach pains and couldn't sleep at all. The next morning I couldn't eat breakfast, and William and his mom kept checking on me. William was an angel. I grew so much fonder of him as he lay next to me, rubbing my stomach and reading stories to me.

He looked thoughtfully at me and said, "Lori, you married a poor man from a poor family."

I smiled. "Well, yes, I suppose I did. But I love you. You are who I love. Money doesn't matter."

He came closer as I rested on the bed, and leaned in, holding my hand. "Will you be happy? I will do everything I can, every day, to make you happy."

"I know you will. I'll do the same for you."

I knew that things would sometimes be hard, but if we were together, we would be happy. So we lay there reading stories, getting teary at some of them. He was just like my dad in that way, very tender-hearted.

汤

That afternoon we decided that we would go to the jewelry store and see if they would at least exchange the ring for two cheaper ones. Mama finally agreed to this after I convinced her that I really didn't mind and that we needed the money worse. This way we could each have one and we could get a refund on the difference.

Well, the trip to the jewelry store proved to be a nightmare. Not only were the people there uncooperative, they were also crazy and rude. It turned into a screaming match between William and the man and woman who owned the shop. Mama had yelled too but was now at the point of fighting back tears. I had never seen that side of William—that anger—but I could tell what was fueling his anger. Clearly, the people were dishonest and had taken advantage of his mom. He was trying so hard to defend his mother, but these people were stone-hearted. They had seen her coming, so to speak. They'd known she had never before set foot in such a store and that she was naïve as to what a ring should actually cost. I felt my heart would break watching this scene.

William is a very tender and patient man who can remain calm and collected when most others cannot. I have seen this side of him a few times since, and it is always when someone has wronged or hurt someone in his family. He is one who truly chooses his battles and when he chooses to fight for something, he does it with all this heart.

As his argument with the shop owners grew more heated, I begged him to just leave the store. He was banging his hand on the glass, and I feared he might break it and then we'd be in worse financial trouble. I also knew that if the police became involved, they would fault William, since he was the once causing the scene. Beyond that, though, he had a foreign wife and they would assume he was rich, which meant that they would expect a bribe. All of this was going through my mind as I pleaded with him to leave. We needed to just cut our losses. Besides, I didn't mind keeping the ring and I knew that would make Mama happy too.

Finally, William agreed to leave.

We'd get the money to get home somehow.

chapter 32

$\mathcal{G}$etting a piece of paper was not quite what either of us had imagined as representing our union as husband and wife. We wanted a wedding ceremony, but time was short and money was even shorter. Although Spring Festival would have been a wonderful time to get married due all William's relatives being together, it just seemed impossible. We planned to live with the anticlimactic nature of getting our marriage certificate until we could plan a May wedding in his hometown and, eventually, a church ceremony with my family in Chicago.

Of course, my real dream would have been to have a temple wedding. In my faith, couples aspire to marry inside one of our Holy Temples, which are different than chapels. They are sacred to us, and a temple marriage symbolizes marrying your sweetheart forever, throughout eternity, not only until death. However, in order to have a temple marriage, both people must be members of the Church of Jesus Christ of Latter-Day Saints, obviously, and even then, there are many preparatory steps. That wasn't going to be possible for us. But somehow, right now, it was okay. If ever there was a day way in the future—if William decided he wanted to learn more about my faith and even adopt it as his own—that would be wonderful, and we could still have a temple ceremony (a sealing, it's called) and recommit to our marriage inside the temple.

Although this was important to me, I somehow knew things would work out for William and me. Call it faith, call it love, but I felt peace taking the steps to marry him, even though it wasn't in the temple. Our circumstances were unique, to say the least, and nothing could have ever prepared me for the reality of meeting the man I would love so deeply, in China.

At that point, William had no interest in learning anything about my religion. He respected that it was important to me, but it was foreign in every way to him. I understood this and respected his feelings. I hoped that he might change his mind at some point, but his lack of religion certainly wasn't a deal-breaker for me. Perhaps if we'd been somewhere other than China, I would have approached things differently. Maybe I would have invited him to church, or asked him to at least meet with missionaries. But here, in China, where I chose to adhere to the laws of the land, I knew religion was a sensitive area and I truly knew in my heart that things would work out. I never felt worried or concerned about William having differing beliefs than I had. It just wasn't an issue at that time, in that context.

汤

William's family knew we were broke and that this was the main reason we were putting off the wedding. One day after lunch at Shi Mu's house, his parents, aunts, and uncles gathered around us and asked if we would consider getting married during Spring Festival if they would help with the cost.

We were completely shocked! First of all, there were only two weeks left in Spring Festival. That would mean planning a wedding immediately. Second, William's family was very poor—that was a fact—and rent collectors and other bill collectors had been hounding them for days. They had so many problems of their own and yet here they were, offering us money so we could have an actual wedding.

We accepted their kind offer and they went to work devising creative ways to come up with the money. Everyone contributed, either financially or with their time. We needed to find a place to have the wedding, make and deliver invitations, plan the food, get some clothes, and, finally, decide on a ceremony. The common practice in William's hometown was to have a big, wonderful dinner in celebration of a couple getting a marriage certificate, but we wanted something more than that—we wanted a ceremony.

When we approached his aunts for advice on this, they smiled and said that they just didn't do that. There was no exchanging of rings, no walking down an aisle. That just wasn't the convention.

Convention hadn't been a part of anything in our relationship, though, so why should our wedding be any different? We sat down one night, pen and notebook in hand, and came up with a plan. We took a little Western tradition and mixed it with things we had read about marriage ceremonies in ancient China. We wanted to include his parents, our wedding rings, walking down the aisle, acknowledging God, and, of course, a kiss. We actually came up with a way to incorporate all of this. Now we had three days to get it all together.

汤

We found a hotel with a room large enough to accommodate our ceremony. The place was not fancy by Western standards— in fact, it was quite run-down—but was the best hotel in this small town. We cleaned it up ourselves, rearranged the tables and chairs to create an aisle we could walk down, and bought a few inexpensive decorations to give it a better atmosphere. William's brother bought invitations, and he and William's father hand-delivered these to all their relatives living in the mountains, the countryside, and the city. We rented some wedding clothes representative of the Qing dynasty era, and came up with some money to hire a chauffeur for the day of the wedding. Two of William's friends agreed to take the pictures. It seemed we had managed to plan everything.

On the day prior to the wedding, we visited a few of the countryside relatives to make sure they had received their invitations. One of the neighbors rushed out to give a present, which she delivered to us with a mix of tremendous pride but also bashful humility. It was a large bag and she placed it directly in front of me, and waited for me to take hold. As I did so, I jumped a bit because the bag was moving. "*Zhe shi yi ge ji*," she said proudly.

I tried to smile and not act completely freaked out. "William is my Chinese really off or did she just say this is a chicken?". "That's exactly what she said," he laughed and then we both did the only thing we could do. We thanked her and took our chicken home. Right as we were leaving, though, another woman from the village, who had been panicked that she had nothing to give, ran back home to get eggs from her own chickens, which she delivered to us as well. So, there we were in village number 2, receiving our first wedding gifts. A few eggs and a live chicken.

When the wedding day had arrived, breakfast that morning seemed quieter—everyone was silent, very unusual for this household. We were all thinking, hoping we'd remembered everything, going over our individual parts. William's brother needed to arrange for fireworks and take care of the music. His mom was incredibly nervous about handing me the ring during the ceremony. His dad had practiced his welcome speech for hours the night before, and I was trying to remember the words I had to say in Chinese. I was so in awe of William's family. What must they be thinking right now? Their son brings home this foreign woman and two weeks later, there's a wedding?

汤

As we waited outside the room where we would have the ceremony, the guests filed in. The guests ranged from local security bureau officials to peasants and farmers from the countryside. Also present were William's former classmates. We were both so nervous, but as I heard my father-in-law begin his welcome speech, I was relieved. We were really doing this.

The aisle we walked down was actually a big red piece of paper, and I held on to my husband's arm for dear life as we passed down it, since I could see nothing through my red veil.

We made it to the front, where we bowed to heaven, his parents, and each other, and sealed it all with a kiss. We had done it.

Never in my life did I imagine that I would get married in a small town in China. Nor could I have imagined a family, other than my own, that would go to such lengths for my happiness. A family that would gather money from wherever they could so that I could have a wedding ceremony, a luxury unheard of in their experience. My in-laws took the money that would have paid bills and used it so that I could wear a dress from the Qing dynasty and little red boots to match. The money Mama had been saving she gave me with her whole heart so that I could get my hair done, buy some earrings, and feel beautiful on my wedding day.

I thought of Mom, and how I should be with her on this day, like I'd always imagined I would be. Who gets married without their mom? Of course, my heart hurt to think of Dad, as I had always pictured that he would walk me down the aisle and that we could take a picture together, him in his suit, looking handsome and happy. He would have loved William. I thought of Chrissy and her laugh and her sarcastic but always hilarious comments. I missed her, and I missed Barb. Two sisters, so different from each other and from me, and yet we'd always stayed connected and close. And my niece Shaleen—she would have been excited to be a part of my wedding. Our family had always been close. My parents had taught us to love one another. They'd known how to have fun, to make light of challenging situations. I thought how strange it was, really, that I'd just gotten married without my family there. I wasn't sad, exactly, but I missed them, and I wished that these two worlds could somehow mesh, even if just for a day.

Our wedding was a significant event in Huang Mei, and was even mentioned on the local television news program. Many people had never seen a foreigner and it was unheard of to them that a Chinese man and an American woman could fall in love and get married in the man's hometown. As I looked around at the guests at my wedding and thought of all the events leading up to today—coming to China alone, meeting William, coming by train back to his small hometown—I was quite amazed myself.

chapter 33

Because we had planned our wedding so quickly, it never occurred to either of us to plan the wedding night. We had both made certain assumptions about how we would spend the remainder of the day after the guests had all gone home. After the wedding, we went back to William's parents' house, where I was surprised to find that most of the wedding guests were there to continue the well-wishing and photo taking. Although this had indeed been the happiest day of my life, I was exhausted. The preparation had been so intense, so incredibly stressful, and now all of that was hitting me. As much as I appreciated the continued love and attention of William's family and friends, I really wanted all of them to leave. I wasn't even thinking of a romantic wedding night. In truth, I was thinking of peace, quiet, a nice talk with William, and an early sleep.

The majority of those guests who had lingered left about an hour later. All the uncles, aunts, cousins, friends, and neighbors went home. I looked around and wondered when this other group—about five of William's classmates—were going to leave.

Then William excitedly ran up to me and asked if I wanted to go to a beautiful temple. His classmates had arranged for a van to take us, and he thought it would be wonderful to go there on our wedding day. Part of me wanted to cry from exhaustion but

I reminded myself of the sweetness of the bitter soup. William hadn't seen these classmates in so long, and they had come quite a ways to be at our wedding. Taking us to this temple was their gift to us.

I put on a smile and off we went.

汤

William's friends were incredibly nice, polite, conversant, and respectful. The temple was indeed beautiful, and so very peaceful. I was glad that we went. I knew I would be more glad, though, when they dropped us off at home and we could finally take off our Qing dynasty clothes, get comfy, and relax.

Again, it was not to happen. When we got home, I expected to say good-bye to everyone, but instead they accompanied us upstairs to the apartment. When we walked in, William's mom invited them to stay for dinner.

Well, fine, that was the polite thing to do. Chinese people won't dare send anyone away without first feeding them. *We'll have a nice dinner*, I thought, *and then they'll go.*

During dinner, however, one of the friends made a statement that almost brought tears to my eyes. He began talking about a tradition they have in their small town. When a good friend gets married, his friends are to honor him and his new bride by planning a party and playing fun games late into the night. "So, tonight, Lori, we will do this for you!" he said with genuine happiness and excitement.

I forced a smile and a "xie xie" upon receiving the news.

William looked at me and for the first time that day, I gave him a look to say, "This is not exactly what I had in mind." His eyes had worry in them, for he wanted nothing more than my happiness, I knew. He had been so happy all day. From his perspective, this was completely normal and was exactly what he had assumed would happen on our wedding night.

Unfortunately, he'd never mentioned anything about this to me. Of all the things we had talked about, we had never discussed how we would spend this night.

汤

After dinner that night, we moved into the living room and a few more guests came—the girlfriends and wives of William's friends. One of them brought a microphone and began to act as a master of ceremonies. The first game, he said, was to tell our love story.

Now, don't get me wrong, I love telling our story and I love hearing William tell it even more. On this particular night, though, under what I felt were forced and unnatural circumstances, the anger was rising in my chest and I thought I might explode.

I didn't want to be mad at William, but this was my wedding day and I was so incredibly sad. I wanted this guy to shut up and I wanted all of them to get out. I tried to smile and talk, but every time I tried to talk, I thought I might cry. William noticed I wasn't happy and was trying to do all the talking and keep things light. At one point, he took me aside and asked me what was wrong. But his friends were waiting in the other room and I didn't want to get into it then, so I simply told him that I was tired and I hoped this party would end soon so we could rest.

"Okay, my sweetheart, let's try to move it along quickly. They are doing this to make us happy, so let's try to go along," he said, earnestly.

"I am trying, William."

"I know, sweetie." He frowned. "You're not happy right now, are you?"

Because I didn't want to hurt him I responded with, "Of course I'm happy, I'm just very tired."

William told our love story and then it was singing time.

This is a very typical custom at Chinese parties. People recite poems, sing a song, or engage in some kind of performance in order to entertain each other. First, William sang a beautiful song—one he had sung months before at a small party we had both attended. He sang beautifully, and then he tried to save me from having to sing by moving on to another game.

I didn't want to be a poor sport. I knew it was expected that I sing too, so I did. I have a terrible singing voice but I belted out my version of "From this Moment" by Shania Twain. I could not have felt more awkward.

After the singing, the night went from bad to worse. Stupid games, some of them humiliating, were next on the agenda. William was feeling uncomfortable too, as clearly his level of maturity had far surpassed that of his friends. The games weren't bad, they were just silly, and I guess for the most part, William and I are not silly people.

One game involved me hiding a coin somewhere on my body and him having to find it. He didn't want to play this game any more than I did. If you were a silly person, an exhibitionist, you would hide the coin in a provocative place and enjoy the cheers of the audience as your new husband searched for it, of course. This was not our style. William nodded toward my foot, and so went I went in the other room, and that's where I hid the coin—in my shoe. This was much to the disappointment of the crowd, but we really didn't care.

There were a few more games before William turned the attention to another new couple and I excused myself to prepare for bed. His friends decided this was their cue to exit. We thanked them for the party and then I went to bed, telling William I wanted to be alone.

When he finally came in, I wasn't ready to talk. I didn't know what to say, so I pretended to be asleep. My heart hurt all night.

汤

When I woke up, William was right there, staring at me. I began to cry. Then he began to cry.

"I hated last night," I said. "I had such different expectations for our wedding night."

At first, he thought it was only about the games. He said that he felt bad too, that he didn't know they'd planned such immature things. When I explained that it was more than that, he honestly didn't get it. He found it extremely hard to believe that I'd actually expected his friends to come for the wedding and then leave directly afterwards. I told him that in America, that was normal. After people get married, they have a reception, and then the newlyweds are off on the honeymoon.

He thought this sounded like a rather selfish custom. "But my friends worked so hard to get here. They had to take a train and a bus and it took them over twelve hours. I could not just tell them to go right away, especially since they had planned a party for us."

Looking at things from his point of view, I could understand what he meant, but my tears flowed anyway. His tears flowed more freely, too, as we both realized it was a true misunderstanding.

"I'm not a good husband," William said. "I can't even make my wife happy on her wedding day. I'm so stupid."

My heart broke at these words, at the sound of his sobs, and as I felt his tears against my cheeks. I just wanted to hold him in my arms and console him forever. It seemed he wanted to do the same for me. As I heard him talk, I realized that he really had tried so hard and it hadn't occurred to him that I could have been hurt by what he thought was normal. As he lay beside me in bed with his fuzzy pajamas, tousled hair, teary eyes, and tender hands, I began to feel very selfish and ashamed. At the same time, I was so grateful that he could see my side, and that he had told me what I needed to hear. That I was the most important person to him and that my happiness meant more than friends, culture, or any other expectations.

We had both brought completely different ideas to this marriage, and we would need to be so careful about communication in the future. We must never take anything for granted. We talked for a long time that morning, and he reassured me that no matter what the cultural expectations were, I was his wife and I came first. He would never purposely do anything to make me feel uncomfortable. He apologized completely and I did too, for not telling him what I'd needed the previous night. He made me promise that if I ever felt uncomfortable again, I would tell him so that he could fix the situation.

汤

That day, we ate a late breakfast and lounged around the house. The sun was shining and I hardly felt cold. My mother-in-law fixed my favorite foods and William and I wrote in our journals about the events of the last few weeks. I'd been an avid journal writer since childhood, and I'd given William a journal after coming home from Christmas break. He'd loved the idea of writing his experiences, and it was something we had started to do together every once in a while.

Neither of us could believe that it had only been three weeks since we'd left Guangzhou. All the trips back and forth to Wuhan, my one-day trip to Guangzhou and back, all the tribulations in getting those blasted red stamps, learning of William's illness, and becoming his wife—all of this happened in about twenty days. The next morning, we would be off to Guangzhou. I was looking forward to getting home and setting up our life together as husband and wife. I had very high hopes for the year 2002. It had begun with an adventure, and I couldn't wait to see what happened next.

chapter 34

The train ride home would take about twenty hours, and I knew I would have plenty to think about along the way. I was happy and exhausted at the same time. It had been such an intense few weeks. I was now a married woman. We were going back to our bubble existence at Clifford School, in Clifford Estates, and I wasn't sure how to feel about that. Overall, I was just happy to be by William's side.

As we found our seats on the train and got settled in, I started to let my mind wander through all the events of Spring Festival.

I remembered the night that William went out to meet friends and I opted to stay home. He had asked me to come, but I was so tired and really wanted to relax and write in my journal. His mom got such a kick out of me always carrying my little journal and pen around the house and almost everywhere else. I don't think any of his family knew what to think of me. I'm sure they wondered what on earth I was writing—and, more to the point, why I was doing it. It was such a novel concept to them, especially to Mama, since she had never even had the chance of learning how to write her own name.

That night, it was only she and I in the house. Well, my niece was there too, but she was sound asleep. Jung-A and Ting Fen had gone out to work, and Baba was at the store. Mama sat working on her knitting. I found it so complicated even to watch. I couldn't keep track of the yarn and which direction it was going in among her three needles. She worked so quickly and precisely, as if she had been doing this her whole life—which, in fact, she probably had.

I purposely stayed in the living room with Mama that evening so it felt as if we were spending time together, even though we weren't really talking. I hadn't made much effort to converse with her since we'd been there. She was most comfortable using the local dialect she'd used her whole life, and I had not yet learned any of that language. For some reason, though, that night I decided to try to use my limited Mandarin to talk with her.

She had gone to the kitchen and peeled an apple for me, which she presented with both hands. I thanked her, put down my journal, and began to eat. She went back to her knitting. I began to talk.

"I'm writing about my father."

She looked up and stopped knitting. "*Shen me?*" She smiled.

I repeated my sentence and gestured toward my journal, which was now sitting on the stool beside me. "*Wo de baba . . . wo zai xie ta . . .*"

She understood my words, but she didn't understand what I could be writing about him. First she just said "oh" and did not resume her knitting but kept looking at me.

I told her that my father had died a few months earlier; I knew she knew that—William had told her—but I said it anyway. I told her that I was writing as much as I could about his life because I didn't want to forget all the stories and all the things that he had taught me. She let out a little laugh, but not as if to make fun of my idea. She just didn't know how to take it—me, writing stories about my father.

I took the chance to ask her something about her own life. She laughed when I asked her. I guess that was even more incomprehensible to her, that I would be interested in her life, in her stories. She had the sweetest dancing eyes when she smiled, but those eyes looked terribly tired, disappointed, and overwhelmed when she was not smiling.

People have asked me if I was nervous about meeting William's mom. The truth is that I really wasn't, and I attribute that to William's attitude. He had made it clear before this trip, both to me and to them, that he loved me, and I guess that was all his parents needed to know. I think his mother loved me before she ever met me. This is the way it should be, I guess. I often hear these stories of someone's parents not approving of the person their child has chosen to love, but William and I were very blessed in a couple of ways. One, we had a strong love; even though it was new then, we knew how we felt and that we would pursue a life together no matter what. Second, we had families who trusted us and showed their support by simply deciding that they would love whomever we had chosen to love.

Mama's childhood had been hard, but was not that unusual for the times she grew up in. Her family were peasants and they all worked hard, with nothing ever coming easily. At one point, she had the chance to attend elementary school for a short time, but eventually she had to quit in order to help her family. The unusual thing was that her sisters didn't have to quit; they got to continue their education. Of course, none of them had the opportunity to go to college or even finish high school, but the basic education they did receive was enough to make a difference in their lives. Mama, in contrast, had simply been working her whole life. She had never looked past the next meal and the next chores in front of her. This made me unbearably sad. I watched her go about her life and I wondered if she ever thought about it, about why things turn out the way they do.

My thoughts drifted to those of my own mother. These two women had had such different lives, but in many ways their experience had been similar. My mother had not had anything come easily either, and I knew that in many ways, her life had been a series of disappointments.

I remember her not having enough money to go to the doctor when she was having health problems, and her being in tremendous pain as she got ready for work and headed out the door before the rest of us had gotten up. She was afraid she'd lose her job if she let her employer know how exhausted and sick she really was. So when most people in her condition were resting and going to doctor's appointments, Mom was working full time, taking care of three energetic kids, and cleaning house. She'd come home in the evenings to see what mess Dad had gotten himself into on that particular day and then she'd begin her work in her own home. It went on like this for years. This was her life.

I had a feeling that if I ever got William's mother and my mom in a room together, they would recognize each other as kindred souls.

chapter 35

The train ride back to Guangzhou was bumpy, to say the least, but I was still able to sleep. I kept waking up to the sound of someone hacking and spitting, but I was able to fall right asleep again. I was obviously tired from all that had happened.

I had been dreaming about part of my childhood. It was that era in which I felt more carefree than I had ever felt in my life. We lived out in the country, on about three acres, in Wisconsin. We had chickens and a garden, but we weren't exactly farmers. Dad worked in town as a janitor, and these were the days when Mom worked at Head Start. She had started volunteering when my sister was enrolled and two years later, they'd given her a job.

During winter months, there were serious snowstorms, and there were days when nobody went to work or school. Those were simply the best days.

We had a wood-burning stove in the living room, on the top of which my mom's bread would sit, waiting to rise. It was the most wonderful feeling in the world to be inside that warm house while looking out at the deep snow. Chrissy and I would play together with toys I could never have let my girlfriends at school know I still played with, things like Barbie dolls and Cabbage Patch Kids. Junior high seemed far away. I was safe in my home with my family. My mom spent her time baking or playing with us. Dad chopped wood for the fire and passed it through the window to us so we could put it in the woodbox. Sometimes we'd go outside, completely bundled up, and play in the snow. Dad would come with us and Mom would watch from the kitchen window.

When I heard the terrible sound of spitting, it mixed in with my dream for just a moment, but then I remembered where I was.

Since those days, I have begged William to never make me take the hard seat trains again, especially during national holidays. It is another world—a world in which people are literally piled on top of each other, in the aisles and on the backs of seats. The railways are the cheapest way to travel in China, and during Chinese New Year especially, everyone goes home. This means that all the peasants, workers, and people just trying to save money (as we were) are all stuffed into the train car together. At least we were lucky enough to have seats; many people, who had paid as much for their tickets as we had, did not. They stood up and leaned on each other the whole time.

With that many people in the car, the body odor was atrocious, and when it was mixed with the stale smell of cigarettes—well, I felt sick the whole time. The bathroom on these long trips absolutely defied description. I tried so hard not to drink or eat anything so that I wouldn't have to use it at all, but this was hard to do, and eventually I always had to use it.

William was great at keeping me involved in conversation to pass the time, though. We still laugh about some of the funny things we witnessed on that train. One guy across from us, in particular, kept bumping his head. He was trying so desperately to sleep and wanted a comfortable position for his head. We watched him bunch up his coat and place it behind his head, but when he laid his head down he missed the coat and bumped his head right on the window ledge. We both winced, knowing that it must have hurt. The odd thing was, he did it again, and then again. By the third time he did this, we could not control our laughter, though we tried to hold it in.

We stood out so much on this train ride. People around us didn't know what to think about this foreign woman with the Chinese guy. Like the people in William's hometown, many of the people on the train likely had never even seen a foreigner before.

Other than laughing and people watching, we talked about our goals for the future during that train ride. They weren't so clearly defined then, and we didn't look very far ahead. Mostly, we looked at the upcoming year. William wanted to get a job in a business situation rather than continuing to teach, but we weren't sure when he would be able to make that change. We talked about whether or not I should continue to do administration the following year.

When we returned to school, we would be starting a new semester. Our talk turned to how people would react to our having gotten married. We also talked about facing the doctor when we got back to Guangzhou.

chapter 36

We arrived in Guangzhou on Thursday and went to the doctor on Friday morning. I wrote the events of that day in my journal.

Right now we are sitting at the tuberculosis hospital. We're waiting for the results of William's X-ray to confirm whether or not he has this disease. Then, we'll figure out what to do about it. So many people in this country have this disease. What is it? Where does it come from? Why haven't I heard about it in America? I am so grateful to be from America and so sad and angry that William may have this condition. It is shocking and overwhelming and it scares me so much. I hope it won't hurt him and I pray we can treat it. I hope it won't stop him from pursuing his dreams, and our dreams. He truly is pure, and good, and kind. There is nobody like him on this earth. His heart is pure. He wants good and noble things in life: a strong marriage, a happy family, a good job, and a safe home. I am tremendously blessed to even know him, let alone be his wife. He has changed everything and I never, ever want to be without him. Please, God, take good care of him. He is my life.

汤

For the next several months William went through torment. He was on nine different medications that, while killing the active tuberculosis, were also wreaking havoc on his general health. He had no appetite and lost a considerable amount of weight. He was almost too weak to hold his head up sometimes. He was sick to his stomach and often vomited or suffered from severe diarrhea. It was all he could do to get through a day of work, and as soon as he got home, he went to sleep. He went to the doctor almost every week, worrying about these side effects, especially the seemingly constant high fever. On some of these days, I would go with him. I couldn't bear to leave him alone and wanted to comfort him, but I knew that when I accompanied him to the doctor, I caused him more stress and pain than comfort.

I hated the hospital and in particular the little exam room where William had to do his checkups. The first time I entered, I was struck by the dull, low-hanging light bulb, which cast a dark shadow over what should have been a bright, sterilized exam room. The walls were not painted—or, if they were, the shade was concrete grey. The sheet on the exam table was stained, and its shade of yellow matched the doctor's coat. I could smell anti-septic, a half-hearted attempt at cleanliness, but that smell was mixed with the sharp scents of mildew, urine, and other unex-plained sources. My shoes stuck to the floor as we entered, and the window was covered with something blurry so you couldn't see clearly outside. I could hear loud voices and Cantonese words and phrases coming from the waiting room. The volume seemed so inappropriate and disorderly for a hospital. What was it about the language that made me feel that everyone speaking it was angry? The eight tones of Cantonese all sounded doubtful, scared, and mad, which is kind of how I felt.

That exam room angered me, just the sight of it. I hated the workers. I hated their dingy medical robes. I hated all those patients whom I feared would make my husband worse. I hated the system. I think I may have even hated China. I cringe as I write that, but it's true. At the time, I couldn't separate everything I loved about China from this disease and the low standard of health care my husband was receiving. I was certain all the doctors were incapable and nothing could be accomplished in this filthy, backward, horrible place.

Unfortunately, I didn't keep these thoughts to myself. Oh no, as poor William was practically hobbling along from one nurse or doctor to another, I was complaining and mumbling under my breath about how we were stuck in this God-forsaken place and how I wanted nothing but to get him to America, where he could get proper treatment.

Of course, we couldn't go to America to get better treatment, because having active TB disqualified William for immigration. We had no choice but to seek treatment right there in Guangzhou.

I did all the research I could and finally found an SOS clinic for expatriates. I thought surely they would be able to help him. All this time, though, William kept telling me that he had faith in his doctor and that just because the conditions were poor didn't mean he couldn't get better right here in China, right at this hospital. I begged him to at least talk to a doctor at the expatriate clinic, just to see if what the Chinese doctors were doing was right.

This was one of the first times that we strongly disagreed with each other. Both of us were sure our position was right and that the other person was well intentioned but simply wrong. It would cost us three hundred American dollars just to have the visit, and William couldn't see the point in that. The thought of wasting all that money when he already had a doctor seemed absurd. On the other hand, I would have given my right arm, let alone three hundred dollars, to go to a clean, "normal" medical building where I had faith in the medical staff. To me, it seemed absurd not to give it a try.

We went back and forth for the next few months, arguing about it and I didn't give up on trying to convince him. Still, he refused.

chapter 37

William had transferred to the secondary school in February, after we had returned from Spring Festival. We were both fine with the change, as it would be more challenging for him. However, there was this assumption from a small minority of people that it was not only good to move William for his own sake but because it would have been a conflict of interest for him to stay and continue working with me.

The thought made me want to laugh. The mere idea that I would somehow show favoritism to William was ridiculous. I directed the language program in which he was a teaching assistant. He worked directly with the teachers, not with me. How on earth this could possibly be a conflict of interest? Did they think we might revert to an eighth-grade mentality and sneak in a make-out session between classes? Would I blow kisses to him during staff meetings? Would I allow him an easier job, saying, "Oh, sweetie, you can just sit in the office and do no work today" or some idiotic thing like that?

We had learned early on, though, to pick our battles, and that even well-intentioned people could sometimes do hurtful or dumb things. There were plenty of thoughtless comments, and even discriminatory actions, following our return home.

At first, coming back after Spring Festival was a honeymoon—

literally—except that we were back at work. Other than dealing with William's illness, we were happy. Every day was just fun. We were together. We made the biggest deal of doing even the most trivial things, and we established a routine very quickly and naturally. We left the house just after seven each day to walk to school—past the market where the farmers were bringing in the vegetables to sell, past the park where the older people were practicing their tai chi, and eventually to the school gate. We always walked hand in hand, never in a hurry, always with something to talk about.

The guards made a habit of smiling and saying, *"Zao shang hao,"* and we always replied in turn. We would pass the cafeteria and then William would head to his classroom and I would make my way to my office.

I was also learning every day just how kind, considerate, and loving my new husband was. One day, we were at a sports meet at school, watching the kids run their races and do the high jump. The weather was particularly sunny and hot that day, and I had been holding a paper at my brow so as to keep the sun off my face and see the kids more clearly. Suddenly, I realized that William had switched positions. He had been standing on my right side, facing the same direction as I was, and now he had turned his body so that it was angled to the left. It was a bit awkward, because now he had to turn his head to the side to watch what was going on. I wasn't sure what he was doing—and then I realized: The sun wasn't hitting me anymore. It was hitting him instead. And he had not made a show of it or said, "Oh, let me block the sun for you." He had done it purely for my comfort, not in order to have me notice and be impressed with his chivalry.

Well, he failed. I continue to marvel at his chivalry and never cease to be impressed by his genuine kindness and humility. He worried about me being warm enough and having enough to eat. He always asked about my sleep, whether I was getting enough.

He genuinely listened as I explained the differences among the myriad of little bottles that sat on our bathroom shelf, showing me his patience and interest. He knew I needed to have my pressed powder and ChapStick available if we were going anywhere. He didn't know why, but he knew it was important to me, so he was always careful to remind me with, "Sweetheart, do you have your ChapStick? Do you have that other thing?"

He did this not because he particularly cared whether or not I used it. He noticed no magical difference in my face after I'd applied pressed powder. He just knew I felt better having those things, and that made him happy.

One day we were walking along in Siqao, a little city near our home, and I was shocked to see a bottle of Clinique moisturizer in the display window.

"Oh my gosh!" I exclaimed. "They actually sell Clinique here. I thought they only had it in Hong Kong."

"They sell what?" he asked, wanting to share my excitement but not knowing what it was for yet.

"It's a really good brand of makeup and facial cleansers."

He gently led me into the store, saying, "Oh, let's take a look."

We looked at this bottle and that and of course he couldn't believe the prices, but he remained calm as I told him a bottle of moisturizer was 250 yuan (about thirty dollars).

He is very concerned about the quality of things, so he examined the bottles and the store itself very carefully. I hadn't planned on buying anything—which is a good thing, because the quality didn't seem quite up to par. I couldn't help but notice that the boxes looked very tattered and the print on the bottles was a bit irregular. These were just throwaway versions of the real product. However, the prices were significantly cheaper than what I usually paid in Hong Kong.

As we walked away he said, "But sweetheart, I'm not so sure about the quality. Maybe those aren't really from America."

I had, of course, thought the same thing.

"If those are important things," he said, "you should have better quality. You can't buy those bad ones because it could hurt your skin. You can buy it in Hong Kong, not Siqao."

I knew that he meant this sincerely and I also know that he appreciated the value of money. He wasn't cheap, just careful. I was just beginning to understand this. He wasn't opposed to us spending money—he was opposed to us *wasting* money.

汤

I soon learned that William would study his receipt and change after buying ten yuan worth of anything, yet he would also encourage me to buy the best. When I asked him about this, I learned even more about him.

"Why is it that sometimes you are so careful about money, trying to get a bargain whenever you can, and yet you encourage me to go to Hong Kong to buy moisturizer or to get my hair done?" I asked him one day.

"Sweetie, some things don't matter as much as others. I do think we need to save money and be careful with our spending. We don't have to buy the most expensive broom or light bulbs or milk or bread—most of these are just as good as others. If we do this, then when you need to buy your . . . what is that stuff again?"

"Moisturizer."

"Yeah, that mois . . . tur . . ." He furrowed his brow.

"Moisturizer," I said with a smile.

"Moisturizer," he said, smiling back. "We will have money for that, or your hair, or to buy pizza . . . we will have that money because we saved it at other times."

"Really? It doesn't seem weird to you that we're careful about how much we pay for noodles, yet we pay a thousand kuai to get my hair done?"

"Not weird," he said smiling because of his extra enunciation to the "r," which he usually had trouble pronouncing. "Not weird, just . . . okay.'"

"You are my sweetheart," I said, hugging him. "How did I get so lucky?"

"I am lucky," he said. "God did that."

I hadn't heard William talk a lot about God, and I felt comforted to hear him begin to make such references. I never expected he would believe exactly what I believed, but I hoped we would always be able to talk about matters of faith and spirituality. If I were being really truthful with myself, yes, I hoped he would see the beauty in my faith enough to want to share it with me, but it wasn't an expectation. I was just happy to hear him acknowledge God's existence. I was beginning to acknowledge God more, as well, and to recognize that my reasons for coming to China were about faith, personal growth, and William.

汤

One Monday morning, Kassie stopped me on my way to my office.

"I need to talk to you," she said.

Wow, her face looked serious. I wondered what was wrong. "Sure," I said, opening the door to my office. "Come on in."

She was breathing quickly and speaking even more quickly. "Look, I'll just come out with it. Mr. Yuen asked me to ask you and William not to hold hands on school grounds."

My heart sank. My gut tightened. I felt sick. "What?"

"I know, I know. It's not fair, but this is what he said. He doesn't want there to be too much talk about this."

What on earth is happening? I wondered. I knew Mr. Yuan. He'd been nothing but kind to me. He'd even come to our wedding reception and given me a dozen roses. I pointed out the hypocrisy to Kassie, and noted as well that married couples who were both Westerners held hands. "Yes," I said, "we wouldn't want the children to get the wrong idea and think that love between cultures was a good thing."

I knew my tone was anything but humble, but this was ridiculous. Were the other Western couples given the same reproach? I wanted to know.

Kassie didn't answer that question. She did say she agreed it wasn't fair, but she emphasized that this was Mr. Yuen's request.

Where was this insulting, random instruction coming from? I asked Kassie that very question.

"I honestly don't know," she admitted. "I'm just the messenger."

"Well, you can tell Mr. Yuenthat I reject his request," I said hotly. "If he feels this way, he can come and say it to my face, and he'd better have an explanation as to why I'm not allowed to hold my husband's hand at school."

He never said a thing, of course.

This was hard on William, because he wasn't used to going against authority, especially at work. He hadn't had the option before. Now, as for Mr. Yuen—I do believe he was a nice man overall, but perhaps he was used to flexing his power. Now people knew they could not mess with Qian Zhi Ming in the ways they had before, or they would be facing us both.

Again, not so humble, but I did sort of enjoy standing up for both of us in this way.

chapter 38

In May we had a week off, during which time William and I were planning to go back to Huang Mei. I was excited about it because this time we wouldn't be running all over trying to get documents or plan a wedding—we would simply get to visit.

Well, there was *one* more thing we needed to do in order to get William's passport, but we didn't anticipate that being a big problem. I planned to take my journal and a good book and just relax with William's family.

The trouble started with the day we were supposed to leave. William had been incredibly sick, and on this particular day he had left his afternoon classes and was sleeping on the floor of my office. He had been throwing up and was running a fever—all of which, according to his doctor, were normal side effects of the medication he was on. This didn't make it any easier to watch him, though.

It was Tuesday afternoon, and I was in a curriculum meeting with the Kassie and Shelly. As I tried to participate in the conversation about English proficiency exams for the students and other administrative details, I just lost it. I was trying so hard to hold it in but as I sat there, I could no longer contain my emotion. I had never been so scared and worried in my entire life. I had mostly been keeping William's health issue quiet because I didn't want people to begin asking questions about his condition. I didn't want to give too much information for fear of how people would react when they heard the word "tuberculosis." It was private, after all. It was our business.

As I sat there sobbing, though, it became their business.

Shelly put her arms around me and held me like the baby I felt I was at that moment. It felt good to cry about it, but when the questions came I wasn't ready. I just said that William preferred to keep it private and not to worry, it was nothing contagious. That was true, although at some point in the past he actually would have been contagious (not that we knew that at the time). Neither of them pushed. They just sat and cried with me. I was really grateful for them at that moment—especially Shelly, with whom I'd never before felt particularly close. She really came through when I literally needed a shoulder to cry on.

I finally left them sitting in Kassie's office and went up to the ELC to check on William. We were scheduled to leave that day, and by this point I was questioning whether we should even go.

He was feeling a little stronger and said he still wanted to go, that a week of rest and relaxation at home would do him good. I didn't feel right about it, but I couldn't necessarily sort out why, so I went along with it. Maybe I hoped that if I didn't question him, his words about feeling stronger would actually come true.

On the bus ride to the train station, I asked him if he would consider getting a special blessing from someone from my church. I had faith and hope that a blessing would help him, even if only just a little—but he kindly said no, he didn't think that would help.

Of course, I understood why he thought that. There was certainly nothing logical about participating in a special prayer, or having someone lay their hands on your head and give you a blessing. It was a foreign concept to him, I knew, and even to many other Westerners. And I knew it seemed illogical to him.

But I also knew that it couldn't hurt and would likely help. I also knew by now, however, that William had a very stubborn streak, and if he said no he meant no. He didn't see the need for it, so I let it go.

I prayed my heart out throughout the entire journey. William slept almost the entire twelve hours and ate nothing except a few bites of bread, and that was with me almost forcing it down him. Without my pushing, he'd have eaten nothing.

汤

The days we spent in Huang Mei were relaxing in some ways, stressful in others. We thought we had completed all the necessary steps to get William's passport, but of course we'd forgotten to expect the unexpected. When we originally visited the security bureau to get the information, we were not exactly given the friendliest of greetings. The officer wanted to know what William wanted a passport for and where did he intend to go and why?

As the words "She has no right to ask you that" were coming out of my mouth, I realized that I was once again operating under an American mindset. In fact, in China a person does not have the inherent right to have a passport. They need to demonstrate where and why they want to travel. And there were, of course, a series of steps and paperwork to be completed. On the final step, we needed to pay a little extra money to get the officers moving. I didn't mind, though, because William absolutely had to have his passport. That was the first step toward us traveling to the States and even eventually immigrating, if we decided on that.

The first couple of days home William's health wasn't too bad but later in the week, his whole demeanor took a different turn. His already thin face became gaunt, his skin looked translucent, and he couldn't eat. I thought I was watching the end of his life. He hadn't had the energy to move all day and he had missed more than three meals—very unusual. In a Chinese household, particularly his mother's, this was a major scare.

I was scared. I wanted so badly to help but for the first time in my life, I didn't have a plan. I had no idea how to help. It scared me that I couldn't. I was used to being resourceful, figuring things out, but this was beyond me. My head hurt and my heart hurt. His mom and I talked about what we could make for him. I helped her make a tomato and egg soup, one that he usually liked.

"Minga," as she called him. "Minga, *he yi dian tang.*" She asked him to drink the broth and brought it to his mouth. His eyes didn't even open all the way and for a second I thought he didn't recognize her.

She started to cry. "He yi dian," she said, her voice quivering and forceful at the same time. He simply couldn't do it. He closed his eyes. She looked at me. I had no answers, no ideas. We spent the next hours just checking on him, putting cool cloths on his head, and sitting by him.

He lay down on the bed and I sat on the chair right next to him. I stared at him, praying he would keep breathing. I watched his chest rise and fall. He was burning up, and every once in awhile he would sit up in a panic and vomit. His mom would get the bin and we would clean him, and within seconds, he would sleep again. Even though he was right in front of me, his weakness made me miss him. It felt like he wasn't even there. He could hardly even talk. My first instinct was to take him to a doctor, but there really wasn't a doctor in this small town. Perhaps we could see one in Wuhan, but it was too late at night for any buses to go. I just started sobbing, again, to which his mother didn't know how to react. I think the fact that I was crying added to her hurt. She started crying too, and sat next to him on the bed, holding his hand, holding mine. She was crying for her son, and for me because she knew. She knew that I loved him with all of me. At that moment, all I could think was that I was going to lose William—in this tiny town, in the middle of nowhere, where nobody could help us.

Without thinking too much about it, I grabbed my mobile phone and called Kassie. I couldn't even get the words out. I just cried into the phone. She kept asking what was wrong. Finally, she asked the right question: "Is it William? Is he sick?"

I cried harder and she knew the answer. When I calmed down a little, I asked her to call the people from church and ask them to please pray for William, and maybe even to fast for him. In our faith, it is not uncommon for the members of a congregation to join together in a special fast when someone's health is at stake.

Although William was weak and sick, I lay next to him on the bed and told him that Kassie and my friends from church would be fasting for him.

"I know you might not think this will help, but I believe that when people unite in prayer and put special purpose behind not eating, sacrificing their comfort for a chance to draw closer to God, things can happen," I told him. "Even miracles."

"Okay, that's nice," he said. He was drifting in and out of sleep. He was sweating a lot, yet he felt cold and clammy when I touched his face. His mother and I just stared at him, not knowing how to help.

At some point during all this, William's mom had left for a short while. When I'd asked her where she'd one, she quietly said she'd gone to pray. Through my basic Huang Mei hua, I came to understand that she had indeed gone to a local temple to pray. It occurred to me that his mother and his wife were both praying simultaneously, pouring our hearts out on his behalf, in whatever way we knew. When she told me this, our eyes locked. And we both understood.

After hanging up with Kassie, I was still worried sick and

counting the hours until the next morning when we could get the earliest bus out of there and go home to Guangzhou. He was less feverish the next morning, still incredibly weak, but I knew somehow that William would be okay. We got him to the bus station, and as soon as we found our seats, he laid his head in my lap and slept. Again. I prayed the whole way home. I tried to think of good things, of a future with him. I didn't want to think any more about losing him.

汤

When we got back to Guangzhou, I called the SOS clinic and made an appointment. William had finally consented to go, more to appease me than because he really thought it necessary. Regardless of the reasons, I was just grateful that he agreed to go.

When we arrived at the office, William asked me to inquire whether or not we could simply talk to a doctor for five minutes without paying and having a formal visit. Luckily, there was a doctor free and she invited us to step into her office. I felt peace and incredible comfort just sitting in her beautiful, spotless office. I took note of everything—the clean, bright walls, the nice waiting room furniture, the neatly pressed nurse's uniforms, the pleasant doctor who spoke English. I was convinced that this place and the doctors in it would make William better.

Dr. Liu was a Chinese-Australian physician who was probably risking her job by consulting with us like this. We'd sort of politely pushed our way past the front desk so we could see the doctor face to face. We were supposed to register, wait for our turn, and pay, but I assured her I just needed five minutes and begged her to make an exception. She nodded hurriedly and showed us into her office, closing the door behind her.

We showed Dr. Liu the medications William was on and explained the situation. To my shock, she said that the hospital where he was already getting treatment was the best in China and that if he were to come to her, she would be prescribing the same things. She even looked at his X-ray for us and, sadly, confirmed that his case was quite advanced. Then she asked us to wait outside, as she really wasn't supposed to be giving advice to non-paying patients.

When she came out, she gave us an article describing the latest TB treatments. She did this in a rush, looking over her shoulder a bit, again going out of her way to help. Thanks to her, we now knew that William's doctor's treatment was in exact alignment with the latest Western medicine.

Well, *I* learned it. I guess William had known it all along.

汤

Eventually, the side effects of the medication wore off and William began to regain his strength. He quit his job at the school and went into business with a friend of ours, which proved to be a good choice. He had wanted to leave the school for a while—mainly because teaching wasn't what he had ever intended to do, but also because the gossip and small-mindedness were taking their toll. We were both ready for him to have some anonymity. The opportunity with KJ would not be about money, but we did hope it would be about experience.

When William quit, I put in a proposal to not continue as the ELC director the following year but rather to take on a more low-key position in the secondary school. It was a bold move for me, and I couldn't have done it without William's support. We made this decision so that I could really give myself a chance to work on my writing, every single day. I hadn't always been a writer, but I'd had the idea to turn some of my experiences in China into a memoir, and I had a few ideas for articles I might want to submit to a magazine as well. I felt great working on my writing, and it was a part of myself I hoped to develop more.

I knew that I had done a great job directing the center and I would probably have had even more career success the following year in that position. But I also knew that remaining there would leave me less time to pursue my dream of getting my ideas down on paper. I really felt it was time to try.

The school agreed to let me transfer departments and position, and even let me choose my replacement, someone to whom I was very comfortable turning over the ELC. I was excited about the upcoming year. I would come to work and do a good job, but I would leave work at work. I would simply teach.

In the meantime, summer was almost upon us and good things were in store there, too.

chapter 31

I hadn't mentioned William's illness to my mom because I didn't want her to worry and the doctors had told us he was not contagious at this point. He was getting used to the medications, and his health was slowly improving.

My mom was coming to visit. I was so thrilled about this that I couldn't stand it. After all, she hadn't met William yet; nobody in my family had. And for her to come to China was just amazing. She had only been on an airplane twice in her life—to Seattle and back—and now she would board a plane for the other side of the world. This was such a luxury for someone in my family. We simply didn't travel, except maybe via the family station wagon when we were all a lot younger. I'd never thought I'd see the day when my mom would come to China, but now that day had come. And I couldn't wait for her to get there.

I picked her up in Hong Kong and we rode the bus together back to Guangzhou. William met us at the bus stop, looking as handsome and sweet as ever. He had a gigantic smile on his face and said, "Hi, Mom," as soon as he saw her.

"Who's this handsome guy here?" Mom said, and gave him a big hug.

I think I started crying right there. We took the bus home together and I remember that William thought Mom was so cute. He loved her gold-studded hat. He just thought she was precious. I guess I did too. She had gotten her nails done and acquired a few new outfits for the trip. Actually, the clothes were hand-me-downs from others, but she'd had them fixed up and cleaned so that they were new to her.

Mom had been doing odd jobs for people from church or neighbors for months in order to build her "China fund." She had even put a notice in the church bulletin announcing that she was available for babysitting, cleaning, errands, or anything else because she was raising money to visit her daughter and son-in-law in China. She'd worked so hard, and in the end she'd saved almost one thousand dollars.

Throughout the trip, Mom kept coming back to her shopping list. Not for herself, but for everyone back home. She had very specific things that neighbors or friends from church, or the clerk at Walgreens, or the girl at the McDonald's drive-thru where she got her Diet Cokes—had requested. And if they hadn't requested something, she had something in mind for them. She looked at the list several times a day and she took such joy in adding to her bag of treasures, every single thing for someone else.

This trip was such a dream for her. She was like a little kid in some ways, more energetic than I'd seen her in years. She worked so hard to learn a few phrases in Mandarin and to truly be open to the experience of being in China. I began to see my mother as the amazing woman that she truly is. I will never forget being at the Great Wall with her. It was entirely magical to see this wonder through her eyes and to feel her excitement. It didn't fully hit me until that moment that my sixty-five-year-old mother had gotten on a plane and taken her first international flight all the way to China to visit me. I couldn't imagine what this meant to her. More than that, I realized what it meant to me. I was filled with so much love for my mom as I watched her and William talking and walking up those steps. I was also filled with so much love for William as I watched how patient he was with Mom.

I, of course, felt rather tense. I know this makes me sound like a terrible person, but it's the truth. It was my natural response to being around my mom. The thought of getting a wheelchair and having William push her around in it stressed me out—but he didn't mind. He put on my little sunhat and pushed her around the Summer Palace and Tiananmen Square, showing her the time of her life. He was the one who made her trip wonderful, not me. He taught her so much and truly listened to her, really trying to get to know his wife's mother. He saw her as she was—a sweet, kind woman who was opening her heart to China. I, meanwhile, mostly saw her as Mom, and couldn't she hurry up a bit? We had a schedule to keep.

汤

Many months later, when we were in Chicago for Christmas, we watched the videotape of her trip. Not only did that give me the chance to see my mom through more objective eyes, it also allowed me to see myself more clearly, too. I watched us on the Great Wall. Mom's face was as red as a tomato. She was sort of hunched over, with sweat dripping from her face, and was holding on to the wall for dear life. Her face had an expression of such agony. I was walking ahead of her and William was taping us both. I actually said in the video, "Okay now, Mom, if you can speed it up a bit, we can totally still get to the Summer Palace before lunch."

At that moment, she looked up, and if looks could kill I would have been catapulted off that great wall and fallen to my death.

As we sat there watching this that night as a family, we were all horrified. But, having the sense of humor that we do, all of us—my mom included—laughed. What a jerk I was! And what a trooper Mom was! I mean, when I think objectively of what I put her through and how well she did, I am amazed. She had joked about how the farthest she had walked in Chicago was from her front door to her van. Now, she was walking all over Beijing and Guangzhou in almost unbearable heat and humidity—with an annoying, pushy daughter who wouldn't stop reminding her of the schedule. She and William had nicknamed me "the pusher" during our Beijing trip, but until I watched the video six months later I didn't realize how true that was.

She did it though. The woman who thought she couldn't walk around the block….did it. She walked up and on the Great Wall. She found something inside herself that pushed her, something even more powerful than her pushy daughter. When I think of everything my mom had been through in her life, I want to rise up and celebrate her achievement that day, and throughout the trip. She did things she never thought she could do. She broke every limit, traipsing around China.

Having my mom visit me in China was wonderful. In some ways it was stressful, but that wasn't her fault. It's just a house-guest thing. However, that got intensified to the hundredth power when William's family came too. We had invited his parents because we thought it would be nice for them to meet Mom, and vice versa. However, William's mom opted to bring her friend and that friend opted to bring her kid. Oh, and they brought William's niece too. Does this sound like a recipe for a cross-cultural utopia or a disaster waiting to happen?

I think if it had just been William's parents, things would have been fine. The friend was nice enough, but her kid was completely annoying—a rather obnoxious nine-year-old boy—and although the baby was cute and I loved her because she was my niece, I still didn't agree with the Chinese toilet training method. Many Chinese parents do not use a diaper. They allow the kids to go to the bathroom on the floor. I realize this sounds insane to outsiders, but that's the way it is in China. The rationale behind it is rooted in poverty, in that people couldn't afford the luxury of diapers, but it has become acceptable no matter one's economic status. It's also deeper than that, though, and seems to have something to do with personal responsibility. Most Chinese children are completely potty-trained by their second birthday, so parents are willing to tolerate their kids going to the bathroom on the floor, should they miss the toilet, in the meantime.

Whatever the rationale was, it really didn't matter. All I knew was that I did object rather strongly to a baby coming into my house without a diaper and freely pooping on my floor!

Needless to say, this caused some tension for me, but I was at least used to the concept. My mom, on the other hand, was completely mortified. In her eyes, here were her daughter's in-laws, waltzing in and allowing a child to go to the bathroom on her floor. In fact, yes, that's exactly what was happening, but when one has no cultural context, it seems rude, backward, and even crazy. Unfortunately, her tension and anger on my behalf made me more tense, and I stupidly directed my anger at her.

That part of Mom's visit was this strange combination of heaven and hell. It was hell when we were all in our tiny apartment together and the friend's kid was running around being obnoxious as the baby pooped on the floor and I thought Mom would jump out of her skin with shock and dismay. But there were also moments of fun and joy, when we sat around together as a family and completely enjoyed each other's company despite the language barrier. William's mom and my mom exchanged knitting methods. We looked at pictures together. When the baby wasn't using the floor as a toilet, she did adorable things that we all watched together. We took the family to the lake on a cool afternoon and I captured photos of William sitting between his mom and my mom, all three of them genuinely laughing and smiling. There were also moments where I could see the sheer pride in William's dad's eyes, so full of love for his son and so proud of the life he had made for himself. When everyone left, I felt a combination of relief and sadness. It's usually after the fact that we realize how amazing our life's experiences are, and this was one of those times. A couple of weeks later, as I looked at the photos from the week when we were all together, I just sat and cried. I thought about how unique our lives really were and about what a special opportunity we'd had. It had begun with me and William finding our common ground, and now we had managed to include our parents. I felt grateful for the chance we'd been given and I felt proud of us for surviving it, despite the challenges, and finding a way to share our lives with them.

Part Three

chapter 40

The start of the new school year reminded us that the carefree days of summer were gone and a new structure would take effect. So many little and not-so-little events had occurred over the summer and now entering autumn (in spite of the heat and humidity) was exciting. William had been studying about my faith and had taken it upon himself to better understand what I believed. He'd even taken a course and had been learning more formally from our friend Harry, another church member.

The laws in China, we learned, were evolving, and William had started coming to church with me, simply out of curiosity. This was allowed by virtue of the fact that he was married to a United States citizen. I hadn't known that he was doing more than studying and accompanying me. He told me later that he had felt more of an emotional desire to learn about this concept of a loving God, a Creator, and what that might mean for him as an individual.

"I had no idea you were taking this so seriously." I'd told him when he shared this one evening as we were preparing dinner. "I guess I thought you were just coming to be nice, and to save me the trip of going alone. Even that, I really appreciated." And than I added. "You know that it was never a condition for me that you join my church. You know that, right?"

For some reason it was important that he knew that. I felt strongly about spiritual matters, and my faith was important to me. So important, in fact, that it was personal and nothing to be taken lightly. I would have never encouraged a superficial conversion, just to make me happy. I wanted to make sure he wasn't doing that, as kind as that may have been.

"No, I really feel something, Lori. I did from the beginning. I feel like there is truth to what you are learning about and there is something really . . . just . . . good about how you live your life. When I'm at church or around those church members, I guess I feel peace. I was curious from the beginning. Once Harry started teaching me more directly about the doctrines, I can't deny that this is something I want to practice and live for myself."

I think I started shaking. I'd been cutting peppers and I put the knife down. I looked intently at him. "What are you saying, exactly?" I'd asked, not wanting to get my hopes up, but already knowing I was about to be very happy, as if it were possible to be any happier.

"I would like to be baptized. I'd like to be a part of this church and learn more and serve others the way I see so many good people are doing."

Tears welled in my eyes and I felt nothing but warm and peaceful all over. I figured this may have happened eventually, but I had imagined it would be years into our future. This was a miracle and I just felt happy.

"What are you thinking?" he asked, looking back at me just as intently as I was looking at him. He'd turned off the stove. We stood facing each other just smiling and really looking into each other's eyes.

"I'm thinking that this makes me so happy and I'm so happy for you, personally. I love that you can see and I guess, feel, this feeling that comes with having a meaningful faith. I'm just happy. I feel like this will bring us even closer."

With that, he reached out and pulled me into the softest and strongest hug ever.

After a more formal process of studying and learning and meeting with members and church leaders, we were able to obtain permission for William to be baptized right in Guangzhou. The building where we met each week had a small gym on the first floor. In that gym was a very small Jacuzzi. On an unforgettable day that fall, William entered the waters of baptism in the most untraditional way I could imagine. Dressed in white, he and Harry stood in that tiny space with friends gathered around. There was a special prayer and then Harry immersed William in the water.

He came up, wiped his eyes, and smiled. The biggest smile I'd ever seen him smile. I was mindful. Very mindful and very grateful. Life has its bitter times, but this was one of the sweetest moments ever. I knew right then that I would never forget this.

chapter 41

$\mathcal{E}$arlier that fall, we'd decided to apply for a tourist visa so that we could travel to the US together for Christmas. Mom would be starting her radiation treatment for breast cancer, and since the rest of the family hadn't yet met William, we thought it would be wonderful to go home for Christmas.

Mom had called the previous week to tell me about her diagnosis. She'd already been through so much, and I was shocked that someone in my immediate family had cancer. Chrissy was so worried; the news had had hit her hard.

"I got some news at the doctor today, Lori," Mom told me almost immediately after I answered the phone that day. "It's not good."

"What did they say?" I asked, full of concern. "Is it your blood pressure?"

"No, that's about the same, but they found a lump in my breast and they've confirmed it's cancer."

Her voice was shaky, but I could tell she was trying to sound calm, probably not wanting to worry me too much.

"I'm sorry, Mom. This is awful. Do you want me to come home?" I hadn't even thought through how that would work, but I meant it. If she needed me, I would go.

"No, no, right now things are okay," she said. "I do need to do radiation treatment and it will start in a week or so."

We went on to talk about the details, and then Chrissy and I talked too. This was one of the times the guilt hit me—but I also knew that I had my own problems. I felt guilty for not being there, but I knew I was also dealing with William's health problems here. My heart felt heavy.

How did my Mom have breast cancer, on top of everything else she has already been through? Cancer. Breast cancer. It hurt deeply and numbed me at the same time. I wanted so badly to be in two places at once. This is a time I should be with my Mom. And yet. And yet I wasn't.

汤

It took us several weeks to get an appointment with the United States consulate. We took turns calling, sitting on hold, and usually getting hung up on. Finally, though, William got through and we had our appointment for October 10.

He worked so hard in preparation for that day—getting all his documents together and writing letters explaining his plans and why he wanted to travel to America. We had done the research; we knew what was expected; and we had a good feeling that we would leave that day with his visa in hand. After all, he was married to a citizen and simply wanted to go home with her for Christmas.

We arrived at the gates of the American consulate in Guangzhou before the sun came up and took our place in line. There was only one person ahead of us, but before long the line behind us extended farther than we could see. The Chinese have a saying that translates to "People mountain, people sea," and on mornings like this, I knew why. There were people everywhere—a mountain and sea of people waiting for their chance to go to America.

The most important factor when determining whether or not an applicant qualifies for a tourist visa is the evidence that the Chinese citizen will return to China. We had more than adequate evidence that both of us planned to return to our jobs and life after visiting the States for a few weeks.

Now, the fact that we were applying for a non-immigrant visa did not mean that my husband never wanted to immigrate. In our minds, these were completely separate issues. Yes, perhaps the following year we would apply for immigration. However, at that moment we simply wanted to go home for Christmas. We saw no reason why we could not do both, and therefore we saw no reason to lie about our plans.

Many friends, however, had advised us to do just that. "When the interviewing officer asks if you ever plan to immigrate, just tell him no!" they told us. They said that once an applicant disclosed the fact that they eventually wanted to immigrate, they would be denied a non-immigrant visa in the meantime. I thought that was crazy. I mean, what if we planned to work overseas for the next five years? By the rationale my friends presented, my husband could never visit the States during that time? It sounded ludicrous, and we saw no reason to believe it. We had nothing to hide! In fact, the embassy's website said not to conceal the fact that you eventually plan to immigrate, as this would not make someone ineligible for a tourist visa. They were completely separate issues. That's what the site said.

Well, when my husband got his chance to interview, we realized that the US consulate did not in fact see them as separate issues. The officer was not interested in any of our compelling evidence of our plans to return to Guangzhou after a short visit. He was interested only in whether or not William ever planned to immigrate, to which William honestly told him that he did— perhaps in the year 2004.

Bam! That was all they needed. A big fat rejection stamp was put in his passport.

When William walked out, he could barely talk. His sadness and hurt made me infuriated. How could they tell have told him no? How could they have not looked at any of his documents? How could they have rejected him for the very reason they claimed they wouldn't?

We stood outside the embassy for what felt like an eternity with tears streaming down our faces and a horrible pain in our hearts. We watched other applicants come out with joy on their faces because they had obtained their visas and were going to visit America. The world was spinning; I couldn't make sense of what had just happened. *Wait a minute*, I thought. *These people get to go to America but William can't come home for Christmas to meet his family? How on earth are they deemed more worthy to go than my husband?* We were frozen with anger and sadness and we both had the sickest feeling—the feeling that although we had been wronged and that clearly a mistake or injustice had occurred, it was not likely to change.

The system was so complicated. It had taken us weeks to even get this appointment, and once you've been rejected once it is much harder to get another appointment, and even harder than that to actually get your visa approved. We also knew that the visa department was indeed the last word and they basically didn't have to answer to anybody. Thirdly, if we didn't know it before, we suddenly knew that we were two "nobodys."

We stood there outside the consulate trying to comfort each other but knowing that no comfort would be found. Our plans to go home for Christmas were destroyed. They had told my husband no. They had unfairly and unjustly said no to our dream.

汤

The American Services office, where I planned to appeal this decision, would not open for another four hours. We spent them in the lobby of a fancy hotel down the street. Normally when we were in this part of town we liked to walk around and look at the shops and have a wonderful lunch. Not this day. On this day we were almost too sad to breathe, let alone eat. We thought and talked for hours, trying to make sense of it. We couldn't. When we realized we couldn't make sense of it we tried to accept it. I wondered if there was perhaps some divine reason we had been rejected. That didn't work for me either. No matter how we looked at it, it was just wrong. William said it best: "They hurt us, and they ruined our plan."

When the time came for us to go to the American Services Unit, I explained my case to the officer at the window and tried very hard to not let the tears and my distressed appearance take away from the validity of my argument. She handed me a complaint form to fill out. I listed two complaints: 1) the interviewing officer had not looked at any of my husband's evidence; 2) the officer—and the system—in fact punished my husband for being honest. At the bottom of the form I said I would be eternally grateful to have the chance to talk for five minutes with someone who could help us. At the very bottom of the form, I wrote the words "help me." I felt like I was at the bottom of a well and that anyone with any power would never hear me and would never have any reason to come down in the well to find me. There were layers and layers of protective bureaucracy between the horrible reject stamp in William's passport and any chance of justice.

My form was given to the American Services Unit supervisor, a nice woman who told me that unfortunately there was nothing she or her office could do. I wanted to scream and sob but I had to hold it together. I knew that she was my link to help, if there was help to be had. I tried to make her understand that I was not simply "sad" because my husband had been rejected.

Rather, someone had made a mistake and William never should have been rejected in the first place. Therefore, taking her suggestion to go through this horrible process of trying again was simply incomprehensible.

I stood there, unsuccessfully fighting back tears, knowing she was my only hope. When there was nothing more to say, I simply said, "Please help me."

After looking right into my eyes for several seconds, she took a big breath, let out a sigh, and said that she would personally take the form to her supervisor. She let me know that she honestly didn't think the situation would change but that she would give the form to him.

I was so grateful—this was at least some action. She said there was really no reason to wait and that I should go home. She explained again that this decision was not likely to change because the visa department really was its own section and their decision was final. Still, I said I would wait. If it was true that the visa department's decision was final, after all, then why was I even here?

I also couldn't face going back outside, back home, back to work, back to our lives knowing that this horrible thing had happened. I didn't know how to make peace with it, how to go on, how to call my family and tell them we weren't coming and that William wouldn't ever be able to come for a visit. I thought about my dad having passed away the previous year just a week before Christmas. It would mean so much to our family for William and me to be home this year, and I couldn't face the fact that he couldn't go.

As I was thinking about spending Christmas here in China, I noticed a man coming toward me.

He made eye contact with me. "Can you come over to the counter?" he asked, beckoning me toward him.

I literally jumped out of my seat and dropped all my papers

on the floor. My head was spinning. He obviously had power and my complaint had gotten his attention. Now he was standing before me asking about my situation. I wanted to jump up and down and hug him simply for talking to me. Instead, I began to calmly explain our situation.

"Is your husband here?" he asked when I'd told him the whole story.

"Yes," I said, "he's waiting right downstairs."

"Let's go get him," he said. I literally grabbed on to the counter to keep from falling down. I could not believe this. This man was helping me, listening to me, and he was going to take me outside to get William. I did not understand what was going on but I suddenly felt significantly lighter.

As I followed him down the stairs and outside, I simply said, "Thank you for helping me," to which he casually replied, "It's all right." I was silently thanking God over and over and over again. I was in awe of what was happening.

We walked outside, past all the guards who had told William he wasn't allowed in, and, with a wave of his arm, the man said, "Go get your husband."

Across the open lot, behind the gate, there was a sea of people—mostly people who had also been rejected—and William was among them. I waved him over and he ran toward me. I ran to meet him. The guards tried to stop him until they saw the man behind me, who I later learned was the chief consul, likely the highest position at the consulate general in Guangzhou.

William and I grabbed hands and began running toward the man.

"I don't know what's going on," I told him, "but it's a miracle." And it was.

As we entered the embassy with this man it was like we were entering a different world. He escorted us to the visa section and then said good-bye. "Thank you" was all we could say as we watched him walk away. He had not told us exactly what was going on and we had not asked. It was clear at that point, though—in both of our hearts if not our heads—that a miracle was taking place. It was as if we didn't want to put it into words at that point, for fear that words would trivialize it and make it disappear. So we just sat there squeezing each other's hands and thanking God for this amazing turnaround.

汤

After a long wait, they called our names and we stood together before an interviewing officer. He was very pleasant but made sure to point out that although my complaint had referred to them as unfair, they in fact were just doing their jobs. I didn't want to argue at that point. I knew that these officers did indeed have a very difficult job to do. I also knew beyond a shadow of a doubt that they had indeed made a mistake with William's case, but I wasn't about to say that now. None of the anger I'd felt earlier that day was with me now. I was just grateful.

After talking with us, the officer did decide to issue the visa. We were overjoyed, to say the least. Although we had been married less than a year, there had already been a number of occasions where we had felt gratitude to a degree we never would have thought possible, usually at the conclusion of some challenge. However, this was the first time in our marriage—and possibly in our lives—that we'd had a day where we'd gone from the depths of despair to feeling on top of the world in less than twelve hours.

How grateful I am for the small things that led to this miracle. The woman in the American Services Unit took my complaint to her boss rather than filing it away. This made it possible for the chief consul to see my complaint immediately upon returning from lunch. He read it and did something about it. This is the miracle. How often do we all look at something and then put it aside to deal with later? For whatever reason, this man read about my problem, got up from his desk, and did something about it right then and there.

Our experience that day taught me a great deal. First and foremost, it is worthwhile to question something that we care about, no matter how overwhelming the issue might feel. I also learned that when we want something done we need to be persistent and visible, so that we are not forgotten. Finally, I was reminded that "the system" is really made up of individuals who have the power to undo an injustice and even make what seems impossible become a reality.

The truth is that although this experience had a happy ending, it still hurts to think about it. It took so much out of us to apply and then to appeal this incredibly unjust decision. It scares me to think that maybe it will always be like this for my husband. Because there are so many people who abuse the system, he'll just have that many more hoops to jump through as he pursues immigration, residency, and perhaps citizenship in the United States of America. I keep telling him that it will be worth it. I often tell myself that too.

chapter 42

William and I knew that at some point we wanted to be parents and we'd been talking about it for a long time. Finally, in August, we'd decided that we would begin to try to get pregnant. For me, this brought so many dreams—so many ideas about being a mother and what that would mean—into focus. I thought about how when I'd come to China, marriage wasn't something I'd even thought about. Motherhood, though, was. The memory of that first day in the orphanage, holding the baby, and how it was so incredibly difficult to leave her. The idea of having a child of my own. The fact that it seemed now, I would have both: a wonderful husband *and* the chance to have a child. A little person to share with, to teach, to love, to pass on my lessons to.

As the months went by, we knew in our hearts that we did indeed want to become parents, and despite the fact that we weren't completely financially ready, we felt good about going ahead with this plan.

Other than that, we were counting down the days until our departure for America. I was so excited that I found it hard to sleep those last few weeks before the trip. William, as well, was counting the days and running through our trip out loud. "Now, tell me again what we'll do on Christmas," he would say. "What is the tradition about the night before? Who's hosting the party for us? Do you think we'll be able to buy noodles in America?" It was so fun to hear his endless questions, and just as fun for me to tell him everything I could about America and Christmas and my family. After all, this would be a trip of so many "firsts" for him, and I couldn't wait to see it all through his eyes.

Every part of our journey was fun simply because we were together. One of the most exhilarating parts for me was leaving mainland China for Hong Kong. I knew then, as William passed through that customs gate, that this trip was real. How many times before had I gone through that gate alone, having to leave William behind? The previous July, when Mom had come, he hadn't been able to come to the airport with me to see her off; he simply hadn't had the right to cross that border.

That fact sickened me. Westerners are quite passionate about personal rights in general but when it hit me personally, the feelings it generated were very unexpected. Now, however, here we were, together on the other side of customs, boarding the ferry for Hong Kong. We were on top of the world.

汤

We hung out in Hong Kong for a couple of days, walking and browsing in the most expensive parts of town and then going home to our hotel room and eating microwave noodles at night. We stayed in a nice hotel right in the center of Kowloon. We took the MTR (Hong Kong's fantastic subway system) to the temple, to the peak on Central, rode the star ferry, and basically just explored and talked and enjoyed every second.

When we finally left for the US, all the flights went smoothly. Neither of us could sit still on the flight from Los Angeles to Chicago. I could not believe that in a few short hours we would be in the same room with my family. William would hug them. They would see him. We would eat together, drive together, spend Christmas together. My family was finally going to meet my husband.

When we landed in Chicago, my family was there, waiting at the baggage area. I saw Chrissy, Barb, all of them. Before I knew it, they were running toward us, everyone hugging William at once. Mom looked so proud, as if to say "I already got to meet him." She gave William a long squeeze and they both smiled at each other. My mom radiated happiness, and I loved that she wanted to hug William. Chrissy started jumping and clapping: "This is so cool! He's finally here." We grabbed our bags and walked toward the car.

"Well, William I've got a good dinner ready for you. I hope you are hungry," Mom said.

"I am. That sounds good. What did you make?"

"Well, Barbara and I worked on it together and Chrissy and Shaleen made the desserts. We've got ham, twice-baked potatoes, and pies, all kinds of great stuff!"

I was looking forward to introducing William to all these yummy American foods. I knew that would be great, but I knew it was just the beginning. This was going to be magical.

The next twelve days were filled with cookies, hot chocolate, caroling, wrapping presents, opening presents, sharing the Christmas story on Christmas Eve, playing games, eating, baking, and more eating. It was filled with laughter and honestly, absolute bliss. There was not a second of tension, not a second of worry. William was embraced by them, and they all loved him. It was perfect.

Christmas eve, a slow snowfall began just as we were inside enjoying the festivities. We got so excited that Chrissy, Shaleen, William, and I ran outside and literally danced around in the falling snow. We laughed and spun each other around like little kids. It felt like a gift from Dad, a hello, his way of welcoming William. I caught a glimpse of William with his arms out-stretched, head back, spinning, taking it all in. I didn't know what was going through his mind, but I knew he was happy. So was I. Truly happy.

William and I also took a road trip to a quaint historical town called Nauvoo. This was one of my favorite places because it's where the early members of our faith established a home. They made it beautiful and successful but were eventually persecuted and kicked out of the city they had literally built. It was at that point that the "Mormon" pioneers went west and ended up settling in Utah. Now, Nauvoo is a darling little tourist town by the Mississippi River in Illinois. I loved every second of sharing this with him, and it could not have been more idyllic. The snow, the horse and carriage ride, the beautiful atmosphere. There's just an incredible spirit about the place, and we soaked in it. When we'd arrived at the little hotel, which was a restored house from the early 1900s, there was a note, our key, and hot cider and cookies. "Welcome Lori and William. Please enjoy the cookies and cocoa. Your room is the top of the stairs on the left. Enjoy your stay."

"What? They just let us in? But we haven't paid or anything?" William said in a voice that communicated both shock and joy.

"Yeah, this isn't usual at all. This is definitely not the norm in America. Maybe it's just that it's this small town. Maybe it's the seasonal 'Christmas spirit,' but whatever it is, this is so cool!"

We hugged, sat by the cozy fireplace and enjoyed our cookies. Best Christmas season ever.

chapter 43

It was almost Spring Festival again, and William and I had been going back and forth for the past few months, trying to decide if we should immigrate to America or stay in China for another year. On paper, it made more sense to stay so that we could save money and be better prepared when we did move to the States. In my heart, though, I wanted to go. I was ready for us to think about a new chapter and was anxious for William to experience America—particularly for him to attend university there.

He had that goal too, but wanted to be absolutely ready. One thing he had learned when we'd gone home for Christmas was that America is a wonderful place . . . as long as you have money. Without money, he'd said, it seemed the life there is miserable. True enough.

We had a long way to go before our savings would be where we wanted them to be, and my student loan debt was still high. No question it made sense to stay, but based on our feelings, we decided to apply for immigration anyway. There was something about getting to America—an unspoken urgency we both felt that we couldn't deny.

After all, we had made it through tough times before, and it would be okay to live the "poor college student" life for a while.

It was all about the process, after all, and learning as we went. Plus, we weren't completely unprepared. We made a plan for how much we could save in China before leaving the following fall. We began getting our paperwork together and studying the process of immigration. We made lists of all the documents we needed to get and devised a plan for how to get them. Clearly, our trip to Huang Mei for Spring Festival would have to involve working on this.

I was already having horrible déjà vu from the year before, remembering how we'd traipsed through the countryside trying to get the first stamp, the second stamp, the third stamp, all the right forms, and all the right signatures. I was not ready to return to that nightmare—so I simply told myself this time wouldn't be so bad.

The main thing we needed to get was William's birth certificate. From a Western perspective, this sounds perfectly natural. Everyone has a birth certificate, right?

Well, no. What if the person is born at home? Before giving birth to William, Xu Shui Xian was outside at the pond doing her wash. When she felt the labor pains she came inside and, with the help of two older ladies, delivered her son. No paperwork was filed. This was the countryside. This was middle China. Beyond that, this was 1976, the tail end of the Cultural Revolution. Even if it had been normal to file paperwork after a birth, during this time, people would not have done it anyway. William had been born under these circumstances and therefore had no birth certificate.

Generally speaking, the birth certificate is not as significant in China as it in the States. The more major document is the registration card we had obtained from the record keeper's attic the year before. With that card, William was able to obtain a Chinese passport. So he had these documents proving his identity—but he didn't have an actual birth certificate.

Of course, I called the consulate and visited them multiple times to try to explain to them how difficult it would be to get a birth certificate that did not exist. I figured, naively, that they would appreciate our honesty (as it would have been easy enough to obtain a fake birth certificate) and say that the birth certificate was not really necessary. However, they didn't. I remember calling a US government official from the countryside and telling him that I would never be able to get the certificate. He told me to get what I could, turn it in with our immigration application, and then we'd go from there.

I felt optimistic at this. This sounded reasonable. We would get what we could and that, combined with William's other documents, should be enough to prove that he was who he said he was.

So with that, we set off for Huang Mei once again. This time, however, we flew there. The first time William had flown was the previous May, when we were in a hurry to get back to Guangzhou and see a doctor. He marveled at the convenience and speed of it, and it was a thrill for me to watch him stare out the window as we took off. It had never occurred to him to fly. After all, he could tolerate almost anything, and taking the train did not bother him one bit. No, he was doing this for me. To him, it was a waste of money, but he knew how much I hated the train at Spring Festival.

As we boarded the plane and found our seats, I thought back to the previous year. Was it already a year ago that I had first gone to Huang Mei? Things were so different then. Our relationship was so new. Everything was unknown. *It's more comfortable now*, I thought, as I grabbed William's hand and squeezed it.

He looked up from his magazine and leaned his head back on the seat, not taking his eyes off me. Then he took both my hands in his and said, "Can you believe this is already our second Spring Festival in Huang Mei?"

"I know." I nodded, smiling. "I was just thinking about that. A lot has happened this year."

"Time passes so quickly." He glanced out the window.

"Are you excited about going home this time?" I asked.

"Well. . . ." He paused for a moment, as if thinking about how to form his ideas. "It's wonderful to go home, but then again I'm not looking forward to the problems there. They have such a hard life and every time we go home, I realize it more and more. And there's really nothing we can do to help them."

It was true. Over the past year, knowing how much his family struggled, we had sent money periodically, but it was never enough, and it almost seemed to cause more contention within the family. At the same time, though, it was hard to do nothing when they had so little and we, comparatively, had so much.

汤

Once we got to Huang Mei, we set about getting statements. We wanted a statement from William's mom and dad, and from the two ladies who had witnessed the birth. Well, the old ladies had since died, so we settled for just his parents. His poor mother didn't quite know what we were up to. After all, it was Spring Festival and everyone else was relaxing, visiting relatives, and eating while William and I were constantly on our mobile phones, trying to get a hold of the consulate or William's classmates, who were helping us gather other documents. We were always taking notes and speaking in English and asking his mom what must have seemed to her crazy questions.

"Now, Mama," I said in my best Chinese, "when Minga"— that's what they called William in the local dialect—"was born, how much did he weigh?" I was trying to gather all the information that would normally be on a birth certificate. My idea was that we could get a blank birth certificate and fill it out, not claiming that it was filled out in 1976 but simply presenting it as an official document that had all the necessary information about his birth. We would get it and his mother's statement notarized, and hopefully that would be adequate proof.

When I asked Mama this question in all seriousness, pencil and paper in hand, ready to write her response, she laughed out loud and, holding her hands about a foot apart, palms facing in, said, "About this much."

I was not amused.

Well, actually, I was kind of amused. But my entire body was aching from stress. My head hurt so bad that I could not see straight. We desperately wanted this information, but I could see this from her point of view. Her son was now twenty-six years old; why was I asking how much he'd weighed as a baby?

William tried to explain that this was what the American government wanted to know so that he could get his visa. "Why do they need to know such a crazy thing?" Mama asked again and again. "So many crazy questions!"

This was after I'd also asked how long William had been at birth and at what time of the day he'd been born. She was right, though. This was crazy. I mean, did they really need this information? Why did every process we went through seem to be so incredibly difficult? When would we ever be able to come to Huang Mei and just rest and enjoy the family without being on some desperate paperwork mission?

There was one moment that stood out as quality family time. In retrospect, there were many, but the biggest was visiting William's grandmother—an experience I won't soon forget. I'd had a special connection with her from the beginning. She was this combination of humility and elegance that is so unusual in any situation, let alone the countryside of China. When I talked with her about her life, I learned just how many difficulties she'd endured. She had faced war and poverty and everything in between yet she still carried herself like a lady and always greeted me with a warm smile and extended hand holding. I just loved her.

During this fourth visit to Huang Mei, though, we saw Grandma in a different light. She had fallen and broken her leg and was confined to her bed. It was difficult to see her like that, unable to move and with very little hope in her eyes. The doctors hadn't put a cast on the leg or given her any medication. Rather, they'd instructed her to stay in bed for about two months, telling her the leg would heal itself. When we saw her, she had been in bed for about a month.

I wanted to badly to do something for her. I wished we could rent a helicopter and take her to the best hospital in Guangzhou and get real help for her. I wished we could make her feel better—but I knew that we couldn't. Knowing that she'd been lying in that same position for all that time made me cringe. I knew how her body must ache, and suddenly it occurred to me that maybe she'd like a massage.

I was holding her hand and I just began to rub her hands and arms a bit, seeing how she'd respond. It made her relax. I moved up to her shoulders a bit and was careful to make sure I wasn't hurting her. Finally, I asked William to ask her if I could rub her back and her other leg a little. She really liked the idea. So, while all the relatives were in the other room, we gently rolled her just a bit so that I could get to her back. Even moving her that little bit, lifting her back a couple of inches and propping her up with pillows, brought her relief. I began to massage her back and she literally moaned with happiness. Those poor muscles. William found some hand cream and we used that to add some moisture to her skin. When the aunts came in, at first I think they thought we were crazy, but when Grandma told them how wonderful she felt they just smiled at me and gave approving nods.

We moved her as much as we could without interfering with the broken leg. I tried to imagine where I would be hurting if I had been lying on that hard bed for a month and decided that she must hurt everywhere. So I did what I could, and I think it really helped both of us: she got a little relief for those aching muscles and joints, and I had found a way to show my love for this dear woman.

It made us sad to leave that day, but having made that connection with her made it less painful. I thought about Grandma a lot over the next few months and was amazed that when we visited seven months later she was her old self again, walking around with the sparkle back in her eyes.

汤

The day before we left for Wuhan to try to get everything notarized, William and his mom sat at the kitchen table practicing her name. I was so humbled by this; I could hardly believe what I was watching. Most of us sign our names or write something every day of our lives, but William's mother had never even had the chance to learn how to write her own name. What reason did she have to do so? Her life was not one of signatures and forms. Her life was one of cooking, cleaning, and hard work that did not involve literacy. As she sat there trying to copy what William had written out for her, I suddenly didn't like myself very much.

I hated that William and I were making her do this— reminding her of something she couldn't do and sending the message that this was an important thing. In doing so, we were discounting all the important things she had done every day throughout her whole life. The way to help her son now was to be able to write her name, something she was trying so hard to do. I watched William's face as he helped her and I knew that he felt it too. *We must really want to go to America to put her through this, to put the whole family through all our craziness, every time we come home*, I thought. At that moment I really wondered if it was all worth it, this idea of going to America. But then I thought,

Of course it is, and William has every right as my husband to go. If we gave up now, all that we had gone through would be for nothing and William would never have a chance to study in America or simply live in the place where his wife was from.

My mind flashed forward to when we had children. If William didn't have permission to go to the States, would we keep the kids from doing so too?

No, all this work was worth it. He had every right to go. I just hated, absolutely hated, that it was so difficult for us. My anger was now directed more at the consulate for having such a stupid requirement. I mean, had they any idea what we were going through here? Why on earth couldn't they accept the registration card or the passport? Why did we have to go back twenty-six years, trying to reconstruct a piece of paper that didn't exist?

Still, we wouldn't give up. After going through all this, especially after watching Mama working so diligently to sign her name, there was nothing we'd let stop us from getting William his immigrant visa.

汤

We got everything notarized in Wuhan—all the documents, all the statements. Now, there was nothing to do except pray that it was enough. If it wasn't, we really had no idea what we would do.

When we got back to Guangzhou, we went to the consulate and turned everything in to INS. They told us that within a month we would hear from them, and either the application would be approved and passed on to the next step, the immigrant visa unit, or they would let us know what else they needed.

With that, we went home. When we walked in the door, the phone rang. It was our friend Stuart, calling to ask us if we'd heard of this terrible disease that was killing people all over the city.

chapter 44

At first we didn't know what the disease was; we just kept getting phone calls asking us if we had heard the latest on the numbers of people affected. It was some type of pneumonia, we knew, but much more serious than the usual kind, since people were dying all over Guangzhou. The media was not openly reporting anything at this time, so all the reports of this came from word of mouth.

Some older ladies in the neighborhood advised me to go out and buy vinegar. They said I should boil it in the house and it would kill germs. People advised one another to stay in their homes and away from other people. We were all so frightened of this disease—the disease we later learned was called SARS (Severe Acute Respiratory Syndrome).

SARS changed people's lives. For the next four months, nothing could be taken for granted. Schools were closed; everyone wore masks; people were afraid to get near each other. The price of vinegar quadrupled and for a while even rice was hard to get. People were panicked, and scared to death that their loved ones would catch this horrible disease for which there was no cure. We knew the symptoms included fever, cough, and diarrhea, so any sign of these symptoms sent a chill though people's bones.

If this had happened six months earlier, when William still

had a fever every day, I would have been even more panicked because in those days, the side effects of his medications were similar to the classic SARS symptoms. Thankfully, now he was almost finished with his TB treatment and was no longer experiencing those side effects.

Finally, the media began to report on the epidemic. Every night, William and I watched to see what the numbers were: how many new cases had been reported and how many deaths had occurred. Of course we knew that the real numbers were much higher, as obviously the government was trying to send the message that things were under control, but even the numbers they reported were astounding. All we could do was to wash our hands frequently, eat well, sleep well, and pray. We tried different vitamins and herbal remedies meant to strengthen the immune system, but beyond that, there was nothing we could do. Everyone felt helpless during those days. It was so scary to have no medicine for this disease and to know that it was just out there, everywhere, anywhere.

During this time in our lives, we did not take a single moment for granted. We watched the news and saw these tragic stories of victims of SARS. Young people, old people—it didn't seem to discriminate. Each week we just prayed that this disease would go away and stop hurting people all over China and in other parts of the world.

By this time it was all over and was getting worse in Beijing than it had been in Guangzhou. We heard reports of cases in Canada, Taiwan, and other parts of the world. People began to leave China, only to be quarantined when they got home. The thought crossed our minds to leave, but in fact even if we'd wanted to, William had no visa and we couldn't. We really didn't want to leave, though, and just kept hoping things would get better. We also worried about the effect this would have on our immigration application. What if China became blacklisted?

What if they decided that since SARS had originated there, no more immigrants from China would be allowed to come to the US? All sorts of thoughts went through our minds. It was a terrible time.

汤

Amidst this SARS scare, William began a new job. This was yet another answer to prayer, another major step for him and toward a brighter future for us. He became the CEO assistant to Brady, a church member who had just moved to China from Utah. His company manufactured computer cables, and he happened to need an assistant around the same time William was looking for a new job. Things just fell into place and in February, William began this new position.

At first, he wasn't sure what his role would be, but as time passed he learned a great deal about management and working with different groups of people. The experience proved invaluable.

Throughout the SARS ordeal, we were still dealing with INS and trying to get William's visa. We received word from them that the documents we had provided were not sufficient to prove William's birth. I felt like screaming, "He's standing right in front of you! Is that not proof enough? He's got a passport and his registration card. What more do you want?"

Well, when I asked, I got an answer. They wanted a birth certificate. When I explained again and again that I would never be able to get that, they said that he needed a notarized letter from the security bureau in his hometown stating why he didn't have a birth certificate.

We had had more challenges with INS before getting this news. They had made a few mistakes, which had caused us a great deal of stress. All of their inquiries were minor but they added up to big headaches. One involved a formal letter from them to William informing him that this was his "final request" for certain documents. The letter claimed their office had been waiting since December for these documents—which was clearly impossible, since we had not even begun this application process until February. They also wanted proof that William had returned from America and had not overstayed his tourist visa. *How about the fact that he was in your office twice last week!?* I wanted to ask them.

I was so furious about all these mistakes on their part that one night I started typing a letter to INS informing them of their errors. That night, William and I had one of the most intense arguments we'd ever had. Neither of us had ever experienced that degree of stress, and it was as though we could barely breathe. We were working so hard to play by their rules and not only were we not winning the game, it now felt like the people responsible for making this decision were not playing fairly. In retrospect, I know these mistakes were unintentional, but at the time, in my exhausted and paranoid state, I felt there was a horrible plot to discourage us from pursuing this visa.

As William read what I wrote, he kept trying to convince me to change it, saying that I would regret using that tone with the consulate. I argued that they had made mistakes, and they needed to acknowledge that fact. He argued that they were the ones with all the power; I could correct them, but my tone was too sharp—I needed to be more humble. We sat there going back and forth, both of us so emotional and frustrated with the other, arguing about each sentence, until three o'clock in the morning. Then, finally—delirious with stress, exhaustion, and regret for having taken out our frustrations and fears on each other—we agreed on a letter with a more humble approach and sent it the next morning.

In the meantime, though, William had no choice but to go back to his hometown, back to the security bureau, to get this form stating why he was never issued a birth certificate. It was all too familiar. Was it just a year ago that I had flown back to Guangzhou from Wuhan for one piece of paper? Now William was heading the opposite direction for, again, one piece of paper. We were just sick about this. After all, we had just returned from there a month earlier after having spent the entire Spring Festival trying to get what the consulate required, and still it wasn't enough.

William wrote the document in English and Chinese, explaining that in the place and time in which he was born, it had not been policy to file a record of birth. On a Tuesday night, he got on the train and headed all the way back to Huang Mei in order to get this piece of paper stamped at the security bureau.

That day, I simply wanted to stay home and cry rather than go to work. I was at my limit. Why was this so hard? I could not believe William was all the way up in Hubei province. I began to feel so bad for him that he had to go through all this in order to be able to go to America with me. It didn't seem fair, and I could hear the tension in his voice as he called me from the security bureau.

"Hi, sweetie," he said quickly. "I only have a couple minutes on my phone card but I need to double-check the English wording with you. . . ." Since there was nobody in Huang Mei capable of translating, he was doing this himself, and since this was our only chance, the words needed to be perfect. As soon as I had said his translation sounded okay, we got cut off. I didn't get to tell him I loved him or to be safe.

As I went about my day at work, I tried to think of other things besides William, but it was of no use. All I could do was imagine each step of his journey and how many hours it would be until he was home with me.

He called me later that night from Wuhan. I felt much better after hearing his voice. The officials at the security bureau in

Huang Mei had signed the document and William had turned it into the notary office in Wuhan. It would be ready the next day, at which time he would get on the train and come home.

I was so amazed at what he had accomplished and I loved him so much for going through all that. He was so matter-of-fact about it. He just knew that it had to be done and did it. Actually, that was always how he was. I was the one to get emotional and freak out over all the challenges that came upon us. I was the one to worry myself sick about all the things I could not control. I was always in a rush to get through the challenge so that we could breathe normally again.

William still is always the one to remind me that life is not like that. We don't rush through the process to get somewhere with no challenges, because there will always be another one. He reminds me of the growth we have experienced since we met. Not too long ago, he asked me if I thought that growth would have been possible without the challenges. He never asks me these things in a condescending way; he does it gently, as if he really doesn't know the answer himself. Of course, we both know that he does, but he is always willing to ask his not-so-patient wife to think with him in those terms. He has said time and time again that all couples have challenges, but we may experience more of them, and of different kinds, because of our different backgrounds and how hard we need to work to understand certain aspects of each other.

Also, because we are trying so hard to grow and develop, we must expect that some pain will come with that. If we were content to just be, and never try to improve, have new experiences, serve others, learn more, or do more, then indeed life would be easy. But then, asks William, what would our relationship be? Would our love for each other be at the level that it is? Would the bitter soup taste so sweet?

chapter 45

INS continued to make us jump through more hoops, but we eventually passed that first step. It was hard to believe that all of those tasks surrounding the birth certificate were only step one.

My friend, Sherry, held a small dinner party for us when we got the news of our INS approval. She had seen me the first night William left for Huang Mei to get documents and had listened to me patiently as I unloaded on her. I had tried that night to act like everything was fine but when someone looks in your eyes with their own kind and concerned eyes, it's hard to hold back emotion. I had gone to yoga that night thinking it would get my mind off things, but seeing Sherry and feeling her hug had just made it all come out. I had made it through yoga but she'd come over afterwards and we'd chatted well into the morning. So now, when we got our INS approval, she was the one to say, "Dinner at my place." We have really been blessed with some good and thoughtful friends who know when it was time for a celebration.

The next steps would prove to be less difficult than the first. We still had more paperwork and more forms to complete, but the main step would be the interview, during which time it would be decided if William would get the visa or not.

We had one more scare when the consulate asked for

documentation from the Huang Mei security bureau proving that William didn't have a criminal record, but it worked out. He was able to ask a good friend to help on that end so that we didn't need to go all the way back in person. I was so amazed at the level of friendship William had established with his former classmates, and that after all these years people were still willing to help. Were it not for that classmate, who was still living and teaching in that small town, William would have had to take another trip back.

This friend had to go to William's former principal at that countryside school we'd visited more than a year earlier and get a certain stamp on a certain piece of paper. Then he had to mail the paper to the notary office in Wuhan—the same office we had gone to at Chinese New Year and where William had gotten his "birth certificate" notarized. Because that man was now familiar with William, he did it.

This, to me, was just short of a miracle. In my experience, things just didn't go that smoothly in China. This part of our process had been so efficient, so convenient, and so not stressful. We got the form and turned it in along with everything else— and a few weeks later, we got the notice saying that William's interview would be June 16.

This was it! We actually had a date. That meant that all the paperwork we had turned in was acceptable, and that as long as things went well at the interview, this could actually happen.

Oh, and he had to pass a medical exam before the interview.

汤

The medical exam was what had caused us so much worry almost two years before. We knew that with active TB, William would never be able to go to America. But now his treatment was complete, and although he would always have scar tissue in his lungs, he was no longer sick. This was so amazing in and of itself; we had been so caught up in everything else that was going on, and William had been so low-key about taking his pills and going to the doctor every month, that we hadn't often stop to recognize those blessings. In fact, we'd done it only once every month, when he came home from the doctor's office with a new X-ray.

That had been our ritual for months now. We would hold up his latest X-ray and compare it to the one from the previous month. Often, we didn't see a significant difference between those two. So then we would compare that day's X-ray with one from a few months back, and we could definitely always see improvement. The last thing we did was to compare it with the very first X-ray, the one we had gotten the first day he began treatment. That seemed so long ago now—and really, it was. As we compared those X-rays, we were very, very aware of how blessed we were.

That first X-ray was completely cloudy. His lungs were all white and it was almost impossible to see any black space in between the ribs. When you look at a normal X-ray, that is what you see—black space everywhere around the ribs. On William's first X-ray, the cloudiness of the TB just blended in with the white of his ribs. We had to really look to find any black space. But as we looked at all the successive X-rays, spanning almost two years, we could see the increase in black space in each one. It was so wonderful. He didn't cough anymore. He wasn't sick.

So now we just had to hope that the consulate recognized this, and that William having had TB in the past wouldn't keep him from going to America. We were so nervous about the health exam because the entire front page of the form was all about TB. Clearly, they wanted to be careful about this disease; we understood that, but we hoped they would see fit to let William in since his TB was no longer active.

汤

Once we were in that hospital going through the process, we felt again like we were back at square one. Most of the tests were routine and William moved right through them, but there was one part—the spitting part—that would prove to be our newest nightmare.

His X-ray showed that the TB had gotten better, but he still needed to prove that it was no longer active. The way to do this was to bring up phlegm and spit into a cup so they could analyze the sample. He needed to do this three times, but he could not do it even once. You know the gesture I'm talking about—the one where a person makes that horrible hacking sound as they bring phlegm up? It is disgusting, of course, and William had never done such a thing in his life. Even that day, as his immigrant visa depended on it, he couldn't do it. He tried—God knows he tried—but all he could bring up was spit, and that wasn't good enough.

So he had to go back the following Tuesday. We practiced until then. We bought honey, which we thought would help him. I didn't really know how to do this, either but I tried to learn so I could help him.

So there we were, sitting in our little apartment desperately trying to learn to hack up phlegm. Again, I was asking myself if it was really worth all of this to go to America. William was so stressed, as he knew this was the last step. Everything we had done would be for nothing if he couldn't hack something up three times at the doctor's office. The pressure he felt was almost unbearable, and of course we couldn't share this with anyone. A few colleagues knew he'd had the interview and everyone just assumed he'd pass the medical exam. Only we knew there was a really good chance he wouldn't.

汤

He went Tuesday and stayed at the hospital the whole morning. Nothing happened. Nothing would come up. I thought of how ironic this was. Chances were, if he had had active TB, it would have been easier to do this. Clearly, he was a healthy man who couldn't manage it. He called to let me know he couldn't do it and then he had to try again the next day. Now it was going on the fourth day that he would be late for work due to these appointments, and because he didn't want to discuss the details with his boss, all he'd been telling him was that he had medical appointments for the consulate—not exactly a lie, but William still didn't feel comfortable with it.

We tried everything. William even went to his former doctor, the one who had treated him through the TB, and asked his advice. That doctor gave him some medicine that was meant to sort of loosen up anything in the chest, making it easier to bring up. But William still needed to somehow learn this movement, this action, of bringing something up from his chest and spitting it out.

Finally, on the fifth day he would have to miss work due to this, he told his boss. Brady was also a friend from church and William had been feeling incredibly guilty not letting him know why he was missing so much work. Once Brady knew what the problem was, he wanted to help. That night, he came over and tried to coach William some more.

The three of us were in our apartment, trying to hack in order to help William. Brady and I were yelling, "Come on, that's too wimpy. Come on, bring it up, let's go!!"

What anyone walking by our place must have thought, I have no idea, and I could not have cared less, because William finally got to a point where something would come up. We shouted for joy. It wasn't quite a full-fledged hack, but it was more than just spit.

That accomplished, William asked Brady to give him a blessing. I thought this took a great deal of faith on William's part. Brady was prepared to give a blessing, as this was not an unusual custom in our faith.

He first asked me to say a prayer. We all sat, bowed our heads, and folded our arms, and I prayed that William would be able to do what he needed to do to pass the test the following day. I expressed thanks and asked that no matter the outcome, we would feel peace. We all said "Amen," and Brady then took his place standing behind William, as William sat. Brady placed his hands on William's head, we again all bowed our heads, and Brady offered a blessing, which is really just a special prayer again asking for God's help, but specifically meant to help William feel sort of an added dose, if you will, of peace. We again all said "Amen."

This is a ritual that my father performed many times for us growing up, any time we were sick or suffering emotionally. It's always brought me peace; I hoped it would do the same for William.

汤

I had taken the next day off to go with William. I had already been approved to have this day off, since it was June 16, the day we were supposed to have had his interview. That was now impossible, but since I had the day off, I wanted to accompany him. As we were crossing the street to get the bus to the doctor's office, Brady drove by. He gave us the "thumbs-up" sign and a big smile. We smiled back and gripped each other's hand tighter. We looked at each other with a look of determination. We would do this.

When we arrived at the doctor's office, they recognized William right away and sent him straight up to the lab. He knew what he had to do. We had found out the previous Thursday that they had counted two of the samples he'd given, so he only needed one more. He went into his little booth and as the lab technician watched, he began the process. I could see him and I was talking to him, even though he couldn't hear me.

"Come on, sweetie, you can do this. You have to do this. Come on, I believe in you!"

As I noticed how hard he was struggling, I knocked on the glass and gave him suggestions—"Maybe stand up, really breathe deeply, sweetie."

He gave me a look that at once said, "I love you and I appreciate your help" and also "You are really making it worse by putting this pressure on me so please, please go sit down and let me try to spit in peace."

I could take a hint. I went and sat down. I prayed silently instead of shouting my helpful tips at him.

When he walked out of the room and handed the cup to the technician, the technician began filling out a piece of paper and asked William for his passport. Okay, this was it! I knew right then we were okay. Why would he ask for his passport otherwise?

Sure enough, he handed William the paper indicating that three acceptable samples had been given and that the results showed no active TB. William's smile covered his whole face. I, of course, started crying. When we walked out of the office, we stood outside for a few minutes, holding tightly on to each other's hands and thanking God again and again. We had passed! We were finished with this step.

We called Brady to tell him the good news and then we began the next step: trying to get an interview.

汤

Our June 16 interview had been cancelled since we were still in the process of trying to spit at that time. Trying to get a new appointment was a confusing and stressful process. We were told by the doctor's office that they had informed the consulate and that we should not attend that interview since the medical portion was not yet completed. They said we should email or phone the consulate to get the new appointment. But we emailed and didn't hear anything. We couldn't get through by phone.

Finally, we went to the consulate and they gave us an interview date for the following week. This was a surprise—so easy. I was glad we went, because the doctor's office had not communicated anything about our situation to the consulate. If we had waited for them to contact us, we would likely still be waiting.

Having the interview date set, we really felt like we could relax a little—but of course we knew there were no guarantees.

chapter 46

$\mathcal{W}$ hile we were going through all this stress of wondering if we would ever be able to leave China and how to plan for the years to come, we got some news that was at once wonderful and stressful: we found out I was pregnant!

We had been trying since the previous August, with no results to speak of. Well, after six months or so of trying and no baby, I began to worry, of course. William, calm as always, said it just wasn't the time.

Well, the months went by, and each month we would get our hopes up only to be disappointed again. Around March we figured something was wrong—and that very same month, I got pregnant! The thing is, though, that we didn't know it at that time. I had been sick off and on and incredibly stressed, so I attributed all the nausea and missed periods to that. Finally, though, on July 1, William said, "Why don't you just go over to Clifford hospital today and check? You have missed two periods now, and I have a feeling."

I really didn't have a feeling, but I think that was just me being pessimistic. I thought it would just be too good to be true. Nonetheless, I went to see the doctor.

When I walked into the hospital, I asked where to register.

(This was a private hospital so not as complicated as typical Chinese hospitals.)

"*Ni hao, zai na li ke yi kan yi sheng. . . .*" I simply asked where I could see a doctor and pointed to my stomach, hoping she would put two and two together.

"*Er luo.*" The woman pointed down the hall.

"Xie xie."

I found the right line, got the right paper, and then found the right room. Now, I just had to wait.

I looked around at the other patients and wondered if any other women were here for a pregnancy test. I felt so calm, as if I already knew I was pregnant and everything was going to change for the better. When was it that I had first imagined being a mother? Probably as a little girl; as far as I could remember, that desire had always been there. I could picture myself as a mom, and I knew exactly the kind of mom I'd be. I hoped.

"Ms. Lori," a voice called from the doorway.

I followed the nurse to the exam room, where I had blood drawn. She then handed me another form and told me to go to another waiting room, where I would get the results. It was all so straightforward.

The other room was down the hall and around a corner. I couldn't even sit down. I was just too excited. I just stood by the counter and hoped I would get the results soon.

A doctor came up to the counter and gestured for me to approach.

"Ni hao, Ni hao," she said as she passed me a paper.

"Xie xie," I said, looking at it and realizing I had no idea what it said. I couldn't read it. I scanned the form, hoping something would pop out as a result. A plus sign? A happy face? As she started to walk away, I quickly called her back.

"Ni hao, *ma fan ni. Zen me yang?*" (*Excuse me, what's the result?*)

She started talking. Quickly. I just wanted a yes or no. I heard "you" (have), so I stopped her.

"*Ni de hise shi wo zhen de huai yun le?*" (Do you mean I am pregnant?)

She smiled. "*Shi, shi! Hui yun le!*" (Yes, yes, you are pregnant!)

I asked the girl standing next to me if I had heard right and she smiled and said "Shi, shi . . . baby," showing me that she knew a little English and could make it clear to me that I was pregnant. I thanked everyone, in English and Chinese. I jumped. I may have squealed. I couldn't believe it, and yet at the same time I'd already known before they told me. I had never been happier.

I called William right away and could hear the excitement in his voice. It just seemed like the most unreal, most incredible dream.

"I got the results," I blurted out. "You were right. I'm pregnant."

"Oh my gosh, my sweetheart. . . ." He was quiet for a few seconds—a wonderfully good quiet, the kind of quiet you are when if you're not, you'll get choked up.

"They gave me another form for a second test. I think it's the ultrasound. I'll call you after."

"Okay. I love you. Can't wait to see you."

I went on to get the ultrasound still not really sure I could believe what was going on. On the one hand, I knew it was real, but I also had this feeling like maybe the doctor would look at the machine and tell me there had been a mistake, that there was no baby there. So as I saw her looking at the machine I watched her eyes closely and I asked her if she saw a baby. She smiled and turned the screen toward me. Not only did she see a baby but she could tell which part was the baby's head. So it was confirmed: I had a baby, and the baby had a head. Now it was real.

When I talked with the doctor, she said that according to the ultrasound, I was over three months pregnant already. That meant I had gotten pregnant right when we decided to seriously try. And all these months I had been feeling terrible, confused, stressed, trying to figure out what to do the next year, there had been a baby inside me who was probably trying to tell me to calm down, that none of my plans were right because he or she would change everything.

汤

As it turned out, July 11 proved to be a very great day. While I was at the hospital learning that we were going to be parents, William was at the US Consulate, having his interview for immigration. He'd had his interview that morning and received his visa with absolutely no problem. Finally, something had gone right in this process. Finally, here was something that didn't require a fight. What a contrast from our experience with the tourist visa.

As we took our evening stroll later that night, we both thought about the day the previous October that had been so terribly miserable. What a difference we felt now. We had accomplished a lot, and we were incredibly grateful. We walked by a lovely park with flowers and bronze statues of important leaders in China's history. We sat there and relaxed for a while, looking up at the stars in comfortable, happy silence.

chapter 47

$\mathcal{M}$iracle number one was that we'd received William's visa. We had the thing we had been working so hard for. The visa was good for six months, which meant that we could leave any time before January 8. Miracle number two was that we were going to have a baby. The baby was due December 18. As we sat and reflected on these blessings, we became keenly aware of the irony of our situation. The timing was—well, sort of impossible. That is, were it not for the baby, we would stay in China one more semester. I would continue teaching, earning a good salary, and William could keep working gaining his experience and getting ready for his graduate school entrance tests. Then we could leave mid-December. It would be perfect.

But with the baby due in December, that plan didn't work. I couldn't get on a plane in the beginning of December and go to America. That meant that if we stayed this semester, I would need to have the baby in China. And this was not a dream-come-true idea for me.

I had hoped to have the baby in America, around my family. They had already missed our wedding, William's baptism, and so many things. I thought this would be something they could share in. Also, while we knew it was possible to have the baby here and then get the paperwork completed, we also knew it was very difficult. The Chinese government had to give their permission, and this took time.

Still, when all was said and done, for financial reasons, it made so much more sense to stay right there in China. The healthcare at the better hospitals was fine and was so incredibly cheap. We could just pay cash and have absolutely no debt or insurance worries. In many ways this made sense, and for a while, we were thinking this was the best option.

But then, what about the visa? It expired on January 8. If I had the baby December 18, could we really get all that paperwork done in two weeks and leave the country? Would the baby and I feel good enough to do so? If we didn't, William would lose his visa.

We thought about extending it, which made us nervous, as we'd learned this could be risky. But if we did go back, when would we go? I couldn't work only half of a semester; my school needed at least a full semester commitment. It was all so incredibly complicated.

We sat one night on our living room floor with our pros and cons lists, insurance information, and my work contract spread out on the floor, trying hard to figure out a solution. After a while there was just silence as we both tried to think our way out of this problem. Every time one of us had an idea, the other one could point out why it wouldn't work. This seemed impossible. Here we were with two of the most important blessings of our lives—a chance to go to America and a baby on the way—and we couldn't find a way to make them both happen.

It seemed no matter what good things happened to us, there was always an accompanying challenge. We walked and talked every night, going over and over every possibility, and what scared us to death was that there really wasn't a good answer. Either way, we were risking something, or at the very least guaranteeing ourselves more challenges.

Finally, one night, William said to me while we were out on a walk, "Haven't we been forgetting something?"

"What?" I braced myself, thinking he was going to add yet another dimension to this puzzle.

"What happened to our scripture study?" he asked. "It seems for a long time we haven't studied the scriptures. We used to read them every night."

"That's true. . . ." I sighed absent-mindedly. "I guess it's been a couple weeks now that we haven't."

I wanted to share his enthusiasm, but at that moment, I was so focused on the tangible, gigantic problem that I couldn't see past it. I have to admit that in that moment I didn't think going inside and reading our scriptures was going to change the world, but I knew that it mattered to William. I sighed and realized that I really appreciated this reminder from William. His faith was reassuring. Despite his fairly recent conversion, he had an unwavering vision of what his baptism meant and he lived it with sincerity every day and in every context. He seemed to take nothing for granted, and considered himself privileged to have learned more about spirituality. He wanted to do everything he could to keep that feeling in his life.

We went home and read our scriptures aloud, alternating back and forth, reading one verse aloud and then listening to the next until we had finished about one chapter. We closed the book and William prayed. He prayed for peace, for guidance, and for God to watch over our families. He also expressed gratitude for all that we already had. We got ready for bed and had a good night's sleep, the first I had had in quite a while.

汤

The next morning we began the day with scripture study and prayer, as we normally did, before going about our routines. There was definitely more peace in both of us throughout that day. As we discussed things that night, we had fresh ideas. It wasn't as if a solution quickly came to us, but at least we were thinking beyond where we had before. It was as if two and two suddenly could equal five or six or seven, rather than only four. There were all these options we hadn't considered before.

Most of them had to do with the graduate programs William would pursue. He had assumed he would pursue his MBA, and to do so required at least six more months of work experience. This was why he'd been feeling that it was so crucial to stay here and continue with his company. However, as he explored and talked with people, new ideas came, new possibilities that were even more in alignment with his professional and academic goals.

Harry and Dana had been such good sounding boards and advisors during these decisions and we always felt grateful that we had them to sort of test out how crazy our ideas sounded. Harry had once remarked that he admired the way we attacked life, but he, like many others, had wondered if it made more sense to stay in China a bit longer. Once we told him that we felt we needed to go sonner rather than later, he was on board and even helped us research programs. In fact, it was Harry who found the graduate program William eventually ended up applying for.

We had been so focused on what we had considered the "best" program that we'd never thought to truly ask ourselves if it was the right fit for us.

Over the next month, I finished teaching summer school and then resigned for the following year. I gave the school plenty of notice and ended things on a good note. We reinstated our health insurance so that we would be prepared to have the baby in America. We decided not to ask the consulate for an extension on the visa. We secured a new place to live, since we were no longer eligible for teachers' housing. We sold our extra things—all the things we wouldn't take to America with us. We moved. We bought airline tickets. We told our families. We told everyone concerned. We began the process of applying to the one school William wanted to attend, Brigham Young University. We put all our eggs in that basket because that was the basket we wanted. We gathered every piece of information we could. William studied day and night. I wrote about all that had happened to us. We prayed. We read our scriptures. We talked. We planned.

Finally, finally, *finally*, everything was okay. We were okay. Our baby was okay. We were happy in this transition period, and that's what it was. It was a transition to what would be the next chapter in our lives.

chapter 48

We went to Wuhan on a quest to get William's transcripts. We were prepared for the worst, having gone through similar processes before. On the day we arrived, we were reminded of how unlikely it would be to get the transcript at this time, because the college was moving locations. Two people, an administrator and a secretary, had told us this.

On a hunch, we decided to go out to the new campus and ask there. The place was completely deserted and the room we were told to go to was locked. We just happened to run into a woman coming out of another room, however, and when we asked her where we could locate his transcript, she said, to our surprise, that it was her office that handled that. We walked in and she began looking through records. Within five minutes, she had located William's transcript and was making a copy of it. This seemed like a good sign.

After getting the transcript, we were in a rush to get back to the hotel because we realized we'd forgotten our money belt that morning. All our cash and credit cards, as well as our passports, were inside. We prayed nonstop on the way there that it was still on the bed where we'd left it. We were actually afraid we wouldn't even have the cab fare to get to the hotel, but then we remembered that William's tithing money was tucked away in one of the zipper compartments of my purse. He'd forgotten to turn it in the previous Sunday. Thank God! With that, we had plenty of money to get back to the hotel.

We burst into our room when we got there—and found that the money belt was right where we'd left it. We felt like this was a day of miracles. It wasn't even lunchtime yet on our first day in Wuhan, and already we had gotten the one transcript and had not lost any money. Absolutely amazing!

汤

We took what we'd gotten to the notary and had him start working on that. Then, for the rest of the day, we just relaxed. I was dealing with a bladder infection, which was not making things very pleasant. It had crept up the morning we left, and although it wasn't severe, it was very uncomfortable. So I rested that afternoon while William studied, and then we watched a movie together on our computer.

We were so excited to be this far along in the process already. The next thing we needed to do was to go to Huang Gang and get William's junior college transcript. We would head for Huang Gang the next morning.

汤

We took a small bus to Huang Gang—the kind of bus where usually people are usually smoking the whole time. Thankfully, William asked everyone on the bus to please not smoke, and they complied. Without that terrible smell choking the air inside, it wasn't a bad trip at all.

Our day in Huang Gang, though, was not to be as successful as was our first day in Wuhan. First of all, the college now had three campuses, and we couldn't figure out which one actually kept the records, as we kept getting different answers from everyone we spoke with. First we went to one campus and found nothing, not even an open records office. Someone there told us the records would likely be at another campus, so we took a taxi there.

The weather was incredibly hot, and between the general discomfort of pregnancy and my progressing bladder infection, I wanted nothing more than to lie down. However, we had very limited time, so I didn't let William know just how miserable I was. Besides, he was trying so hard to make me comfortable. We were taking taxis everywhere, which usually we didn't do because of the cost, and he was really going out of his way to make sure I was okay. And it wasn't his fault that this was the way things were done in China. We could not simply make a phone call and order his transcript. We had to go in person and track it down.

Well, we found the records office, but by that time the people who worked there had already gone to lunch. We were told they'd be back at two thirty and it was now about eleven. We shrugged and decided to get some lunch ourselves.

The only place nearby was totally disgusting, but it was food, so we ate and made the best of it. We found a clinic next door where we looked at medicine for my infection, but we were really afraid to take anything for fear that it might hurt the baby. We had looked in Wuhan, too, but we had been told there that not all antibiotics are safe during pregnancy, and we just didn't want to take a chance. I was in pain but we decided to go without the medicine for now. We went back to the college to wait until two thirty.

汤

It felt like an eternity that we had waited, and nobody was being very helpful. At three, the girl who was supposed to work in the records office still hadn't shown up, so William decided to walk to the other side of campus to get some information as to where she, or anyone who could help us, might be. He returned ticked off because he had been informed that she was right in the basement of the building where we'd been waiting.

We headed down to her office, and the nightmare continued: she simply could not find any record of William—or of anyone in his class, for that matter. We went with her to the room where all the transcripts were kept, but there was nothing on him. Her attitude was blasé and unapologetic.

William told her this was unacceptable. He had spent three years at that college and they must have a record of his being there. All she could do was to recommend he talk to another administrator at the other campus.

I'd like to say I couldn't believe this—but actually, it was exactly what I'd expected when we came in search of the transcript. Unhelpful people and irresponsible record keeping—that was status quo here.

We went back to the first campus again and found the office of the guy who supposedly could help. He leaned back in his chair, chain smoked, and talked to everyone else that came in as we were trying to tell him about our dilemma. Finally, he casually said this was not his area and referred us to someone else. At the other campus.

We jumped in a taxi, went back to the other campus for the third time that day, and found this guy's office. No, he knew nothing. No, he couldn't help. No, this wasn't his problem. He did give us the phone number for a dean whom he said might be able to help.

William called him on the spot. The dean was surprisingly friendly and said he would try to help the next morning. We were relieved, but still skeptical that anyone would help. We found a hotel and got some rest. Our hotel was decent and even had a view of the lake. We ordered room service and read, enjoying a peaceful night.

汤

The next morning, we met the dean, who instructed the school driver to give us a ride to the old campus—the one where William had actually attended school. He was very kind and promised that the people there had been instructed to help us.

This campus was in the middle of nowhere and we had to take a very bumpy dirt road to get there, but we made it there in one piece. We got off the bus ready to begin to tell our story and try to find someone to help us—but to our surprise, none of that was necessary, because a man was waiting for us with a stamped transcript on his desk.

We couldn't believe it! Of course, they hadn't really found his original transcript, but the dean must have informed them to put something together showing that William had indeed attended and had done well, and they had done so. We were so grateful and so excited that we hardly gave it a second look. We stuck it with the rest of our papers, and headed back to Wuhan.

汤

The bus ride to Wuhan took about an hour and a half. As soon as we arrived back, we checked into our hotel and then headed to the notary public guy. He sent us down to the translation place to get everything translated first. While there, we noticed that on William's Huang Gang transcript, there were no dates showing when William had attended.

We were so upset. How could we have been so stupid? How could we have left without carefully checking this over? So careless! As we looked back on those few days in Wuhan and Huang Gang, in fact, we noticed several careless mistakes that we had made, all because we had gotten too excited. But we knew there was nothing to be done about it now. We just hoped the transcripts would be acceptable to BYU.

Once we'd turned everything in to the notary, we headed back to our hotel. We kept trying to get ahold of the dean of William's college, who seemed to be purposely avoiding us. I personally think she was somewhat bitter about William heading off to America and didn't want to be bothered with signing his recommendation form. I hoped I was wrong, but she couldn't spare five minutes for us during those days. I also think she thought we were going to cause her a lot of trouble in asking for the transcript. Little did she know that we'd gotten it, no problem, without her help.

When we finally got a hold of her, she said she could meet with us when we got back from Huang Mei. Of course.

汤

We arrived in Huang Mei on a Saturday around lunchtime. It was ridiculously hot, but it was wonderful to be reunited with William's parents and Little Ling. We basically just hung out with them at home and at the store, and everything went really well. William's parents were getting along a lot better and had developed their own system and routine that seemed to work for them. They shared the responsibilities of taking care of Ling and managing the store, and there didn't seem to be tension between them. Every other time we'd come back, they'd had major problems getting along, and major financial stresses as well. However, the business was doing okay now and they seemed to be all right. I was grateful.

They did not have air conditioning, of course, and that was hard. The first day and a half was really bad for me. I had forgotten how dusty things were there and how high up we really were on the seventh floor. I had definitely forgotten what it was like to be without the comforts of home. William was an absolute angel to me, though, getting me ice and drinks and even carrying a huge, heavy fan up the seven flights of stairs so that I could be more comfortable. I don't even know where he got the ice, now that I think about it. He'd always been attentive, but my being pregnant seemed to have brought this out even more. So I knew it was going to be a hard week in some ways, but with cold drinks, the fan, and William doting on me as best he could, I figured I could survive.

汤

The next day, unexpectedly, it began to cool off—drastically. I mean, it was like it went to fall weather all of a sudden, with nice breezes and everything. I could not believe it. The days we were out visiting relatives were so comfortable. If it had been hot, I would have been so crabby and miserable and I'm sure I would have made William miserable too. I had never been so grateful for cool weather as I was on those days. Everything was easier for me. Part of it was that we didn't spend a super long time at each person's house; we just had nice, brief visits with everyone and saw everyone we had hoped to. I didn't have as hard a time getting used to the food and other conditions this time, either, which again I was so grateful for.

Every time I felt tempted to complain about things during this visit, I reminded myself that this was William's last trip home for a long time. It was going to be incredibly hard for him to leave his family and go to America, knowing they were so far away and that it would be a long time before he saw them again. I still let out a couple of complaints, but I tried hard to go with things and make him happy. His family loved us so much and they were so proud of him. I just wanted this to be a wonderful memory for all of them. After another day in Huang Mei, we would head back to Guangzhou.

chapter 49

We had one more month in China, and I wanted to make the most of it. William would spend that time preparing for his GMAT (Graduate Management Admission Test), which he would take a month after we got to Chicago. I planned to spend the time writing and enjoying every moment of my pregnancy. It was so nice to have this transition time, where we were ending one important era and moving on to another.

I often found my thoughts turning to America and what we hoped to find there. There was so much that was still unknown. How would William adjust? How would I, for that matter, after having lived in China for more than three years? How would it be to live with Mom and Chrissy? Would William actually get into BYU? It was hard to believe that dream could come true, but it was there. How would it be for William to attend church in America? How might his faith change once we no longer had the security of our little congregation and we were in a new, much larger church group? How would it be to live the simple life now that neither of us would be working and we'd be living off our savings? How would our marriage handle all the changes? And most importantly, we were to become parents within the next two months. What would little Abraham or Annabelle teach us? How would this little person change our lives?

I felt nervous, but joyful. I felt proud of us. We had worked incredibly hard to get this far and we were finally taking this next step. Together.

汤

We'd spent our last night in Guangzhou walking around Clifford Estates, visiting all the places that had meant something to us. The dorm William had lived in when he'd first come. My first apartment. Our first apartment together. The school where we'd met and worked together. The little store we always visited to get milk or bread, sometimes ice cream. The wet market where we knew all the ladies at the vegetable stalls, the fruit stands, and where we went to buy chicken or fish. The lake. The lake we'd walked near so often. The mountain where we'd first climbed up to the tower. That night when everything fell into place.

The next morning, we carried our suitcases down and headed toward the bus stop. William was holding the huge envelope of X-rays documenting his TB journey. He was about to put it in the suitcase when we caught each other's eye.

"Do we actually need these?" he asked me.

"No, we don't."

We both smiled, and with that he folded the big envelope in half and stuffed it in the trash can. I couldn't help but wonder if we'd need them any time in the future, but it felt too good to place them in the trash and leave that memory behind to worry too much about it.

We needed to take a small bus to the larger bus station in the front of Clifford Estates, so we dragged our three suitcases down the block and began the journey.

We bought our tickets and found our bus. We'd bought a few snacks for the bus ride to Hong Kong, where we would spend two days before heading to America. The plan was to go to the Latter-Day Saint temple there, and I was so looking forward to showing William around Hong Kong and just watching him experience that wonderful place since he'd only had a glimpse the previous Christmas.

He put our suitcases underneath the bus in the storage compartment and we found our seats. He was fighting back tears, and the bus hadn't even pulled out of the station. There were no words to offer him, but I understood. He was leaving his country. We linked arms, facing out the window.

Tears streamed down his face. They fell right off his chin, and he made no attempt to stop them or wipe them away. So much love and emotion, just freely pouring out of him.

"I never knew China was so beautiful," he said.

My tears came too then, more slowly, but they came. And they came for all kinds of reasons, mostly relief, I guessed. And reverent awe, too, of all that had happened since I'd boarded that plane in Chicago three years earlier. I thought of that girl who'd calmly set foot in China, knowing she was supposed to be there. My mind replayed scenes from the early days—meeting my students, trying to get a phone cord that first week in China, the orphanage, the friendships, those beautiful Sundays at church, running out on the track after school, learning to cook and appreciate food in a new way, all the travel adventures. Figuring things out, helping my family, understanding them. Connecting with my mom, saying good-bye to my dad. Finding myself. Realizing my strength and independence, and finally feeling peace.

And then there was William. I had come from the other side of the world to find him. How I loved him! He had already changed my life, and I had a clear, almost tangible feeling there would be many good days ahead.

I looked out the window as we drove over a bridge. Looking down at the river, I noticed how the water was calm but seemed purposeful at the same time—moving steadily and beautifully. The water reminded me of all the small lakes in the midwestern

United States. That water also seemed calm and purposeful. So often I'd gone fishing with my dad when we lived in Wisconsin. On one particular day, it was just the two of us. I couldn't have been more than ten years old. We sat side by side on a pier, him teaching me how to thread my hook and toss my line out just like he had done. Both of us had our feet hanging over the edge. Blue sky, sunshine, my dad.

"Daddy, I want to do this forever." It wasn't that I loved fishing. In fact, I didn't. What I loved were those quiet moments, just the two of us. "Can we go fishing again tomorrow?"

My dad smiled. "Well, we'll have to see. But we'll be out here again soon, that's for sure. Hey, looks like you got one!" I laughed as he helped me reel it in.

Dad. I remembered the fishing trips. I remembered everything about him—the stories, the prayers, the music, his faith, his humor. His cowboy boots. His guitar. And yes, I remembered the globe. That day in Chicago when he had shuffled out of his bedroom with something to tell me. He'd given his assurance that he knew me, and he knew what I needed to do. He gave me the courage to take that step, that leap, to China, and toward myself.

As I held William's hand, the bus moving further away from Guangzhou, it became clearer than ever how profound Dad's words had been, and how—without them—perhaps I would not have come to China. His words were a gift.

"I think you should go to China."

"You do, Dad?"

"I really do."

About the Author

Lori Qian holds a BA in anthropology and philosophy and an MA in applied linguistics, and has advanced graduate training in school leadership, literacy instruction, and elementary education. She is a regular contributor to *Urban Family Magazine* in Guangzhou, China, and enjoys presenting around the world on topics ranging from cultivating creativity to pedagogical approaches to writing. She is passionate about education, multiculturalism, and self-improvement. After living in China for ten years, she recently relocated to Alpine, Utah, with her family, ready to embrace an entirely new adventure. Qian is currently working on her second book, *Fighting for Fitness*, a self-help memoir of her own health transformation.

SELECTED TITLES FROM SHE WRITES PRESS

She Writes Press is an independent publishing company founded to serve women writers everywhere. Visit us at www.shewritespress.com.

Accidental Soldier: A Memoir of Service and Sacrifice in the Israel Defense Forces by Dorit Sasson. $17.95, 978-1-63152-035-8. When nineteen-year-old Dorit Sasson realized she had no choice but to distance herself from her neurotic, worrywart of a mother in order to become her own person, she volunteered for the Israel Defense Forces—and found her path to freedom.

Learning to Eat Along the Way by Margaret Bendet. $16.95, 978-1-63152-997-9. After interviewing an Indian holy man, newspaper reporter Margaret Bendet follows him in pursuit of enlightenment and ends up facing demons that were inside her all along.

Filling Her Shoes: Memoir of an Inherited Family by Betsy Graziani Fasbinder. $16.95, 978-1-63152-198-0. A "sweet-bitter" story of how, with tenderness as their guide, a family formed in the wake of loss and learned that joy and grief can be entwined cohabitants in our lives.

Renewable: One Woman's Search for Simplicity, Faithfulness, and Hope by Eileen Flanagan. $16.95, 978-1-63152-968-9. At age forty-nine, Eileen Flanagan had an aching feeling that she wasn't living up to her youthful ideals or potential, so she started trying to change the world—and in doing so, she found the courage to change her life.

Gap Year Girl by Marianne Bohr. $16.95, 978-1-63152-820-0. Thirty-plus years after first backpacking through Europe, Marianne Bohr and her husband leave their lives behind and take off on a yearlong quest for adventure.

This is Mexico: Tales of Culture and Other Complications by Carol M. Merchasin. $16.95, 978-1-63152-962-7. Merchasin chronicles her attempts to understand Mexico, her adopted country, through improbable situations and small moments that keep the reader moving between laughter and tears.